THE EVOLUTION OF UAE FOREIGN POLICY

The Evolution Of UAE Foreign Policy

PRINCIPLES, COMPONENTS, AND GOALS

GEW Intelligence Unit

Hichem Karoui (Ed.)

Global East-West (London)

Copyright © 2024 by GEW Intelligence Unit
GEW Reports & Analyses (The Voice of the Mediterranean)
Editor: Hichem Karoui
Global East-West (London)

All rights reserved. No part of this book may be reproduced in any manner whatsoever without written permission except in the case of brief quotations embodied in critical articles and reviews.

First Printing, 2024

Contents

Introduction		**1**
Sources and References		20
I	The Historical Foundations of UAE Foreign Policy	25
References		42
II	The Role of Leadership in UAE Foreign Policy	44
References		59
III	Economic Diplomacy: A Pillar of UAE Foreign Policy	61
References		109
IV	Soft Power and Cultural Diplomacy	111
References		127
V	Security and Defense in UAE Foreign Policy	129
References		144
VI	Regional Dynamics: The UAE and the Middle East	146

References	163
VII Global Partnerships: The UAE on the Global Stage	165
References	182
VIII Energy Diplomacy: A Core Component of UAE Foreign Policy	184
IX References	199
X The UAE's Diplomatic Approach to Regional Conflict Resolution	201
XI References	216
XII Public Diplomacy: Shaping Perceptions of the UAE	218
XIII References	244
XIV Climate Diplomacy: Addressing Global Environmental Challenges	246
XV References	262
XVI Cybersecurity and Digital Diplomacy: Protecting National Interests	264
XVII References	280
XVIII The Future of UAE Foreign Policy: Opportunities and Challenges	282
XIX References	298
XX Conclusion - Defining the UAE's Foreign Policy	300

Introduction

SECURING THE NATIONAL INTERESTS OF THE UAE AND ITS PARTNERS

The United Arab Emirates has maintained a modern foreign policy since its founding in 1971, reflecting its leadership's determination to root the UAE's renaissance in the global policy framework. The UAE's foreign policy utilizes a set of ethical and professional standards that differentiate that policy from the policies of many countries, allowing for greater respect for the UAE's positions and the effective, positive participation of Emirati political leadership and diplomats in international and regional forums. Since the UAE's founding, preserving the State's independence, safeguarding its sovereignty, and maintaining its territorial integrity have been key principles of its foreign policy. The policy, which is guided by the vision of the nation's leadership, its principles, and its objectives, also supports the UAE's friendly international relations, cooperation, and interconnectedness, in line with the objectives of the country's people, their heritage and culture, and the requirements of overall sustainable development. (Al Suwaidi, 2021)(Al-Darmaki et al., 2023).

The United Arab Emirates (UAE) has made significant strides in foreign policy, especially in recent years. Here are some key points:

1. FOREIGN POLICY SHIFTS:

- Over the past decade, the UAE's foreign policy has substantially changed. It has de-escalated and normalized relations with major regional players, including Iran, Israel, Turkey, and Qatar (UBF publications).

- Notable developments include ending the rift with Qatar, re-establishing diplomatic relations with Iran, concluding agreements with Israel, and opening the door for Syria's return to the Arab fold (Krasna, 2023).

2. ECONOMIC RECOVERY AND REGIONAL ENVIRONMENT:

- The UAE has made a strong recovery from the COVID-19 pandemic, with economic growth restored by the beginning of 2023.

- Strong oil prices have enabled high government spending, contributing to a positive economic outlook.

- The regional environment has improved, with several disputes resolved during 2021 and 2022(Krasna, 2023).

3. TRUST INDEX:

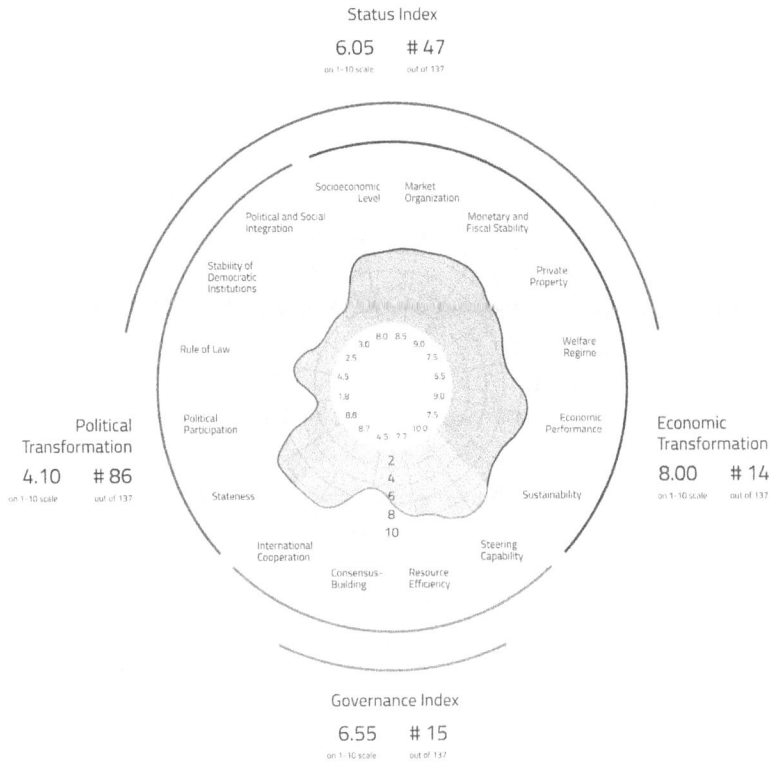

BTI Transformation Index

- The UAE has implemented a "Trust Index" to gauge trust among the country's banking customers. This index reflects how customers view banks over time.
- According to the UAE Banking Federation (UBF), trust in the UAE banking sector has shown a strong year-on-year increase, reaching 74% in 2022 (BTI 2024).
- Additionally, the 2021 UAE Trust Index revealed that 85% of UAE consumers see their main bank as "honest, trustworthy, and fair" – an all-time high perception of banks (EdelmanTrust Barometer 2023). It says:

"The latest report, which surveys 32,000 respondents in 28 countries, found that despite global challenges such as conflict, food insecurity, and climate change resulting in a polarized society, there is unshakable trust in the UAE.

The UAE is ranked the third most trusted country in the world, and all four institutions the index measures trust in (government, business, NGOs, and media) saw significant trust levels. Government once again topped the list as the most trusted institution at 86 percent, followed closely by business at 78 percent. In comparison, business is the only trusted institution globally.

The driver of this high levels of trust in the UAE is a reflection of respondents believing that the government, businesses and NGOs are seen as competent and ethical. As a result, UAE ranks high amongst economic optimism – 72% of respondents believe they will be better off economically in five years' time, while only 40% of global respondents say they and their families will be better off in five years, a 10-point decline from 2022."

4. GLOBAL TRUST RANKING:

- The UAE is ranked as the third most trusted country globally, according to the 2023 Edelman Trust Barometer.

Trust levels in institutions (government, business, NGOs, and media) are significant, with government being the most trusted institution at 86%, followed closely by business at 78% (Almezaini, 2019).

In 2024, trust remains high in the UAE, as shown below:

Trust Index 2023 to 2024: Trust Remains High in the UAE

Trust Index
(average percent trust in NGOs, business, government, and media)

Distrust (1-49) — Neutral (50-59) — Trust (60-100) — Significant change

2024 Trust Index among
Developing countries 63
Developed countries 49

	2023 General population		2024 General population	Greatest changes in	
55	Global 28	56	Global 28		
83	China	79	China		
75	Indonesia	76	India	S. Korea	+7
74	UAE	74	UAE	Malaysia	+6
73	India	73	Indonesia	Nigeria	+5
71	Saudi Arabia	72	Saudi Arabia	Thailand	+4
68	Singapore	70	Thailand	Australia	+4
66	Thailand	68	Malaysia	China	-4
63	Kenya	67	Singapore	Colombia	-4
62	Malaysia	64	Kenya	UK	-4
61	Mexico	61	Nigeria		
56	Nigeria	59	Mexico		
54	Netherlands	56	Netherlands		
53	Brazil	53	Brazil		
52	Canada	53	Canada		
51	Colombia	52	Australia		
50	Italy	50	Italy		
49	Sweden	49	S. Africa		
48	Australia	49	Sweden		
	Ireland		Ireland		
48	U.S.	47	France		
47	France	47	Ireland		
46	S. Africa	46	Spain		
46	Germany	45	U.S.		
45	Spain	45	Germany		
43	UK	43	S. Korea		
42	Argentina	39	Argentina		
38	Japan	37	Japan		
36	S. Korea		UK		

2024 Edelman Trust Barometer

In summary, the UAE's foreign policy has adapted to changing circumstances, and its trust index reflects positive perceptions in both the banking sector and overall institutional trust. In 2024, the UAE society focuses on shaping the country's policymaking and preparing it for 2030.

Principles of the UAE Foreign Policy

Mediation programs that have proven effective for the future are perceived as priority issues in foreign policy. Notably, along with strengthening relations with the world's largest international actors, the country's diplomatic missions provide constructive work in international organizations, providing their support. This has reached historical importance and naturally makes it possible to state the change in the balance of world forces.

Given the importance of nonviolent crisis solutions, separate programs and projects affecting the population's interests are continuously conducted. These are a building block for stabilizing societies, ensuring their continuation, and providing equal opportunity for personal fulfilment, namely, for the future generation.

Implementing preventive and humanitarian programs on international platforms aimed at resolving regional and global issues through diplomacy, cooperation, and active dialogue with partners is crucial in the context of foreign policy activities.

The UAE's strategic interest in ensuring regional and global peace and security, regardless of the financial burdens of such treatment, contributes to creating its unique model of conducting foreign policy actions. The fundamental principles and goals of the UAE foreign policy primarily include the promotion of confidence in the international market, strengthening sustainable development, attracting investments, and providing comfortable living conditions for future generations. (Krzymowski, 2022)(Salisbury, 2020)(Ibrahim and Al-azzawi, 2022).

Co-existence aims to create favorable external conditions for sustainable growth of the UAE's economy, its comprehensive development and strengthening social, political, gender and ethnic harmony in the society. The ultimate objective is to create conditions for the quality and happy life of citizens. The main goals of this direction are: to contribute to the development of an inclusive, open and international nationwide economy, stimulate the role of multilateral and plurilateral institutions in the area of regulation of international relations, create favorable conditions for comprehensive development in the fields of education, culture, science and art. (Krzymowski, 2020)(Alketbi, 2023)(Aminjonov, 2020).

Another aspect is humanitarian direction (the symbiosis of state and non-governmental diplomacy). The main objectives of this element are the construction and development of a great "horizontal" humanitarian potential network, the delivery of humanitarian aid, the mobilization of the international community resources around implementing development goals, increasing states' awareness of the need to consolidate capabilities in the area of human security, creating conditions for cultural communication and intellectual development of society, attracting the attention of the world community to the problems of the state and establishing constructive communication with the epistemic community. (Al Suwaidi, 2021)(Litsas2023).

Objectives of the UAE Foreign Policy

The cluster approach practiced by the United Arab Emirates describes the fundamental principles of the country's foreign policy. Respect for the sovereign rights of states is considered the basic principle and the basis for cooperation. The approach combines the defense of national interests and adherence to the principle of non-interference with respect and support for other states' sovereignty and territorial integrity. UAE respects states and governments. The cluster approach has a disciplining effect. It urges to exclude violence and violating the principles enshrined in the UN Charter. At the same time, these foreign policy principles are operationalized in the cluster format, based on ensuring a comprehensive understanding of international problems and mobilizing resources to address them. With respect to the first principle, the cluster is used to consolidate states for collective actions and for pursuing the UAE's efficient foreign policy. According to the second principle, the mobilization of resources within the cluster occurs through various coalitions and formats. UAE's foreign policy is focused on a dozen major coalitions, which have different objectives, membership, and scope of activities, and can be used to solve various problems. For example, there is a coalition of wealthy states and a coalition of humanitarian aid donors which works in crises. In 2011, the UAE sent humanitarian aid to 38 countries, with the total assistance amounting to about USD 19.9 billion. (Gökalp, 2020)(Cochrane, 2021)(Krzymowski, 2022)

The analysis of UAE foreign policy provides evidence of the dynamics observed in the decision-making and implementation. It is characterized by an active pragmatic approach, combining extensive diversity and multipolarity of partners with effort focusing on key aspects. The latter include the commonality of values and principles, as well as the specifics of the goals set in the regions of the Persian Gulf and the Arab world. Moreover, the nature and focus of the foreign policy have been influenced by the strategy adopted by the United States in the region and the decisions of the Russian Federation, which returns to the region both as an actor and an arbiter. (El-Dessouki and Mansour2023)(Borck, 2024).

Economic Diplomacy

Economic diplomacy remains a cornerstone of UAE foreign policy in 2024. The UAE has concluded 10 comprehensive economic partnership agreements and is negotiating with several other countries, aiming to boost its exports by 33%(El Ketbi, 2024). The UAE's Ministry of Foreign Affairs plays a crucial role in attracting foreign investments and promoting trade through its global network of missions and embassies(MoFA, 2024). Additionally, the UAE's sovereign wealth funds, particularly ADQ, are actively used to exert the country's influence abroad, with significant investments in Africa and strategic deals with countries like Turkey and Egypt(The Economist, 2024).

Considering the core priority of Emirati business diplomacy, the MoFT implemented a foreign policy designed for the digital age, relying on a "trust" index. This is how the ministry and its homologues collect and analyze precise data daily relating to the confidence that market operators in the country have in the Emirati market. This index still kept secret, then informs the decisions of the MoFT and its homologues. The objective of the rulers is to ensure that the country retains a minimum level of confidence with foreign companies, to continue attracting foreign direct investment. The country's economic diplomacy has thus gone a step further than marketing its products, relying on economic intelligence at the heart of its action. (Albaity et al.2023)(Ibrahim and Al-azzawi, 2022)(El et al.2024)(Alshamlan et al.2021).

The economy stands as a priority for Emirati foreign policy, especially with the desire of the federation to diversify its sources of foreign investment and its emerging activities somewhat beyond traditional sectors such as finance and the military industry. The financial priority is also an opportunity to enhance the image of the UAE abroad. The logic being summed up in the words of the Minister of State for Foreign Trade: marketing matters in the business world; that's what diplomacy is all about. In terms of the promotion of trade exchanges since 2007, given the difficulties of the 2008 crisis and the Arab uprisings since 2011, the UAE's economic diplomacy was also, as in the Arab countries, to support the development of entrepreneurs, the young, women, in other words, segments of society threatened by these shocks. The institution has also been the driving force in establishing this emergency response. (Crupi and Schilirò2023)(Due-Gundersen and Al Suwaidi, 2024)(Shahrour, 2020).

Security and Defense Cooperation

At the same time, to secure the UAE maritime borders, it is important to carry out effective inland and offshore maritime security operations in cooperation with the international community. The UAE also continues security training and cooperation programs with friendly countries and organizations, with a view to the business of military experience, analyzing and drawing lessons from the latest military developments and innovations, and understanding and assessing the latest requirements for the fight against terrorism and military operations (Vetter)(Kaye et al., 2021).

As the UAE government works collectively to address regional and global security threats, it fully supports international efforts to manage conflict, restore security and stability, ensure effective regional security mechanisms, and bring peacekeeping to a successful conclusion. The strengthening of regional and international security and defense cooperation emerged to guarantee access to the country's critical infrastructure and maritime trade routes, and to protect supply chains and energy and food security. Therefore, cooperating with regional and international partners to ensure alliances' sustainability and protect strategic facilities and targets is imperative. (Krieg, 2023)(Brehony2020)(Al-Ansari et al., 2021).

There are expectations that security and defense cooperation with external partners will continue on its upward trajectory. The foundations are already solid. The G20 collective action remains a key mechanism through which the government pursues international security and defense cooperation. The principle of collective action animates defence diplomacy in light of the mutual benefit of collaboration to meet the challenges of peace and security (Colombo and Dessì, 2022)(Janardhan, 2022).

Bilateral and Multilateral Relations

The UAE continued its diplomatic efforts in 2024 to achieve regional peace and security. This was consistent with its historical experience in managing various regional crises. The UAE believed in cooperation and sought to create opportunities for growth and prosperity for all. It aimed to work with all states to find solutions and convince them to fulfill their respective commitments. Notably, the UAE cooperated with some countries in some international cases. It also promoted economic cooperation in such a way as to generate development possibilities, in turn providing cross-border business opportunities that could act as a stabilizing force in the region. For instance, it signed an agreement with Israel to normalize relations and aimed to promote wider Arab-Israeli normalization in order to achieve a two-state solution. It also endeavored to remove the obstacles to development that the Iranian elite created, to the detriment of the Iranian people, by undermining international stability (Kertcher and Schiff, 2024)(Hallward and Biygautane2024)(Ali and Uzzaman2023).

By 2024, the UAE aimed to strengthen existing bilateral relations to form new partnerships and alliances that could contribute to development and progress. The UAE aimed to reduce the dependence on oil and diversify the national economy. Consequently, it concentrated significant efforts on stimulating innovation and attracting investment. The country also aimed to conduct an energetic foreign policy to provide an attractive and reliable political and economic environment, in turn attracting business that could benefit from the UAE's wide-ranging regional and global networks. The UAE saw the future sustainable economy and its global networks as essential tools in consolidating its soft power and enhancing the UAE's role at the regional and global levels in achieving international peace and security (El Amine, 2023)(Mason, 2023)(Krzymowski, 2020)(Puri et al., 2022)(Schiff and Kertcher, 2024).

The UAE's multilateral relations in 2024 are highlighted by its active participation in global forums and its contributions to international organizations. The UAE has contributed to multilateral organizations such as UNICEF, UNDP, and the Office of the UN High Commissioner for Refugees.

Diplomatic Initiatives and Mediation Efforts

In connection with multilateral and international issues, the UAE has continued to exercise its mediation and diplomatic initiatives to preserve peace and address global issues – such as Energy Security, Humanitarian Affairs and the Refugee crisis, Organized Crime, Corruption, and Terrorism, Conventional and Non-Conventional Pollution, Outer Space Security, International Institutional and Law Reform, Reinforcement of Supra-National Public Affairs, and Forced Labor, Modern-Day Slavery, and Peonage. During the period of review, the UAE has also made persistent efforts to sensitize the international community, through high-level international meetings in Abu Dhabi, to some other important strategic issues, such as Chemical, Biological, Radiological, and Nuclear Security, Gulf regional security, and Food Production and Security. In the second semester of the year, Gulf rivalry with Iran has substantially flamed during an open confrontation manifested by the attacks on oil tankers, war in Yemen, etc. (Antwi-Boateng and Alhashmi, 2022)(El-Dessouki and Mansour2023)(Al et al.2020).

Despite its absence in international alliances and defense agreements, the UAE has developed an extensive diplomatic network and, within the last decade, managed to expand its economic and diplomatic influence around the world. Besides the strategic bilateral ties – with the United States of America, the main preferential trade partner, the United Kingdom, as well as some of the largest and historically influential countries such as Russia, New Zealand, Switzerland, and Australia – the UAE has forged vital strategic and economic partnerships with medium and smaller countries, such as South Korea, Afghanistan, and Portugal. This year provided two significant examples of those relations. In January 2019, Afghan authorities executed a set of agreements with the UAE, including launching a joint investment fund to tackle stunting and malnutrition successfully, two of Afghanistan's most pressing public health issues. A few months later, the UAE promised a direct grant of $3 billion to Pakistan as fiscal aid for its foreign exchange reserves' increase – sustaining the deep but discreet partnership with a key country for the region (Antwi-Boateng and Alhashmi, 2022)(El-Dessouki and Mansour2023).

Soft Power and Public Diplomacy

It is possible to distinguish another area where the UAE is gaining success and thus increasing its soft power - the tourism industry. The UAE is rapidly developing its tourism potential. Dubai has almost become a tourist brand thanks to attracting many of this sector's consumers. The answer to why the country has chosen the tourism industry is quite simple, and it is reflected in its foreign policy. The fact is that the success of foreign policy is primarily determined by its attractiveness to other states and the public of other countries. UAE's leadership is well aware of this. Moreover, it believes that these critical factors lie in big wealth and economic prosperity and the historical, regional, and religious uniqueness of GA or Emirate. (Antwi-Boateng and Alhashmi, 2022)(Locke et al., 2023).

In 2017, the United Arab Emirates (UAE) Cabinet of Ministers made a significant decision that marked an important milestone in the country's development. Recognizing its youth's immense value and potential, the UAE decided to establish a dedicated Youth Ministry. To ensure this initiative's success, a Minister of State for Youth Affairs was appointed to lead and guide the ministry's endeavors. Two years later, in 2019, the UAE's Cabinet of Ministers once again demonstrated their commitment to enhancing the nation's economic prospects and global standing. With a strategic vision in mind, they appointed a Minister for Foreign Trade, entrusted with the vital task of developing UAE exports. This appointment served as a testament to the country's firm belief in the power of international trade and its determination to harness it effectively. By actively nurturing and investing in the capabilities of its young population, the UAE has embraced the notion that human capital and soft power resources play an essential role in driving the country's progress. This realization has propelled the nation towards creating and cultivating a modern economy and a prosperous society united in their pursuit of welfare and well-being. The UAE's vision for the future is built upon the foundations of empowering its youth, fostering international trade, and leveraging its vast potential to achieve unparalleled growth and development. (Alkhaldi et al.2023)(Saradara et al., 2023)(Massouti et al., 2024)(El Khatib et al., 2022).

Climate Change and Environmental Diplomacy

New norms and standards in environmental protection and climate action and worldwide promotion of global and regional green initiatives are crucially important to the UAE. Numerous projects being implemented in the area of renewable energy and climate change adaptation have created favorable results, including growing interest in expert opinions voiced by the country's representatives on the one hand and the provision of assistance and capacity building to different countries on the other. High-quality environmental, nature protection, and environmental sustainability standards, supported by environmental certification programs and information campaigns to ensure that freshwater resources are untapped - an important part of the environmental and climate policy toolkit - have significantly contributed to the position of the UAE in international rankings. Such contribution has been increasing in recent years thanks to existing and newly created global, regional, and international initiatives in climate change and the environment. (Alkhaldi et al.2023)(Afzal et al., 2022)(Locke et al., 2023).

In 2024, the UAE significantly improved its environmental diplomacy tools and developed the climate change agenda due to the long-term visionary goals set by its leadership. The UAE's foreign policy community has not only been effectively promoting its national interests at the global and regional levels but also assumed a great responsibility to contribute constructively to the development of collective actions aimed at addressing challenges to the environment, biodiversity, climate change, and other urgent global issues. The concept has been significantly altered through joint efforts to implement the Strategy of Environmental Diplomacy, with the main purpose primarily directed at turning global challenges into national opportunities. (Saradara et al., 2023)(Bluemenau and Müller, 2024)(Alnaqbi and Alami, 2023).

What is the regional impact of the Abraham Accords?

Some observers of the Middle East scene note that the impact of the Abraham Accords on that scene is geopolitically equal to zero. All the Arab countries that signed those accords do not weigh in the geopolitical balance regarding the Arab-Israeli conflict. Bahrain's current population is roughly 1,496,529. Bahraini citizens account for around 11.5% of the total population. This would amount to approximately 172,000 citizens. The UAE has over 1 million citizens, accounting for around 10.4% of the total population. Sudan did not ratify the deal due to the country's ongoing civil conflict. Morocco is so far from the Middle East that joining the accords makes little difference in the regional power struggle. None of these four countries have ever posed a threat to Israel. So, whether or not they agree on a peace deal with Israel will not impact the power balance. Furthermore, Israel has been exposed as utterly defenceless since October 7, and much more so following the Iranian counter-attack. If Israel is unable to defend its own population, how can it protect other nations? If any Abraham Accords signatories looked for a dissuasive element, this is no longer credible.

The analysis provided raises several points about the Abraham Accords' geopolitical impact, questioning their significance in altering regional power dynamics in the Middle East. To evaluate this perspective, it is essential to consider the accords' motivations and implications for the signatory countries and the broader regional context.

1. Motivations of the Signatory Countries

Bahrain and the UAE: Both countries have strategic reasons for entering the Abraham Accords, primarily concerning their security concerns with Iran. The UAE and Bahrain view the accords as a means to strengthen their international alliances, particularly with the United States, which they perceive as a counterbalance to Iranian influence in the region. The UAE, being the first Gulf state to normalize relations with Israel, sees this as a strategic alignment against a common perceived threat from Iran. Bahrain, following suit, likely views its participation similarly, given its geopolitical vulnerabilities and close ties with Saudi Arabia and the US.

Sudan: The government agreed to normalize relations with Israel primarily to be removed from the US list of state sponsors of terrorism, which was a significant step towards alleviating its international isolation and economic difficulties. However, the deal has not been ratified, reflecting Sudan's complex internal dynamics and ongoing civil conflict, complicating its foreign policy decisions.

Morocco: The government's motivation includes the US recognition of its sovereignty over Western Sahara, which is a significant diplomatic gain. While geographically distant from the Gulf region, Morocco's decision is part of a broader realignment under US auspices, which it views as beneficial for its international standing and bilateral relations with the US and Israel.

2. Geopolitical Impact and Regional Power Dynamics

- Limited Direct Threat to Israel: It is accurate that none of the signatory states posed a direct military threat to Israel prior to the accords. The primary impact here is not about neutralizing a threat but rather about reshaping diplomatic relationships and creating new economic and security collaborations. If we ask, did the UAE need the accords to enhance its economy and security? The answer would probably be Israel and the USA need it much more.

- Iranian Counter-Attack and Israeli Defense: The recent events, including the Iranian counter-attack, have indeed put a spotlight on Israel's security challenges. However, even if Israel is not "completely defenseless", the Iranian counter-attack destabilised it and showed that it is as vulnerable as any regional state. Besides, the USA did not dare strike Iran directly and tried to restrain Israel, fearing an expansion of the war. Many suspect Iran to have the capacity to reach Israel with non-conventional weapons. Israel, lacking the strategic depth that Iran enjoys, would not survive in an all-out war. Saudi Arabia has well understood the stakes and its recent agreement with Iran reflects a new strategic thinking. As the proverb goes, "if you cannot stop them, join them." This means that the UAE, traditionally an ally of KSA, could be the next to join the "party": an agreement with Iran could ease the relations, while impacting the regional power balance. This was not the case with Abraham Accords.

- Credibility of the Dissuasive Element: The effectiveness of the Abraham Accords as a deterrent is debatable. While they signify a shift in regional alignments, they have no strategic value in forming a broader coalition that might deter hostile actions from adversaries like Iran, as the actual military effectiveness and mutual defense capabilities provided by these accords are not clearly defined. The accords are more symbolic and diplomatic rather than military alliances.

Conclusion

The Abraham Accords represent an insignificant shift in regional diplomacy rather than an immediate alteration in the military balance of power. While the direct military impact may be limited, the strengthening of diplomatic ties with the US and among the signatory states themselves carries limited implications for regional politics and security arrangements. The effectiveness of these accords should be viewed through the lens of diplomacy and international relations rather than pure military capabilities.

In summary, the UAE's foreign policy in 2024 is characterized by robust bilateral and multilateral relations, strategic economic diplomacy, a focused security and defense posture, and a strong commitment to humanitarian aid. Viewed from the UAE, these elements collectively enhance the state's standing on the global stage and contribute to regional stability and prosperity.

This book is a research-based exploration of the UAE's most important national decision-making topics related to foreign policy.

Sources and References

Almezaini, Khalid, 'The Transformation of UAE Foreign Policy since 2011', in Kristian Coates Ulrichsen (ed.), *The Changing Security Dynamics of the Persian Gulf* (2018; online edn, Oxford Academic, 21 Feb. 2019), https://doi.org/10.1093/oso/9780190877385.003.0011, accessed 5 May 2024.

El Ketbi, Ebtesam. "In 2024, diplomacy and economic co-operation will define UAE foreign policy", The National. https://www.thenationalnews.com/opinion/comment/2024/01/18/in-2024-diplomacy-and-economic-co-operation-will-define-uae-foreign-policy/

Krasna, Joshua (2023). "Big Changes in United Arab Emirates Foreign Policy". https://www.fpri.org/article/2023/04/big-changes-in-united-arab-emirates-foreign-policy/

MoFA, (2024). https://www.mofa.gov.ae/en/The-Ministry/The-Foreign-Policy/Economic-Diplomacy

UAE Banking Federation Publications. https://www.uaebf.ae/en/publications/trust-index

The Economist (2024)."The UAE is using a wealth fund to gain diplomatic sway". https://www.economist.com/finance-and-economics/2024/04/25/the-uae-is-using-a-wealth-fund-to-gain-diplomatic-sway

EdelmanTrust Barometer 2023. UAE. https://www.edelman.ae/trust-barometer-2023-uae

United Arab Emirates Country Report 2024 - BTI. https://bti-project.org/en/reports/country-report/ARE

Al Suwaidi, A. M. S. J. "THE UNITED ARAB EMIRATES SOFT POWER IN THE INTERNATIONAL RELATIONS CONTEXT." (2021). uaeu.ac.ae

Al-Darmaki, F., Yaaqeib, S. I., and Partridge, S. "Ethical standards for psychological practice in the UAE: current status and aspirations." Ethics & Behavior (2023). [HTML]

Krzymowski, A. "Role and significance of the United Arab Emirates foreign aid for its soft power strategy and sustainable development goals." Social Sciences (2022). mdpi.com

Salisbury, P. "Risk perception and appetite in UAE foreign and national security policy." (2020). chathamhouse.org

Ibrahim, R. A. R. A. and Al-azzawi, S. J. "... soft power and its indicators to build the country's reputation an analytical study of the website publications of the UAE Ministry of Foreign Affairs and International ...." RES MILITARIS (2022). resmilitaris.net

Krzymowski, A. "The European Union and the United Arab Emirates as civilian and soft powers engaged in Sustainable Development Goals." Journal of International Studies (2020). ceon.pl

Alketbi, M. S. A. H. "Sustainable development: influence of economic decisions taken at the state level in the United Arab Emirates (UAE)." (2023). openrepository.com

Aminjonov, F. "Policy innovations and rationale for sustainable energy transition in the UAE." Social Science Quarterly (2020). academia.edu

Litsas, Spyridon N. "Smart States Act Positively in the International Arena: The UAE Case." In Smart Instead of Small in International Relations Theory: The Case of the United Arab Emirates, pp. 99-126. Cham: Springer Nature Switzerland, 2023. [HTML]

Gökalp, D. "The UAE's humanitarian diplomacy: Claiming state sovereignty, regional leverage and international recognition." (2020). cmi.no

Cochrane, L. "The United Arab Emirates as a global donor: What a decade of foreign aid data transparency reveals." Development Studies Research (2021). tandfonline.com

El-Dessouki, Ayman, and Ola Rafik Mansour. "Small states and strategic hedging: the United Arab Emirates' policy towards Iran." Review of Economics and Political Science 8, no. 5 (2023): 394-407. emerald.com

Borck, T. "Seeking Stability Amidst Disorder: The Foreign Policies of Saudi Arabia, the UAE and Qatar, 2010-20." (2024). [HTML]

Albaity, Mohamed, Ray Saadaoui Mallek, Hussein A. Hassan Al-Tamimi, and Philip Molyneux. "Do trust and country governance affect credit growth in GCC countries?." International Journal of Islamic and Middle Eastern Finance and Management 16, no. 3 (2023): 516-538. [HTML]

El Khatib, Mounir, Abdulrahman Ahmed AlMansoori, and Saeed Alsuwidi. "The importance of Trust in digital transformation and SMART Government initiatives." International Journal of Business Analytics and Security (IJBAS) 4, no. 2 (2024): 16-38. gaftim.com

Alshamlan, Mariam Abdalla, Vania Maria Fernandez, and Manuel Fernandez. "Foreign direct investment in the United Arab Emirates: A study on the main contributors." European Journal of Business and Management Research 6, no. 1 (2021): 97-101. ejbmr.org

Crupi, Antonio, and Daniele Schilirò. "The UAE Economy and the Path to Diversification and Innovation." INTERNATIONAL JOURNAL OF BUSINESS MANAGEMENT AND ECONOMIC RESEARCH (2023): 2286-2300. ijbmer.com

Due-Gundersen, N. and Al Suwaidi, K. "Potential for the UAE as a Model for Coordinating GCC-Wide Economic Diversification." (2024). researchgate.net

Shahrour, K. "The evolution of Emirati foreign policy (1971-2020): The unexpected rise of a small state with boundless ambitions." Paris: Science Po (2020). sciencespo.fr

Vetter, D. "Soft Power in the United Arab Emirates: Their Quest for Reputational Security." phaidra.univie.ac.at . univie.ac.at

Kaye, D. D., Robinson, L., Martini, J., Vest, N., and Rhoades, A. L. "Reimagining US strategy in the Middle East: Sustainable partnerships, strategic investments." (2021). dtic.mil

Krieg, A. "Security assistance to surrogates–how the UAE secures its regional objectives." Mediterranean Politics (2023). tandfonline.com

Brehony, Noel. "The UAE's role in the Yemen crisis." Global, regional, and local dynamics in the Yemen crisis (2020): 131-147. [HTML]

Al-Ansari, M. M. H., Aras, B., and Yorulmazlar, E. "The new gulf order: Crisis, mediation, and reconciliation." Middle East Policy (2021). researchgate.net

Colombo, S. and Dessì, A. "Collective Security and Multilateral Engagement in the Middle East: Pathways for EU Policy." (2022). iai.it

Janardhan, N. "Asia in an emerging Gulf collective security framework." Asian perceptions of Gulf security (2022). taylorfrancis.com

Lootah, M. S. "The United Arab Emirates as a leading country in tolerance." Pt. 2 J. Legal Ethical & Regul. Isses (2021). [HTML]

Baycar, H. "Promoting multiculturalism and tolerance: Expanding the meaning of "unity through diversity" in the United Arab Emirates." Digest of Middle East Studies (2023). wiley.com

Alhashmi, M., Bakali, N., and Baroud, R. "Tolerance in UAE Islamic education textbooks." Religions (2020). mdpi.com

Dazi-Héni, F. "The war in Ukraine and Arab Gulf states' foreign policy shifts." European Review of International Studies (2023). [HTML]

Kirmanj, S. and Tofik, R. "The UAE's Foreign Policy Drivers." Middle East Policy (2023). [HTML]

Borck, T. "Seeking Stability Amidst Disorder: The Foreign Policies of Saudi Arabia, the UAE and Qatar, 2010-20." (2024). [HTML]

Kertcher, C. and Schiff, A. "Unpacking Unofficial Normalization: Israel's Unofficial Relations with the UAE and the Abraham Accords." Journal of Asian and African Studies (2024). sagepub.com

Hallward, Maia Carter, and Taib Biygautane. "Arab State Narratives on Normalization with Israel: Justifying Policy Reversal." Contemporary Review of the Middle East (2024): 23477989231220444. [HTML]

Ali, Nawazish, and Muhammad Saeed Uzzaman. "Capitalizing on Geo-economics: Opportunities for Israel and UAE in Post-Abraham Accords Era." INTERNATIONAL JOURNAL OF HUMAN AND SOCIETY 3, no. 4 (2023): 328-340. ijhs.com.pk

El Amine, R. "The GCC countries diplomatic approaches and its impact on economic development: a comparative study of the UAE, Saudi Arabia, Qatar, and Kuwait." (2023). ndu.edu.lb

Mason, R. "Saudi Arabia and the United Arab Emirates: Foreign policy and strategic alliances in an uncertain world." Saudi Arabia and the United Arab Emirates (2023). [HTML]

Puri, A., Teckchandani, J., and Rahman, A. "India-UAE Relations: Emerging Dynamics." CEMJP (2022). archive.org

Schiff, A. and Kertcher, C. "Silent alliances and shifting tides: unveiling the hidden pathways to resolving interstate rivalries–the UAE-Israel case." International Journal of Conflict Management (2024). [HTML]

Antwi-Boateng, O. and Alhashmi, A. A. "The emergence of the United Arab Emirates as a global soft power: current strategies and future challenges." Economic and Political Studies (2022). researchgate.net

Al Rashedi, Naser, Fatima Al Shamsi, and Hamda Al Hosani. "UAE approach to space and security." In Handbook of Space Security: Policies, Applications and Programs, pp. 621-652. Cham: Springer International Publishing, 2020. [HTML]

Locke, J., Dsilva, J., and Zarmukhambetova, S. "Decarbonization strategies in the UAE built environment: An evidence-based analysis using COP26 and COP27 recommendations." Sustainability (2023). mdpi.com

Alkhaldi, Mohammed, Immanuel Azaad Moonesar, Sahar T. Issa, Wissam Ghach, Ahmad Okasha, Marina Albada, Sabrina Chelli, and Aseel A. Takshe. "Analysis of the United Arab Emirates' contribution to the sustainable development goals with a focus on global health and climate change." International Journal of Health Governance 28, no. 4 (2023): 357-367. emerald.com

Saradara, S. M., Khalfan, M. M. A., Rauf, A., and Qureshi, R. "On the path towards sustainable construction—the case of the United Arab Emirates: a review." Sustainability (2023). mdpi.com

Massouti, A., Al-Rashaida, M., and Alhosani, M. "A qualitative study on Dubai's inclusive education policy from school leaders' perspectives." Sustainability (2024). mdpi.com

El Khatib, M., Al Mulla, A., and Al Ketbi, W. "The role of blockchain in e-governance and decision-making in project and program management." Advances in Internet of Things (2022). scirp.org

Afzal, M. S., Tahir, F., and Al-Ghamdi, S. G. "Recommendations and strategies to mitigate environmental implications of artificial island developments in the Gulf." Sustainability (2022). mdpi.com

Bluemenau, B. and Müller, J. A. "More similarities than (initially) meet the eye? The international community and the evolution of antiterrorism and climate change governance." (2024). fondation-pierredubois.ch

Alnaqbi, S. A. and Alami, A. H. "Sustainability and Renewable Energy in the UAE: A Case Study of Sharjah." Energies (2023). mdpi.com

I

The Historical Foundations of UAE Foreign Policy

The Emergence of the UAE: Tracing the Formation of the United Arab Emirates

The Emergence of the UAE: Tracing the Formation of the United Arab Emirates The United Arab Emirates (UAE) is a nation born out of a unique blend of history, culture, and geopolitical realities. The formation of the UAE was not a sudden event but rather a process that evolved over time, shaped by the complex interactions of tribes, sheikhs, and regional dynamics. In the early 19th century, the area now known as the UAE was a collection of loosely affiliated tribes, each led by their own sheikh and existing within a decentralized political landscape. These tribes engaged in trade, hunting, and pearl diving, shaping their identities and networks of influence. As the region began to experience increased external influence from European powers and the Ottoman Empire, the tribes realized the need for unity and cooperation to safeguard their interests and maintain stability. This realization culminated in the formation of the Trucial States in the early 19th century, a loose confederation of sheikhdoms that sought to manage external relations and protect their territories. The signing of the General Treaty of Peace in 1820 with the British government marked a turning point in the region's history, formalizing the relationship between the Trucial States and the British Empire. This treaty protected the sheikhdoms in exchange for exclusive British control over their foreign affairs. Over the years, the Trucial States continued to navigate the complexities of regional politics, including interactions with neighboring states and the changing dynamics of world events. The discovery of oil in the region in the 20th century brought newfound wealth and opportunities but posed challenges in governance and development. In 1971, the seven emirates of Abu Dhabi, Dubai, Sharjah, Ajman, Umm Al-Quwain, Fujairah, and Ras Al Khaimah came together to form the United Arab Emirates, with Ras Al Khaimah joining shortly after. This union represented a significant milestone in the history of the region, symbolizing a commitment to unity, progress, and shared prosperity. The emergence of the UAE as a sovereign nation was a testament to its founding fathers' vision, leadership, and perseverance, who recognized the importance of cooperation and collaboration in navigating the complexities of the modern world. This spirit of unity and determination continues to shape the UAE's identity and foreign policy strategies to this day.

Pre-Independence Diplomacy: The Role of Tribes and Sheikhs in Shaping Foreign Relations

In the years preceding the formation of the United Arab Emirates, the Arabian Peninsula was a patchwork of tribes and sheikhdoms, each with its own unique identity and allegiances. These tribes and sheikhs played a crucial role in shaping the diplomatic landscape of the region, laying the groundwork for the foreign relations of the future UAE. The tribal dynamics of the region were complex, with alliances and rivalries shifting based on historical ties, trade relationships, and shared cultural heritage. Tribes often formed the backbone of social and political structures, with a system of traditional governance in place that relied on consensus-building and mediation. Sheikhs, as the leaders of these tribes, held great influence over their people and territories. Their decisions and actions carried weight not only within their own community but also in the broader regional context. By forging alliances and treaties with neighboring tribes and external powers, sheikhs played a key role in safeguarding the interests and security of their people. Pre-independence diplomacy in the region was characterized by a delicate balance of power and shifting allegiances. Sheikhs navigated a complex web of relationships with neighboring tribes, the British colonial authorities, and emerging regional powers. They engaged in strategic negotiations, trade agreements, and conflict resolution efforts to maintain stability and secure favorable outcomes for their communities. The role of tribes and sheikhs in shaping foreign relations laid the foundation for the future diplomatic endeavors of the UAE. Their deep understanding of local dynamics, traditional governance structures, and intricate networks of alliances provided invaluable insights that would inform the diplomatic strategies of the newly formed federation. As the UAE embarked on its journey towards independence, the legacy of pre-independence diplomacy remained a crucial element in shaping the country's foreign policy priorities. The role of tribes and sheikhs in navigating the complexities of regional politics and forging strategic partnerships set the stage for the UAE's emergence as a key player on the global stage.

Early Diplomatic Engagements: Establishing Relationships with Key Regional and Global Players

As the tribes and sheikhs in the region laid the groundwork for future diplomatic engagements, the emerging United Arab Emirates focused on establishing relationships with key regional and global players. In the early stages, the UAE sought to solidify ties with neighboring countries in the Gulf region, recognizing the importance of cooperation for security and economic prosperity. Efforts were also made to engage with major powers on the global stage, with a focus on building alliances that would support the young nation's development and stability. Through diplomatic channels, the UAE worked to forge partnerships with countries such as the United States, the United Kingdom, and France, seeking to leverage their political and economic influence for mutual benefit. These early engagements laid the foundation for sustained cooperation and collaboration in areas such as trade, defense, and security. The UAE also sought to enhance its diplomatic presence in international organizations, showcasing its commitment to multilateralism and global governance. Joining forums such as the United Nations and the Arab League allowed the UAE to voice its perspectives on key issues and contribute to shaping international policies. Moreover, the UAE prioritized building relationships with countries in the Middle East and North Africa region, recognizing the interconnectedness of regional dynamics and the need for cooperation to address shared challenges. By fostering ties with countries such as Egypt, Jordan, and Saudi Arabia, the UAE positioned itself as a key player in regional diplomacy and a stabilizing force in a volatile geopolitical environment. In navigating the complex landscape of international relations, the early diplomatic engagements of the UAE emphasized the importance of dialogue, cooperation, and building trust with key partners. These efforts laid the groundwork for a foreign policy that would continue to evolve and adapt to the changing dynamics of the global arena.

The Influence of Pan-Arabism: Nasser and the United Arab Republic

The concept of Pan-Arabism, championed by Egyptian President Gamal Abdel Nasser, had a significant influence on the formation and early foreign relations of the United Arab Emirates. Nasser's vision of Arab unity and solidarity resonated with many leaders in the region, including the founding fathers of the UAE. The establishment of the United Arab Republic between Egypt and Syria in 1958 further underscored the importance of pan-Arab ideology in shaping political alliances and cooperation in the Middle East. The United Arab Republic's dissolution in 1961 did not diminish the appeal of Pan-Arabism in the region. As newly independent states like the UAE sought to navigate the complex dynamics of post-colonial politics, the principles of unity and cooperation espoused by Nasser remained influential. The UAE's leaders understood the strategic value of aligning with other Arab nations to enhance their collective strength and influence on the global stage. Despite some differences in approach and priorities, the UAE maintained a cordial relationship with Egypt and other Arab states that shared a commitment to Pan-Arab ideals. This alignment helped the UAE navigate regional challenges and forge alliances that advanced its interests in promoting stability and cooperation in the Middle East. The legacy of Pan-Arabism continues to inform the UAE's diplomatic engagements with Arab countries, underscoring the importance of shared history, culture, and strategic objectives in shaping foreign policy decisions.

The Gulf Cooperation Council: Strengthening Regional Cooperation and Unity

Following the formation of the United Arab Emirates and the regional geopolitical landscape shaped by Pan-Arabism, the Gulf Cooperation Council (GCC) emerged as a pivotal institution in strengthening regional cooperation and unity. Established in 1981, the GCC aimed to enhance economic, political, and security ties among its member states – Bahrain, Kuwait, Oman, Qatar, Saudi Arabia, and the United Arab Emirates. The formation of the GCC marked a significant step towards promoting collective security and stability in the Gulf region. Through mutual cooperation and collaboration, member states sought to address common challenges and promote shared interests. The GCC's collective security framework provided a platform for dialogue and coordination on regional security issues, contributing to the maintenance of peace and stability in the Gulf. Economically, the GCC promoted intra-regional trade and investment, fostering economic integration and diversification. The establishment of the Gulf Common Market in 2008 aimed to create a unified economic space, facilitating the flow of goods, services, and capital across member states. This economic integration bolstered the region's competitiveness and resilience in the global market. Moreover, the GCC played a crucial role in promoting cultural exchange and social cohesion among member states. Cultural initiatives and educational programs supported cross-cultural understanding and cooperation, nurturing a sense of shared identity and heritage within the Gulf region. These cultural exchanges not only strengthened social ties but also promoted a sense of unity and solidarity among member states. In the realm of diplomacy, the GCC served as a platform for collective engagement with external partners, amplifying the voice of Gulf countries on the international stage. Through coordinated diplomatic efforts, member states were able to advocate for their interests and positions on key regional and global issues, enhancing the GCC's influence and visibility in the international arena. Overall, the Gulf Cooperation Council's commitment to strengthening regional cooperation and unity has been instrumental in fostering a sense of solidarity and partnership among its member states. By promoting economic integration, collective security, cultural exchange, and diplomatic coordination, the GCC has played a significant role in shaping the Gulf region's dynamics and advancing shared objectives for the benefit of its member states.

The Iran-Iraq War: Navigating Regional Conflicts and Alliances

The Iran-Iraq War: Navigating Regional Conflicts and Alliances Amid the turbulent landscape of the Middle East, the Iran-Iraq War presented a significant challenge for the United Arab Emirates as it sought to navigate regional conflicts and alliances. The war, which lasted from 1980 to 1988, was characterized by intense hostilities between two key regional powers, Iran and Iraq. For the UAE, the Iran-Iraq War posed a complex diplomatic dilemma. On the one hand, the country maintained close economic ties with both Iran and Iraq, making it imperative to balance its relationships with the warring parties carefully. The UAE's strategic location in the Gulf region further heightened the challenges posed by the conflict as the country sought to ensure its security and stability amidst escalating tensions. Throughout the war, the UAE pursued a neutral foreign policy stance, emphasizing the importance of dialogue and diplomatic engagement in resolving regional conflicts. This approach reflected the country's commitment to promoting peace and stability in the region while safeguarding its own interests. Despite the complexities of the Iran-Iraq War, the UAE's diplomatic efforts during this period played a crucial role in de-escalating tensions and fostering dialogue among key regional players. By leveraging its position as a neutral and trusted mediator, the UAE demonstrated its commitment to conflict resolution and peacebuilding in the Middle East. As the Iran-Iraq War drew to a close, the UAE's diplomatic leadership in navigating regional conflicts and alliances laid the foundation for its continued engagement in promoting peace and stability in the region. This pivotal period underscored the importance of dialogue, diplomacy, and strategic decision-making in addressing complex geopolitical challenges and advancing the UAE's foreign policy objectives.

The First Gulf War: The UAE's Role in the International Coalition

The First Gulf War marked a turning point in the history of the United Arab Emirates, as the country actively participated in the international coalition formed to liberate Kuwait from Iraqi occupation. The UAE's decision to join the coalition reflected its commitment to upholding regional stability and security. The leadership of the UAE recognized the importance of standing against aggression and supporting international efforts to maintain peace in the region. The UAE's involvement in the First Gulf War was multifaceted, encompassing both military and humanitarian contributions. The country deployed troops to support the coalition's military campaign, demonstrating its willingness to take a stand against threats to regional security. Additionally, the UAE played a key role in providing humanitarian aid to the people of Kuwait, reflecting its commitment to supporting its neighbors in times of need. The First Gulf War showcased the UAE's capabilities as a regional player and highlighted its commitment to promoting peace and stability in the Middle East. The country's active participation in the international coalition underscored its willingness to collaborate with other nations to address shared security challenges. By standing shoulder to shoulder with its allies, the UAE demonstrated its readiness to defend common values and principles in the face of adversity. Overall, the UAE's role in the First Gulf War underscored its position as a responsible and reliable partner in the international community. The experience of participating in the coalition helped shape the country's foreign policy approach and reinforced its commitment to promoting peace and security in the region. The lessons learned from the First Gulf War continue to inform the UAE's engagement with the global community and its efforts to contribute to a more stable and prosperous world.

The Arab Spring: Challenges and Opportunities for UAE Foreign Policy

The Arab Spring presented a complex set of challenges and opportunities for UAE foreign policy. As popular uprisings and protests swept across the Arab world, the UAE faced the need to navigate its response to these regional developments carefully. While the UAE leadership expressed concern about the potential for instability and the rise of radical elements in the region, it also recognized the demands for political reform and social change voiced by the Arab Spring movements. The UAE government responded by emphasizing the importance of stability, security, and development in the region. It sought to balance its support for stability with a commitment to addressing the legitimate grievances of the people. The UAE engaged in diplomatic efforts to advocate for peaceful resolutions to the conflicts arising from the Arab Spring while also promoting dialogue and reconciliation among the warring factions. Moreover, the Arab Spring underscored the importance of economic diversification for the UAE. As the unrest in the region disrupted traditional markets and supply chains, the UAE recognized the need to expand its economic reach beyond oil and gas. The government initiated policies to attract foreign investment, promote entrepreneurship, and foster innovation in non-oil sectors. In light of the Arab Spring, the UAE reevaluated its foreign policy approach, recognizing the need to adapt to the changing dynamics in the region. By engaging in dialogue, supporting stability, and pursuing economic diversification, the UAE sought to position itself as a key player in shaping the future of the Middle East amidst the challenges and opportunities presented by the Arab Spring.

Economic Diversification: The Shift towards a Trade and Investment-based Foreign Policy

The United Arab Emirates' strategic shift towards economic diversification has played a pivotal role in shaping its foreign policy approach. In response to the challenges posed by the Arab Spring and the evolving global economic landscape, the UAE has increasingly focused on fostering trade and investment partnerships to ensure sustainable growth and stability. This move towards a trade and investment-based foreign policy reflects the country's commitment to diversifying its economy and reducing reliance on oil revenues. By leveraging its economic strength and strategic location, the UAE has positioned itself as a key player in the global marketplace. The country has proactively sought to attract foreign investment, promote entrepreneurship, and facilitate trade through the development of world-class infrastructure and business-friendly policies. This emphasis on economic diversification has not only enhanced the UAE's economic resilience but has also strengthened its diplomatic relationships with countries around the world. Through initiatives such as the UAE Vision 2021 and the UAE Centennial 2071, the government has outlined a clear roadmap for transitioning to a knowledge-based economy driven by innovation and technology. These ambitious goals have propelled the UAE onto the global stage as a hub for innovation, research, and development, attracting foreign expertise and investment in key sectors such as renewable energy, healthcare, and technology. Furthermore, the UAE's proactive engagement in international trade agreements and economic forums has enabled the country to forge mutually beneficial partnerships with a diverse range of countries. By promoting free trade and investment, the UAE has demonstrated its commitment to fostering economic growth and prosperity not only for itself but also for its global partners. As the UAE continues to pursue its economic diversification agenda, its trade and investment-based foreign policy will remain a cornerstone of its diplomatic efforts. By harnessing the power of economic diplomacy, the UAE seeks to build bridges, create opportunities, and contribute to a more interconnected and prosperous world for all.

The Vision of the Founding Fathers: Shaping the Core Principles of UAE Foreign Policy

The vision of the founding fathers of the United Arab Emirates has played a crucial role in shaping the core principles of the country's foreign policy. The late Sheikh Zayed bin Sultan Al Nahyan and his fellow rulers envisioned a nation that would be built on principles of tolerance, diplomacy, and cooperation. These foundational values have guided the UAE's approach to international relations since its formation in 1971. Sheikh Zayed's commitment to diplomacy and peaceful coexistence has been a cornerstone of UAE foreign policy. His belief in the importance of dialogue and negotiation as tools for resolving disputes and building alliances has been instrumental in establishing the UAE as a key player on the global stage. This commitment to diplomacy has helped the UAE navigate complex regional and international challenges while promoting stability and prosperity in the region. Another key principle of UAE foreign policy is economic diversification. The founding fathers recognized the importance of moving beyond reliance on oil revenues and prioritized the development of trade and investment partnerships as a means of ensuring long-term economic sustainability. This shift towards a trade and investment-based foreign policy has allowed the UAE to enhance its economic competitiveness and establish itself as a hub for global business and innovation. Furthermore, the founding fathers of the UAE placed a strong emphasis on cultural diplomacy as a means of promoting understanding and cooperation between nations. They understood the power of cultural exchange in fostering ties between people from different backgrounds and beliefs. This commitment to cultural diplomacy has seen the UAE host numerous cultural events, festivals, and exhibitions that showcase the country's rich heritage and promote dialogue and mutual respect among nations. In conclusion, the vision of the founding fathers continues to play a vital role in shaping the core principles of UAE foreign policy. Their commitment to diplomacy, economic diversification, and cultural exchange has helped the UAE establish itself as a respected and influential player in the international arena. By staying true to these principles, the UAE will continue to navigate the complexities of the global landscape while promoting peace, prosperity, and cooperation.

In a Nutshell

The formation of the United Arab Emirates (UAE) in 1971 significantly shaped its foreign policy by establishing a framework for unity, security, and international engagement among the federation's seven emirates. This historical context has influenced the UAE's approach to regional and global affairs, driven by the need to secure its position and interests in a volatile region.

HISTORICAL CONTEXT AND FORMATION

The UAE was formed from the Trucial States, a collection of sheikhdoms along the southern coast of the Persian Gulf. The federation was established in response to the withdrawal of British forces from the Gulf region, creating a vacuum that the new country needed to fill quickly to ensure its survival and sovereignty. The last emirate, Ras al Khaimah, joined in 1972, completing the federation[1][16].

EARLY CHALLENGES AND SECURITY CONCERNS

Initially, the UAE faced significant security challenges, including territorial disputes with neighboring countries such as Iran and Saudi Arabia. The early foreign policy was heavily focused on establishing the UAE's legitimacy and securing its borders. The resolution of the Buraimi dispute with Saudi Arabia in 1974 was a critical early success in this regard[1].

ROLE OF FOUNDING LEADERS

The UAE's foreign policy has been profoundly influenced by its founding father, Sheikh Zayed bin Sultan Al Nahyan, who was the principal architect of the federation and its foreign policy until his death in 2004. His vision emphasized unity among the emirates and peaceful coexistence with neighboring countries. Sheikh Zayed's policies were characterized by pragmatism and a focus on development and humanitarian issues[1][12][19].

INFLUENCE OF TRIBAL DYNAMICS

Tribal dynamics have also significantly shaped the UAE's foreign policy. The country's political structure is deeply intertwined with its tribal makeup, and each emirate is governed by a ruling family. This structure has influenced the UAE's diplomatic approach, which often reflects the consensus among these ruling families[4].

REGIONAL ALLIANCES AND THE GULF COOPERATION COUNCIL

The formation of the Gulf Cooperation Council (GCC) in 1981 was a significant development in the UAE's regional policy. The UAE has used the GCC platform to enhance security cooperation and economic integration with its Gulf neighbors. This alliance has been crucial in coordinating policies regarding regional issues such as the Iran-Iraq War and the Qatar diplomatic crisis[1][12].

ECONOMIC AND STRATEGIC SHIFTS

Over the years, the UAE's foreign policy has evolved to include a stronger focus on economic diplomacy and global engagement. The discovery of oil and the subsequent economic boom transformed the UAE into a significant player in global energy markets, expanding its diplomatic reach. The UAE has leveraged its economic success to build a robust network of global partnerships[1][5][10].

MODERN DIPLOMATIC ENGAGEMENTS

In recent years, the UAE has adopted a more assertive foreign policy stance, as seen in its military involvement in Yemen and its normalization of relations with Israel through the Abraham Accords. These actions reflect a shift towards a more proactive foreign policy that seeks to secure the UAE's strategic interests while also positioning it as a key player in regional and global affairs[2][3][13].

CONCLUSION

The formation of the UAE set the foundation for a foreign policy characterized by pragmatism, strategic alliances, and an increasing openness to global engagement. From securing its initial legitimacy and territorial integrity to becoming a dynamic global player, the UAE's foreign policy continues to be shaped by its foundational experiences and the vision of its leaders[1][12][19].

References

[1] https://www.chathamhouse.org/2020/07/risk-perception-and-appetite-uae-foreign-and-national-security-policy-0/2-uaes-foreign-and
[2] https://academic.oup.com/book/8975/chapter-abstract/155312223?redirectedFrom=fulltext
[3] https://www.fpri.org/article/2023/04/big-changes-in-united-arab-emirates-foreign-policy/
[4] https://info.publicintelligence.net/MCIA-UnitedArabEmiratesCulture-Guide.pdf
[5] https://icwa.in/pdfs/DrLakshmiSHP.pdf
[6] https://www.mofa.gov.ae/en/The-Ministry
[7] https://repositorio.ual.pt/bitstream/11144/5671/1/08-EN-vol13-n2-art05.pdf
[8] https://sgp.fas.org/crs/mideast/RS21852.pdf
[9] https://www.cmi.no/publications/file/7169-the-uaes-humanitarian-diplomacy-claiming-state-sovereignty.pdf
[10] https://scholarworks.uaeu.ac.ae/cgi/viewcontent.cgi?article=1854&context=all_theses
[11] http://etheses.dur.ac.uk/3448/1/electronic_version_of_my_thesis.pdf
[12] https://www.mofaic.gov.ae/en/Missions/Paris/The-UAE/Foreign-Policy
[13] https://onlinelibrary.wiley.com/doi/full/10.1111/dome.12286
[14] https://uaecabinet.ae/en/uae-vision
[15] https://www.uae-embassy.org/discover-uae/foreign-policy
[16] https://www.marines.mil/Portals/1/Publications/UAE%20Profile.pdf
[17] https://www.washingtoninstitute.org/policy-analysis/uae-after-sheikh-zayed-tensions-between-tribe-and-state
[18] https://carnegieendowment.org/sada/86130
[19] https://www.uae-embassy.org/discover-uae/sheikh-zayed-bin-sultan-al-

nahyan
[20] https://www.thecairoreview.com/essays/the-rise-of-the-united-arab-emirates/

II

The Role of Leadership in UAE Foreign Policy

Leadership Influence in UAE Foreign Policy

The United Arab Emirates (UAE) has emerged as a key player in the global arena, with its foreign policy decisions attracting widespread attention and scrutiny. At the heart of the UAE's foreign policy framework lies the significant influence of its founding fathers and visionaries. The visionary leaders who laid the foundation of the UAE played a crucial role in shaping the country's approach towards international relations and diplomacy. Sheikh Zayed bin Sultan Al Nahyan, the founding father of the UAE, was a visionary leader who emphasized the principles of tolerance, diplomacy, and cooperation in the country's foreign policy. His commitment to building strong relationships with neighboring states and the international community set the tone for the UAE's diplomatic endeavors. Sheikh Zayed's vision of a united and prosperous UAE guided subsequent rulers and leaders in their foreign policy decisions. His emphasis on dialogue, peaceful coexistence, and economic development as tools of diplomacy continues to influence the country's approach to global affairs. The legacy of Sheikh Zayed is embedded in the foreign policy initiatives of the UAE, with his principles of mutual respect, cooperation, and non-interference serving as guiding principles for the country's interactions on the world stage. The foundation laid by the UAE's founding fathers continues to shape the leadership's influence on foreign policy, reinforcing the country's commitment to stability, security, and prosperity in the region and beyond.

Founding Fathers and Visionaries: The Influence of UAE's Founding Rulers

The founding fathers of the United Arab Emirates, including Sheikh Zayed bin Sultan Al Nahyan and Sheikh Rashid bin Saeed Al Maktoum, played an instrumental role in shaping the country's foreign policy foundations. Their vision, leadership, and strategic outlook laid the groundwork for the UAE's approach to international relations. Sheikh Zayed, in particular, espoused principles of tolerance, diplomacy, and peaceful coexistence, which continue to influence the UAE's foreign policy to this day. His emphasis on building strong relationships with neighboring countries and the international community set a precedent for the country's engagement on the global stage. Sheikh Rashid also contributed significantly to the UAE's foreign policy landscape, focusing on economic development, infrastructure growth, and regional stability. His pragmatic approach to governance and diplomacy helped establish the UAE as a key player in the Middle East and beyond. The founding rulers' commitment to unity, progress, and prosperity for the UAE and its people served as a guiding light for the nation's foreign policy objectives. Their legacy of leadership continues to inspire a forward-thinking and proactive approach to international relations, anchored in the values of cooperation, solidarity, and mutual respect.

Contemporary Leadership: The Role of the Current Ruler in Shaping Foreign Policy

The contemporary leadership of the UAE, exemplified by His Highness Sheikh Mohammed bin Zayed Al Nahyan, plays a pivotal role in shaping the country's foreign policy. As the President of the UAE and the ruler of Abu Dhabi, Sheikh Mohammed's leadership style and strategic vision have considerable influence on how the UAE engages with the international community. His commitment to maintaining the legacy of the founding fathers while adapting to the realities of the modern world demonstrates a continuity of purpose and a steadfast dedication to advancing the interests of the UAE on the global stage. Sheikh Mohammed's leadership is characterized by a pragmatic approach that blends traditional values with a forward-looking mindset. His emphasis on economic diversification, innovation, and sustainability has propelled the UAE onto the world stage as a hub for trade, investment, and technological advancement. Under his guidance, the UAE has forged strategic partnerships with key international players, positioning the country as a reliable and dynamic partner in addressing global challenges.

Moreover, Sheikh Mohammed's leadership style is marked by a commitment to stability, security, and prosperity for the UAE and the wider region. His engagement in diplomatic efforts to promote peace and dialogue underscores the UAE's role as a responsible member of the international community. By prioritizing dialogue, cooperation, and mutual respect in its foreign relations, the UAE, under Sheikh Mohammed's leadership, has earned a reputation as a bridge-builder and a peacemaker in a turbulent region. In navigating the complex geopolitical landscape of the 21st century, Sheikh Mohammed's leadership has been instrumental in steering the UAE toward a future defined by innovation, resilience, and global engagement. His vision for the UAE as a thriving, diverse, and forward-looking nation has shaped the country's foreign policy agenda, inspiring confidence and fostering trust among its partners around the world. Sheikh Mohammed's leadership legacy is a testament to the enduring values of the UAE and its unwavering commitment to shaping a brighter future for generations to come.

Institutional Framework: How Leadership is Manifested in Government Structures

The institutional framework within the United Arab Emirates plays a crucial role in translating the leadership's vision into tangible foreign policy outcomes. At the core of this framework is the Ministry of Foreign Affairs and International Cooperation, which serves as the primary governmental entity responsible for formulating and implementing the country's foreign policy objectives. The Ministry is headed by a Minister of Foreign Affairs who oversees a team of dedicated diplomats and foreign policy experts. These individuals work closely with other government agencies, including the National Security Council and the Presidential Court, to ensure a coordinated approach to foreign affairs. The UAE's Federal National Council also provides a platform for parliamentary oversight and input on foreign policy matters. Through debates, discussions, and consultations with government officials, members of the Federal National Council contribute to shaping the country's external relations agenda. Furthermore, the diplomatic corps, consisting of ambassadors and diplomatic missions worldwide, serve as essential conduits for advancing the UAE's diplomatic goals. These representatives maintain close ties with their host countries, engage in bilateral and multilateral negotiations, and promote the UAE's interests on the global stage. In aligning with the leadership's directives, the institutional framework of the UAE emphasizes efficiency, effectiveness, and adaptability in responding to evolving geopolitical challenges. By fostering collaboration among various government entities and leveraging the expertise of dedicated professionals, the institutional framework ensures that the UAE's foreign policy remains agile and responsive to the dynamic international landscape.

Decision-Making Processes: Understanding How Leadership Directs Foreign Policy Actions

Decision-making in UAE foreign policy is a complex and nuanced process that is heavily influenced by leadership. The government structures in the UAE play a crucial role in facilitating these decisions, providing a framework within which leadership can direct foreign policy actions. A combination of institutional mechanisms, consultative processes, and the personal involvement of key leaders characterizes the decision-making process. At the institutional level, the UAE's government structures are designed to facilitate coordination and coherence in foreign policy decision-making. Key institutions such as the Ministry of Foreign Affairs and International Cooperation, the National Security Council, and various specialized committees are central in advising leadership and formulating policy recommendations. These institutions serve as the backbone of the decision-making process, providing expertise and analysis to inform key policy choices. Consultative processes are another important aspect of decision-making in UAE foreign policy. Leadership regularly engages with various stakeholders, including government officials, experts, and representatives from key sectors such as business and academia. These consultations help ensure that policy decisions are well-informed and reflect a diversity of perspectives. By soliciting input from a wide array of sources, leadership can better understand the implications of different policy options and make decisions that are grounded in both expertise and stakeholder feedback. Personal diplomacy, particularly leader-to-leader interactions, also plays a significant role in shaping foreign policy decisions in the UAE. The personal relationships that leaders cultivate with their counterparts worldwide can directly impact the direction and outcomes of foreign policy initiatives. Leaders leverage their personal networks to build trust, forge alliances, and navigate delicate international dynamics. By engaging directly with other world leaders, UAE leadership can influence decision-making processes at the highest levels and advance the country's strategic interests on the global stage. Overall, the decision-making processes that drive UAE foreign policy are multifaceted and dynamic, reflecting the interplay of institutional frameworks, consultative practices, and personal diplomacy. Leadership's role in directing these processes is central, shaping the direction and outcomes of foreign policy actions in accordance with the country's strategic priorities and long-term vision for international engagement.

Personal Diplomacy: The Importance of Leader-to-Leader Interactions

Personal diplomacy plays a crucial role in shaping the course of international relations and foreign policy. When leaders engage directly with their counterparts on the global stage, it can have a significant impact on the direction and outcomes of diplomatic initiatives. In the case of the UAE, leader-to-leader interactions have been central to advancing the country's interests and building strong relationships with key partners. The personal diplomacy of UAE leaders involves not only formal state visits and diplomatic summits but also informal meetings and conversations that take place behind closed doors. These interactions provide an opportunity for leaders to establish rapport, build trust, and communicate directly about complex issues facing their countries. Through personal diplomacy, UAE leaders can influence the decision-making processes of other nations, forge alliances, and promote shared interests. By engaging directly with world leaders, they can convey the UAE's strategic vision, priorities, and commitment to collaboration on global challenges. Furthermore, personal diplomacy allows UAE leaders to project an image of stability, competence, and vision on the world stage, enhancing the country's reputation and credibility in international affairs. Building strong personal relationships with other leaders can also help mitigate misunderstandings, resolve disputes, and navigate complex geopolitical dynamics effectively. In an increasingly interconnected and interdependent world, personal diplomacy remains a powerful tool in the arsenal of foreign policy. By prioritizing leader-to-leader interactions, the UAE can continue strengthening its position as a key player in global affairs and advancing its long-term strategic vision for foreign policy.

Vision 2030: Leadership's Long-Term Strategic Vision for Foreign Policy

Under the visionary leadership of the late Sheikh Khalifa bin Zayed Al Nahyan, the previous president, the UAE has set a comprehensive and ambitious roadmap for its foreign policy objectives with Vision 2030. This long-term strategic vision aims to position the UAE as a global leader across various dimensions of international relations. Vision 2030 encapsulates a proactive approach to diplomacy, emphasizing strategic partnerships, economic diversification, and sustainable development. The UAE seeks to enhance its influence and promote stability in the region and beyond by leveraging its soft power assets and fostering mutually beneficial relationships with other nations. Central to Vision 2030 is the concept of forward-thinking leadership that anticipates and adapts to evolving geopolitical challenges. By investing in human capital, innovation, and technology, the UAE aims to secure its position as a hub for knowledge-based industries and a driver of economic growth in the region. Through Vision 2030, the UAE underscores its commitment to promoting peace, tolerance, and prosperity on the global stage. By championing initiatives that address pressing global issues such as climate change, cybersecurity, and humanitarian aid, the UAE seeks to build a more resilient and interconnected world. As the UAE continues to navigate the complexities of the international arena, Vision 2030 serves as a guiding framework that embodies the country's aspirations for a more prosperous and peaceful future. By aligning its foreign policy goals with this long-term strategic vision, the UAE remains steadfast in its pursuit of excellence and leadership in the global community.

Crisis Management and Conflict Resolution: How Leadership Responds to Challenges

Crisis Management and Conflict Resolution: How Leadership Responds to Challenges The leadership of the UAE plays a critical role in effectively managing crises and resolving conflicts both domestically and internationally. When faced with challenges, the leadership adopts a proactive and strategic approach to address the root causes and find sustainable solutions. One key aspect of the UAE leadership's crisis management strategy is its emphasis on swift decision-making and decisive action. Leaders quickly assess the situation, consult relevant stakeholders, and implement measures to mitigate the impact of the crisis. This proactive approach helps maintain stability and security within the country and the region. Furthermore, the leadership's commitment to multilateralism and diplomacy is instrumental in resolving conflicts peacefully. The UAE actively participates in regional and international mediation efforts, leveraging its diplomatic relations and soft power to facilitate dialogue and negotiation between conflicting parties. The leadership aims to build bridges and foster cooperation among nations by promoting dialogue and understanding. In times of crisis, the leadership also demonstrates resilience and unity, rallying the population behind a common goal and providing reassurance during challenging times. This sense of national cohesion and solidarity strengthens the country's ability to weather crises and emerge stronger from adversity. Moreover, the leadership's commitment to upholding international law and promoting human rights is central to its conflict resolution strategy. By adhering to principles of justice, equality, and respect for sovereignty, the UAE leadership sets a positive example for the global community. It strengthens its reputation as a responsible international actor. Overall, the leadership's proactive, multilateral, and conscientious approach to crisis management and conflict resolution underscores its commitment to peace, stability, and prosperity at home and abroad.

International Reputation: The Impact of Leadership on UAE's Global Standing

The international reputation of the United Arab Emirates (UAE) is intricately linked to the leadership at the nation's helm. UAE leaders' actions, decisions, and behaviors profoundly impact how the country is perceived globally. Leadership plays a critical role in shaping the narrative surrounding the UAE, influencing how other nations and international organizations interact with the country. UAE leaders represent the nation in diplomatic engagements, trade negotiations, and international forums. Their conduct and statements carry weight and can either enhance or detract from the country's global standing. By demonstrating leadership qualities such as integrity, diplomacy, and strategic thinking, UAE leaders can bolster the nation's reputation as a reliable and responsible member of the international community. Furthermore, the vision and values of UAE leaders contribute to shaping the country's image and reputation. Leaders prioritizing innovation, sustainability, and social development project a forward-thinking and progressive image of the UAE. By championing initiatives that promote tolerance, diversity, and cultural exchange, UAE leaders showcase the country as a beacon of openness and inclusivity in a rapidly changing world. In times of crisis or conflict, the response of UAE leadership is closely scrutinized by the international community. How leaders navigate challenges, demonstrate resilience, and seek peaceful resolutions can significantly impact the perception of the UAE's commitment to stability and security. UAE leaders can strengthen the country's reputation as a responsible and constructive player in global affairs by showcasing leadership qualities such as decisiveness, empathy, and a commitment to dialogue. The smooth transition of leadership in the UAE from the late Sheikh Khalifa to Sheikh Mohammed bin Zayed has probably implications for the country's international reputation. Soft leadership transitions, continuity in foreign policy objectives, and a clear vision for the future are essential in maintaining the UAE's standing as a dynamic and influential player on the world stage. By ensuring strong leadership succession mechanisms and upholding the values of innovation, tolerance, and prosperity, the UAE will continue to enhance its international reputation and assert its position as a leading global player.

There is a recognition of the significant impact these changes can have on the country's foreign policy direction. The leadership dynamics within the UAE, particularly the succession process and the emergence of new leaders, inevitably shape the country's external relations and strategies on the global stage. The ability of Sheikh Mohammed bin Zayed to build upon the established foundations while also introducing new perspectives and approaches would determine the continuity and evolution of the UAE's diplomatic agenda. Leadership transitions can shift priorities, alliances, and strategic partnerships. The new leader's ability to navigate regional and global challenges is critical in shaping the country's position and influence in the international arena. Moreover, the transition process allowed the UAE to redefine its role in global affairs, adapt to changing geopolitical dynamics, and seize new opportunities for growth and influence. The leadership dynamics during the transition set the tone for the country's engagement with key partners, as well as its response to emerging threats and opportunities. In conclusion, the new leadership dynamics in the UAE will play a pivotal role in determining the country's foreign policy direction and shaping its international reputation.

In a Nutshell

The role of leadership in shaping the foreign policy of the United Arab Emirates (UAE) is profound and multifaceted. It reflects the vision and strategies of its founding rulers as well as contemporary leadership. This influence permeates the institutional framework, decision-making processes, personal diplomacy, the UAE's response to international crises, and its long-term strategic vision.

1. FOUNDING FATHERS AND VISIONARIES: THE INFLUENCE OF UAE'S FOUNDING RULERS

The UAE's foreign policy foundations were laid by Sheikh Zayed bin Sultan Al Nahyan, the principal architect of the federation and its first President. His leadership was committed to building strong bilateral and multilateral relationships, fostering regional stability, and promoting economic development. Sheikh Zayed's policies emphasized peaceful coexistence and non-interference, which have remained central tenets of UAE foreign policy[4][19].

2. CONTEMPORARY LEADERSHIP: THE ROLE OF THE CURRENT RULER IN SHAPING FOREIGN POLICY

Sheikh Mohamed bin Zayed Al Nahyan, the current President, has continued to shape the UAE's foreign policy in significant ways. His leadership is marked by a more assertive foreign policy stance, reflecting a shift towards greater international engagement and regional security initiatives. This includes the normalization of relations with Israel under the Abraham Accords and active participation in regional security matters such as the military involvement in Yemen[1][3][13][19].

3. INSTITUTIONAL FRAMEWORK: HOW LEADERSHIP IS MANIFESTED IN GOVERNMENT STRUCTURES

The UAE's foreign policy is deeply embedded in its institutional framework, where the President, as the head of state and the Supreme Council of Rulers, plays a central role. The Ministry of Foreign Affairs, under the guidance of the President and in coordination with other key ministries, executes the UAE's foreign policy. This structure allows for a centralized but flexible approach to foreign policy, aligning it closely with the national interests and leadership's vision[4][7].

4. DECISION-MAKING PROCESSES: UNDERSTANDING HOW LEADERSHIP DIRECTS FOREIGN POLICY ACTIONS

Decision-making in UAE foreign policy typically involves a top-down approach, where the President and senior advisors make key decisions. This process is influenced by strategic assessments of national security, economic interests, and international relations dynamics. The leadership's direct involvement ensures that foreign policy actions are closely aligned with the broader goals of national development and security[3][4].

5. PERSONAL DIPLOMACY: THE IMPORTANCE OF LEADER-TO-LEADER INTERACTIONS

Personal diplomacy plays a crucial role in the UAE's foreign policy, with the country's leaders often engaging directly with other world leaders to forge strong bilateral relationships. This approach has been evident in Sheikh Mohamed bin Zayed's interactions with global leaders, which have helped to elevate the UAE's international profile and secure strategic partnerships[13][19].

6. VISION 2030: LEADERSHIP'S LONG-TERM STRATEGIC VISION FOR FOREIGN POLICY

The UAE's Vision 2030 is a strategic framework to reduce the country's dependence on oil and diversify its economy. This vision influences foreign policy by prioritizing economic diplomacy, international trade, and investment. The leadership's commitment to this vision directs foreign policy towards fostering an environment conducive to achieving these long-term economic goals[4][19].

7. CRISIS MANAGEMENT AND CONFLICT RESOLUTION: HOW LEADERSHIP RESPONDS TO CHALLENGES

The UAE leadership has demonstrated adeptness in crisis management and conflict resolution, often opting for diplomatic solutions and multilateral engagements. This is reflected in its active role in mediating regional conflicts and participating in international peacekeeping efforts. The leadership's pragmatic approach in these matters aims to maintain regional stability and protect national interests[3][16].

8. INTERNATIONAL REPUTATION: THE IMPACT OF LEADERSHIP ON UAE'S GLOBAL STANDING

The UAE's leadership has significantly influenced its international reputation, positioning it as a reliable partner in global affairs. This reputation is bolstered by the UAE's commitment to humanitarian aid, its active role in international organizations, and its adherence to international law. The leadership's strategic decisions have enhanced the UAE's standing as a progressive, stable, and influential country on the world stage[16][19].

In summary, the leadership of the UAE, from its founding fathers to the current rulers, has been instrumental in shaping a dynamic and forward-looking foreign policy. This policy reflects the country's internal values and aspirations and its proactive engagement in addressing global challenges.

References

[1] https://academic.oup.com/book/8975/chapter-abstract/155312223?redirectedFrom=fulltext
[2] https://icwa.in/pdfs/DrLakshmiSHP.pdf
[3] https://www.chathamhouse.org/2020/07/risk-perception-and-appetite-uae-foreign-and-national-security-policy-0/2-uaes-foreign-and
[4] https://www.mofa.gov.ae/en/The-Ministry
[5] https://studies.aljazeera.net/en/reports/2017/06/transformations-uae-foreign-policy-170608095838131.html
[6] https://academic.oup.com/cairo-scholarship-online/book/22844/chapter-abstract/183329983?redirectedFrom=fulltext
[7] https://www.uae-embassy.org/discover-uae/governance/political-system-governance
[8] https://books.google.ca/books/about/The_Making_of_UAE_Foreign_Policy.html?id=YeCPrgEACAAJ&redir_esc=y
[9] https://www.fpri.org/article/2023/04/big-changes-in-united-arab-emirates-foreign-policy/
[10] https://www.expatica.com/ae/living/gov-law-admin/the-government-and-political-system-in-the-uae-71501/
[11] https://www.uae-embassy.org/discover-uae/governance
[12] https://ivypanda.com/essays/leadership-culture-in-the-united-arab-emirates/
[13] https://usuaebusiness.org/resources/his-highness-sheikh-mohammed-bin-zayed-al-nahyan-president-of-the-u-a-e-ruler-of-abu-dhabi-and-supreme-commander-of-the-u-a-e-armed-forces/
[14] https://arabcenterdc.org/resource/reflections-on-mohammed-bin-zayeds-preferences-regarding-uae-foreign-policy/
[15] https://www.tandfonline.com/doi/full/10.1080/23739770.2020.1845067
[16] https://www.uae-embassy.org/discover-uae/foreign-policy

[17] https://www.rand.org/pubs/commentary/2016/02/the-next-generation-of-leaders-in-the-persian-gulf.html
[18] https://foreignpolicy.com/2023/08/07/saudi-arabia-uae-emirates-nationalism-mbs-mbz/
[19] https://www.uae-embassy.org/discover-uae/governance/about-uae-president-sheikh-mohamed-bin-zayed
[20] https://www.proquest.com/openview/05721c0b251d54d52cc2e935673cc1df/1?cbl=135362&pq-origsite=gscholar

III

Economic Diplomacy: A Pillar of UAE Foreign Policy

Economic Diplomacy

Economic diplomacy is a strategic tool nations use to advance their economic interests and achieve their foreign policy goals. It involves the intersection of economic and diplomatic activities, leveraging economic resources and relationships to enhance a country's global standing. Economic diplomacy plays a crucial role in shaping a nation's foreign policy agenda, as it allows countries to strengthen their international partnerships, promote trade and investment opportunities, and influence global economic systems. At its core, economic diplomacy seeks to utilize economic assets to achieve diplomatic objectives. By engaging in economic negotiations, trade agreements, and investment partnerships, countries can bolster their economic ties with other nations while furthering their political goals. Economic diplomacy is instrumental in fostering international cooperation, resolving conflicts, and promoting economic development on a global scale. The importance of economic diplomacy cannot be overstated in today's interconnected world. With the increasing interdependence of economies and the rise of global trade networks, economic diplomacy has become a critical tool for countries to navigate the complexities of the international arena. By leveraging economic resources and engaging in strategic economic initiatives, nations can enhance their diplomatic influence, foster economic prosperity, and safeguard their national interests in an increasingly competitive global landscape. In the UAE context, economic diplomacy has been a cornerstone of the country's foreign policy strategy, driving its economic diversification efforts, fostering international trade partnerships, and promoting its position as a key player in the global economy. Through a strategic focus on economic diplomacy, the UAE has strengthened its economic ties with key partners, attracted foreign investment, and positioned itself as a hub for trade and commerce. As we delve deeper into economic diplomacy in the following sections, we will explore the historical foundations of the UAE's economic diplomacy, its key economic partnerships and agreements, and the role of economic statecraft in advancing the country's foreign policy objectives. By examining the multifaceted aspects of economic diplomacy, we can better understand how economic tools and strategies are employed to shape the UAE's global engagement and enhance its diplomatic influence on the world stage.

Definition and Importance

Economic diplomacy is a strategic tool countries use to advance their national interests through economic means. It involves negotiating and implementing economic agreements, trade relations, investment strategies, and other economic activities to achieve foreign policy goals. The importance of economic diplomacy lies in its ability to leverage a country's economic strength to influence and shape its relationships with other nations. Using economic incentives, sanctions, or other measures, countries can pursue their foreign policy objectives and secure their national interests in a globalized world. Economic diplomacy plays a crucial role in fostering economic growth, promoting trade and investment, enhancing competitiveness, and creating opportunities for cooperation and partnerships with other countries. It helps countries navigate the complexities of the global economy and build strong and resilient economic relationships that benefit their citizens and businesses. In today's interconnected world, economic diplomacy has become a key pillar of foreign policy, offering countries a powerful tool to navigate the challenges and opportunities of the global economy. As the UAE continues to expand its economic footprint and strengthen its international partnerships, economic diplomacy will remain a central element in shaping its foreign policy goals and enhancing its influence on the world stage.

Role in Shaping Foreign Policy Goals

Economic diplomacy plays a pivotal role in shaping the foreign policy goals of the United Arab Emirates (UAE). As a key component of its diplomatic strategy, economic diplomacy serves as a powerful tool for advancing the UAE's national interests on the global stage. By leveraging economic resources, trade agreements, and investment partnerships, the UAE can strengthen its diplomatic relations, promote economic growth, and enhance its international influence. The UAE can pursue various foreign policy objectives through economic diplomacy, including fostering a conducive environment for sustainable development, promoting trade and investment opportunities, and enhancing economic competitiveness. Using economic incentives and leverage, the UAE can attract foreign investment, forge strategic partnerships, and enhance its role as a regional economic powerhouse. Moreover, economic diplomacy enables the UAE to proactively address global challenges like climate change, cybersecurity, and economic instability. The UAE can work towards common goals, promote cooperation, and contribute to developing global solutions by engaging in economic dialogue with international partners. Economic diplomacy's role in shaping the UAE's foreign policy goals cannot be overstated. The UAE can strengthen its diplomatic relations, enhance its economic resilience, and advance its national interests worldwide by strategically using economic tools and initiatives. In doing so, the UAE reinforces its position as a dynamic and forward-thinking player in the international arena.

Historical Foundations of UAE's Economic Diplomacy

The historical foundations of the UAE's economic diplomacy can be traced back to the region's early trade routes and economic networks. The UAE has a rich commerce and maritime trade history, serving as a crucial link between East and West. Even before the formation of the modern nation-state, the region that would become the UAE was a hub for trade, connecting the Indian Ocean region with the Arabian Peninsula and beyond. The strategic location of the UAE along major trade routes contributed to its economic significance and laid the groundwork for future economic diplomacy efforts. The historical trade networks of the UAE were shaped by the ingenuity and resilience of its people, who engaged in trading activities both regionally and internationally. Merchants from the UAE traveled far and wide, establishing trade relationships with neighboring regions and distant lands. This early economic engagement not only bolstered the economy of the UAE but also fostered diplomatic ties with various civilizations and cultures. The UAE's economic diplomacy evolution can be seen in how traditional trade practices transformed into modern economic strategies. With the establishment of the United Arab Emirates as a unified nation in 1971, economic diplomacy became an integral part of the country's foreign policy approach. The UAE sought to leverage its economic resources and expertise to enhance its diplomatic relations and strengthen its position on the global stage. The UAE established itself as a key player in the global economy through strategic investments, trade agreements, and economic partnerships.

The historical foundations of the UAE's economic diplomacy continue to shape its approach to international trade, investment, and economic cooperation. By building on its rich trading heritage and embracing modern economic principles, the UAE has successfully positioned itself as a dynamic and influential player in economic diplomacy.

Early Trade Routes and Economic Networks

The early trade routes spanned the region and significantly influenced the UAE's economic diplomacy. Dating back to ancient times, the Arabian Peninsula served as a key crossroads for trade between continents, with merchants from various cultures converging to exchange goods and ideas. The bustling ports along the Arabian Gulf facilitated maritime trade, linking the region to Asian, African, and European markets. These trade routes facilitated the flow of goods and fostered cultural exchanges and diplomatic interactions. The economic networks that emerged from these trade routes laid the foundation for the UAE's economic diplomacy in the modern era. The traditions of commerce and exchange ingrained in the region's history continue to shape the country's approach to economic diplomacy today. By leveraging its strategic location and heritage as a trading hub, the UAE has established strong economic ties with countries worldwide. The early trade routes also underscore the importance of connectivity and openness to foreign trade in shaping the UAE's economic diplomacy. The country's leadership recognizes the value of engagement with global markets and the benefits of embracing a diversified economy. Drawing inspiration from the historical trade legacy, the UAE has positioned itself as a dynamic player in the global economy, seeking mutually beneficial partnerships and opportunities for economic growth. As the UAE evolved from a region of traditional trade to a modern hub of commerce and finance, the principles of openness, cooperation, and innovation have remained central to its economic diplomacy. Building on the legacy of the past, the UAE continues to forge ahead, navigating the complexities of the global economy with a strategic and forward-looking approach firmly rooted in its rich history of trade and economic exchange.

Evolution Towards Modern Economic Diplomacy

The evolution towards modern economic diplomacy was characterized by a strategic shift in the UAE's approach to economic relations on the global stage. The UAE has become a key player in the international economic landscape from its historical roots in early trade routes and economic networks. Embracing a proactive and multifaceted strategy, the UAE has leveraged its economic resources and partnerships to advance its national interests and bolster its global influence. This evolution has been marked by a deliberate focus on diversification and innovation as the UAE seeks to position itself as a trade, investment, and economic cooperation hub. Developing world-class infrastructure, cutting-edge technologies, and a business-friendly environment has propelled the UAE onto the radar of global investors and partners. By fostering a conducive economic growth and entrepreneurship ecosystem, the UAE has successfully attracted foreign investments and established strategic economic partnerships with countries worldwide. Furthermore, the UAE's commitment to international trade liberalization and free market principles has driven its modern economic diplomacy efforts. Through active participation in regional and international trade agreements, the UAE has sought to expand its economic reach and enhance its competitiveness in the global marketplace. The UAE has positioned itself as a key player in regional and global economic integration by opening up its economy and embracing trade liberalization. In addition to its robust trade and investment policies, the UAE has prioritized economic diversification and the development of knowledge-based industries as part of its modern economic diplomacy agenda. By investing in technology, renewable energy, and healthcare sectors, the UAE aims to transform its economy and create new opportunities for sustainable growth and development. This strategic focus on economic diversification not only strengthens the resilience of the UAE economy but also enables the country to adapt to evolving global economic dynamics. Overall, the evolution towards modern economic diplomacy represents a strategic shift in the UAE's approach to economic relations, driven by a proactive and forward-thinking vision. By leveraging its historical trade roots and proactive economic policies, the UAE is well-positioned to navigate the complex challenges and opportunities of the global economic landscape and emerge as a key player in shaping the future of international economic relations.

Key Economic Partnerships and Agreements

The UAE's commitment to economic diplomacy has paved the way for key economic partnerships and agreements that have significantly shaped its global relations. These partnerships are essential in driving economic growth, fostering innovation, and enhancing the competitiveness of the UAE on the global stage. One of the cornerstones of the UAE's economic diplomacy strategy is its focus on establishing strong bilateral trade relations with key partners worldwide. Through these bilateral agreements, the UAE aims to strengthen economic ties, expand market access, and promote mutually beneficial trade partnerships. The UAE has forged deep-rooted economic relationships built on trust, shared values, and common goals by engaging in open and transparent dialogue. Furthermore, the UAE has proactively leveraged multilateral agreements and economic alliances to advance its economic diplomacy goals. By participating in regional and international forums, such as the Gulf Cooperation Council (GCC) and the World Trade Organization (WTO), the UAE has harnessed collective efforts to address global economic challenges, promote free trade, and enhance economic cooperation. These alliances provide a platform for the UAE to advocate for its interests, negotiate trade agreements, and collaborate on key economic issues with like-minded partners. In addition to trade partnerships, the UAE has made significant strides in attracting foreign investment and fostering investment partnerships with countries worldwide. By creating a conducive business environment, implementing investor-friendly policies, and offering strategic incentives, the UAE has positioned itself as a preferred destination for foreign investors looking to capitalize on the country's dynamic and diversified economy. These investment partnerships drive economic growth and job creation and facilitate technology transfer, knowledge exchange, and innovation collaborations that benefit both parties. Overall, the UAE's focus on key economic partnerships and agreements underscores its commitment to economic diplomacy as a strategic tool for advancing its national interests, enhancing its economic competitiveness, and fostering prosperity for its people. By cultivating strong economic relationships with key partners and championing a rules-based international trading system, the UAE is well-positioned to navigate the complexities of the global economy and capitalize on emerging opportunities for sustainable growth and development.

Bilateral Trade Relations

The UAE has cultivated strong bilateral trade relations with key partners across the globe, underlining its commitment to fostering economic cooperation and mutual prosperity. These bilateral trade relationships are the foundation for expanding trade volumes, enhancing market access, and promoting business opportunities for the UAE and its partner countries. Through sustained diplomatic efforts and strategic engagement, the UAE has established fruitful trade ties with a diverse range of countries, spanning various regions and economic sectors. These bilateral trade relations are underpinned by a shared commitment to promoting trade liberalization, enhancing economic diversification, and facilitating cross-border investments. The UAE's proactive approach to bilateral trade relations has resulted in signing numerous trade agreements and memoranda of understanding (MoUs) with partner countries aimed at streamlining trade procedures, reducing trade barriers, and fostering a conducive business environment for companies operating in both markets. These agreements cover a wide array of sectors, including agriculture, industry, services, and technology, reflecting the breadth and depth of the UAE's trade engagements on the global stage. Moreover, the UAE's emphasis on bilateral trade relations extends beyond traditional trade partnerships, encompassing emerging markets and frontier economies seeking to leverage the UAE's strategic location, advanced infrastructure, and business-friendly ecosystem. By forging strong bilateral trade relations with diverse countries, the UAE positions itself as a hub for regional and international trade, attracting foreign investments, stimulating economic growth, and enhancing its global competitiveness. As the UAE continues to deepen its bilateral trade relations with key partners worldwide, it remains steadfast in its commitment to advancing economic diplomacy as a cornerstone of its foreign policy strategy. Through sustained dialogue, cooperation, and collaboration with partner countries, the UAE seeks to navigate the complex geopolitical landscape, seize new business opportunities, and chart a prosperous path built on shared economic goals, mutual benefits, and enduring partnerships.

Free Trade Agreements and Economic Alliances

Free Trade Agreements and Economic Alliances are crucial in shaping the UAE's economic diplomacy strategy. By entering into strategic partnerships through free trade agreements and economic alliances, the UAE seeks to enhance its economic competitiveness, expand market access for its goods and services, and foster stronger economic ties with key trading partners. These agreements are important to promote economic growth, attract foreign investment, and create a conducive environment for trade liberalization. The UAE has actively pursued negotiations for free trade agreements with various countries and regions around the world. These agreements aim to eliminate trade barriers, such as tariffs and quotas, and facilitate the smooth flow of goods and services between the UAE and its trading partners. By lowering trade barriers and enhancing market access, free trade agreements help to stimulate economic growth, promote job creation, and increase bilateral trade volumes. In addition to bilateral free trade agreements, the UAE has forged economic alliances with regional and international organizations. These economic alliances strengthen economic cooperation, promote investment flows, and facilitate economic integration among member countries. The UAE gains access to shared markets, resources, and expertise by participating in economic alliances, which can further drive economic development and enhance its global competitiveness. Furthermore, free trade agreements and economic alliances provide a platform for the UAE to engage in dialogue and negotiate on various economic issues, including investment protection, intellectual property rights, and market access. By leveraging these agreements and alliances, the UAE can advance its economic interests, promote a more open and transparent trading environment, and position itself as a key player in the global economy. Overall, free trade agreements and economic alliances serve as key pillars of the UAE's economic diplomacy efforts, enabling the country to navigate the complexities of international trade, enhance its economic resilience, and forge stronger partnerships with countries and regions worldwide.

Investment Partnerships

The UAE has strategically formed investment partnerships with key countries and organizations to foster economic growth and development. These partnerships provide opportunities for collaboration, technology transfer, and mutual benefit in various sectors, contributing to the UAE's diversification efforts and enhancing its global presence. One prominent example of investment partnerships is the UAE's collaboration with African, Asian, and European countries to support infrastructure development projects. Through joint ventures and strategic investments, the UAE has played a pivotal role in enhancing connectivity, promoting sustainable development, and fostering economic cooperation in these regions. Furthermore, investment partnerships in key sectors such as technology, healthcare, and education have allowed the UAE to leverage expertise and resources from international partners, driving innovation and knowledge exchange. By forging strategic alliances with leading global companies and institutions, the UAE has transformed its economic landscape and positioned itself as a hub for innovation and entrepreneurship. The UAE's investment partnerships extend to strategic industries such as aerospace, defense, and advanced manufacturing. Through joint ventures and strategic acquisitions, the UAE has strengthened its capabilities in these sectors, diversifying its economy and enhancing its competitiveness on the global stage. In sustainable development, the UAE has championed investment partnerships focusing on renewable energy, water conservation, and environmental sustainability. By collaborating with international partners, the UAE has implemented cutting-edge technologies and best practices to address pressing environmental challenges and promote a greener future for future generations. Overall, investment partnerships play a crucial role in the UAE's economic diplomacy efforts, enabling the country to harness external resources and expertise to drive economic growth, innovation, and sustainable development. By nurturing these strategic alliances, the UAE continues to enhance its position as a global economic powerhouse and a key player in the international investment landscape.

Economic Diplomacy in the Energy Sector

The UAE has strategically positioned itself as a key player in the global energy sector, leveraging its abundant energy resources and expertise to forge strong partnerships with countries worldwide. The UAE has become a leading energy exporter and a significant player in global energy markets through proactive economic diplomacy. With vast oil and natural gas reserves, the UAE has established itself as a major player in the global energy landscape. The country's energy sector is critical in driving economic growth and development, both domestically and internationally. Through proactive engagement with energy markets and stakeholders, the UAE has been able to maximize the value of its energy resources and enhance its strategic position on the world stage. The UAE's energy diplomacy efforts extend beyond just resource extraction and exportation. The country has significantly invested in developing renewable energy sources, such as solar and wind power, as part of its long-term energy strategy. By diversifying its energy portfolio and embracing sustainable practices, the UAE aims to position itself as a pioneer in transitioning to a greener and more sustainable energy future. Through strategic partnerships with key energy players, the UAE has tapped into new markets and forged alliances that strengthen its energy security and resilience. By collaborating with other energy-producing nations and participating in regional and international energy organizations, the UAE has shaped global energy policies and enhanced its influence in the energy sector. The UAE's economic diplomacy in the energy sector is guided by a long-term vision of promoting sustainable development, fostering innovation, and ensuring energy security for future generations. By adopting a forward-thinking approach to energy diplomacy, the UAE is well-positioned to navigate the complexities of the global energy landscape and contribute to shaping a more sustainable and secure energy future for the world.

Energy Resources and Global Energy Markets

The UAE is strategically positioned as a key player in the global energy landscape due to its abundant energy resources, primarily oil and natural gas. The country's vast reserves have enabled it to significantly contribute to global energy markets, influencing supply and pricing dynamics. The UAE's energy sector plays a pivotal role in shaping the country's economic development and foreign policy priorities. With over 90% of its exports attributed to oil and gas, the UAE holds a critical position in the global energy market. As one of the largest producers of oil in the world, the country's energy resources have fueled its economic growth and established it as a key supplier to international markets. The UAE's strategic location in the Gulf region, a major energy production and transportation hub, further enhances its influence in global energy markets. The UAE's energy sector is characterized by its state-of-the-art infrastructure and advanced technology, enabling it to efficiently extract and process energy resources. This technological edge has positioned the country as a leader in the energy industry, attracting partnerships and investments from global energy players. By leveraging its technological capabilities, the UAE has been able to maximize the extraction and production of energy resources, ensuring a steady supply to meet domestic and international demand. In addition to its production capacity, the UAE has focused on diversifying its energy sources and investing in renewable energy initiatives. The country's commitment to sustainability and environmental stewardship has led to the development of renewable energy projects like solar and nuclear power plants. By expanding its energy mix and embracing clean energy solutions, the UAE aims to reduce its carbon footprint and contribute to global efforts to combat climate change. The UAE's energy resources and global energy markets are crucial in shaping its foreign policy objectives and economic strategy. As a key player in the energy sector, the country's decisions and actions have ripple effects across the global energy landscape, influencing market trends, investment decisions, and geopolitical dynamics. By effectively managing its energy resources and engaging in strategic partnerships, the UAE continues to assert its influence and leadership in the international energy arena.

Strategic Partnerships in Energy Industry

The UAE has strategically cultivated strong partnerships within the global energy industry, leveraging its abundant energy resources and expertise to establish mutually beneficial relationships with key players in the sector. These strategic partnerships have enhanced the UAE's energy security and contributed to its influence in shaping global energy markets. One of the key strategic partnerships in the energy industry for the UAE is with major international oil and gas companies. Through collaborations and joint ventures, the UAE has tapped into advanced technology and expertise to maximize the production and value of its energy resources. These partnerships have played a crucial role in advancing the UAE's energy sector and positioning it as a key player in the global energy market. Furthermore, the UAE has forged strategic energy partnerships with key energy-consuming countries, ensuring a stable and reliable energy supply to meet growing demand. The UAE has secured its position as a trusted energy supplier in the international market by establishing long-term supply agreements and investment partnerships. These partnerships have strengthened the UAE's energy security and provided a platform for economic cooperation and development. Moreover, the UAE has actively engaged in energy diplomacy through participation in international energy forums and organizations. By contributing to global energy dialogue and policy discussions, the UAE has been able to shape international energy agendas and promote sustainable energy practices. These diplomatic efforts have elevated the UAE's profile in the global energy arena and reinforced its commitment to responsible energy management and sustainability. As the UAE continues expanding its energy partnerships and influence in the global energy industry, it remains committed to fostering cooperation and collaboration with key stakeholders. By leveraging its strategic energy assets and diplomatic acumen, the UAE is poised to play a leading role in shaping the future of the global energy landscape.

Economic Diplomacy in Infrastructure Development

The UAE's strategic partnerships in the energy industry have paved the way for significant infrastructure investment, fueling economic growth and regional connectivity. These infrastructure developments enhance the UAE's position as a regional economic hub and strengthen its diplomatic ties with key partners. The UAE's commitment to investing in infrastructure projects extends beyond its borders, focusing on developing vital sectors such as transportation, telecommunications, and urban development. Through strategic partnerships and collaborations, the UAE has played a pivotal role in transforming the infrastructure landscape of various regions, promoting sustainable development and economic prosperity. Infrastructure projects in key sectors such as transportation have been a priority for the UAE, with initiatives like the Dubai Metro and Abu Dhabi's Integrated Transport Center setting new benchmarks for efficiency and connectivity. These projects improve residents' quality of life and position the UAE as an innovative urban planning and sustainable development leader. Telecommunications infrastructure has also been a key focus for the UAE, with initiatives like 5G networks and smart city technologies driving digital transformation and enhancing connectivity. These investments support the UAE's economic diversification efforts and strengthen its diplomatic relations with countries looking to leverage advanced technologies for their own development. Urban development projects in the UAE, such as the Masdar City sustainable urban development initiative, showcase the country's commitment to sustainable infrastructure practices and green technologies. By promoting environmentally friendly infrastructure solutions, the UAE demonstrates its leadership in addressing global challenges such as climate change and sustainable development. Overall, the UAE's strategic investments in infrastructure projects as part of its economic diplomacy efforts have contributed to its economic growth and regional influence and enhanced its reputation as a forward-thinking and proactive global player in shaping the future of infrastructure development.

Investments in Infrastructure Projects

With the UAE's strategic focus on infrastructure development, investments in key projects have played a pivotal role in shaping the country's economic landscape. The UAE has actively invested in infrastructure projects, from transportation networks to urban development initiatives. These investments have improved the country's physical infrastructure and contributed significantly to job creation and economic diversification. The transportation sector is one of the key areas of infrastructure investment in the UAE. The country has substantially invested in building modern airports, seaports, and road networks, enhancing connectivity within and with international markets. These investments have facilitated smoother movement of goods and people and positioned the UAE as a major transportation hub in the region. In addition to transportation infrastructure, the UAE has also focused on developing its urban infrastructure to support its growing population and economy. Investments in projects such as residential complexes, commercial centers, and industrial zones have provided essential amenities for residents, attracted foreign investment, and spurred economic growth. The development of world-class cities like Dubai and Abu Dhabi stands as a testament to the UAE's commitment to building sustainable and modern urban spaces. Furthermore, the UAE has invested in renewable energy projects in its infrastructure development strategy. The country has made significant strides in harnessing solar and wind energy, reducing its dependence on fossil fuels, and promoting environmental sustainability. These investments in clean energy infrastructure contribute to the UAE's commitment to eco-friendly practices and position the country as a leader in the global shift towards renewable energy solutions. Infrastructure investment has been a cornerstone of the UAE's economic diplomacy efforts, driving economic growth, enhancing regional connectivity, and attracting foreign investment. By strategically investing in key infrastructure projects, the UAE has positioned itself as a dynamic and forward-thinking player in the global economy, setting the stage for continued growth and prosperity in the years to come.

Impact on Economic Growth and Regional Connectivity

The UAE's investments in infrastructure projects have played a pivotal role in driving economic growth and fostering regional connectivity. These strategic investments have boosted the UAE's economy and had a ripple effect throughout the region. By developing state-of-the-art infrastructure, the UAE has created a conducive environment for businesses to thrive and for trade to flourish. The modern infrastructure network, including world-class airports, seaports, roads, and telecommunications systems, has enhanced the ease of business in the UAE. This has attracted domestic investors and foreign businesses looking to establish a regional presence. The efficient transportation and communication systems have significantly reduced business operations' costs and time, further stimulating economic growth. Furthermore, the UAE's focus on building sustainable infrastructure has positively impacted regional connectivity. The country has emerged as a key hub for trade and commerce, serving as a gateway between East and West. The well-connected infrastructure has facilitated the movement of goods, services, and people, strengthening economic ties with neighboring countries and beyond. Infrastructure development has also bolstered the UAE's position as a regional and global trade player. The country's strategic location and world-class infrastructure have made it an attractive destination for businesses seeking to tap into diverse markets. The infrastructure investments have driven economic growth within the UAE and elevated the country's stature as a key player in enhancing regional connectivity and promoting economic integration.

Trade Promotion and Investment Attraction

UAE's strategic investments in key sectors have bolstered its economic growth and facilitated regional connectivity. These initiatives have positioned the UAE as a hub for trade, investment, and innovation in the Middle East and beyond. By fostering strong partnerships with global players and promoting a business-friendly environment, the UAE has attracted significant foreign direct investment and diversified its economy. The UAE's commitment to trade promotion is evident in its proactive approach to fostering international trade agreements and partnerships. Through participation in trade fairs, exhibitions, and business forums, the UAE showcases its products and services to a global audience, attracting potential investors and trading partners. Moreover, the UAE's emphasis on digital transformation has led to developing e-commerce platforms and initiatives that facilitate cross-border trade and enhance market access for businesses. In line with its vision for economic diversification, the UAE has implemented robust investment attraction strategies to attract foreign investors across various sectors. By offering attractive incentives, streamlined procedures, and a favorable business environment, the UAE has positioned itself as a preferred destination for foreign investment. The country's investment promotion agencies play a pivotal role in facilitating investment opportunities and supporting investors seeking to establish their presence in the UAE. Furthermore, the UAE's focus on innovation and entrepreneurship has attracted a thriving startup ecosystem, fostering collaboration and knowledge exchange with global partners. Through initiatives such as specialized economic zones, research and development centers, and entrepreneurship hubs, the UAE has created a conducive environment for innovation and investment in emerging industries. Overall, the UAE's trade promotion and investment attraction efforts underscore its commitment to fostering economic growth, enhancing bilateral relations, and positioning itself as a leading economic powerhouse in the region. By leveraging its strategic location, business-friendly policies, and investment-friendly environment, the UAE continues to attract foreign investment and promote trade opportunities that drive sustainable economic development and regional connectivity.

Trade Promotion Initiatives

Trade promotion initiatives are crucial in advancing the UAE's economic diplomacy agenda. The UAE strongly emphasizes trade promotion as a key strategy to enhance its global trade relations and boost economic growth. Through various initiatives and programs, the UAE aims to showcase its competitive advantages, attract foreign investment, and facilitate trade partnerships. One of the primary trade promotion initiatives is the organization of trade missions and exhibitions both domestically and internationally. These events provide a platform for UAE businesses to showcase their products and services, network with potential partners, and explore new market opportunities. The UAE government actively supports and promotes these initiatives to drive economic diversification and enhance the country's global trade presence. Another key aspect of trade promotion initiatives is the establishment of free trade zones and economic clusters. The UAE has strategically developed free trade zones such as Dubai International Financial Centre (DIFC) and Jebel Ali Free Zone (JAFZA) to attract foreign investment and foster a business-friendly environment. These zones offer attractive incentives, streamlined regulations, and state-of-the-art infrastructure to facilitate trade and investment activities. Moreover, the UAE government works closely with international trade organizations and partners to promote trade liberalization and strengthen economic ties. Membership in organizations like the World Trade Organization (WTO) and participation in trade agreements like the Gulf Cooperation Council (GCC) demonstrate the UAE's commitment to promoting open and fair trade practices. In addition to trade missions and free zones, the UAE leverages digital platforms and e-commerce initiatives to expand its global reach and connect with a wider audience. Digital trade promotion strategies create new avenues for businesses to engage with international markets, increase visibility, and drive export opportunities. Overall, trade promotion initiatives are vital to the UAE's economic diplomacy efforts, enabling the country to position itself as a global trade hub, attract foreign investment, and foster economic growth. By implementing strategic trade promotion initiatives, the UAE strengthens trade relations, enhances competitiveness, and drives sustainable economic development.

Investment Promotion Strategies

The UAE employs various investment promotion strategies to attract foreign investors and bolster its economic development. One key strategy is the establishment of free trade zones, which offer incentives such as tax exemptions and streamlined regulations to encourage foreign investment. Additionally, the UAE actively participates in investment promotion events and international forums to showcase its investment opportunities and attract potential investors. Another important strategy is the promotion of public-private partnerships, which leverage private sector expertise and resources to drive infrastructure development and economic growth. The UAE also focuses on creating a business-friendly environment through regulatory reforms and investment incentives, fostering a conducive climate for domestic and foreign investment. Moreover, the UAE's investment promotion strategies often target key sectors such as renewable energy, technology, and tourism, aligning with the country's vision for economic diversification and sustainable growth. By actively promoting these sectors and offering investment incentives, the UAE aims to attract strategic investments that support its long-term economic goals and enhance its global competitiveness. Overall, these investment promotion strategies play a crucial role in the UAE's economic diplomacy efforts, helping to strengthen its economic partnerships, attract foreign investment, and drive sustainable economic growth. Through targeted and strategic initiatives, the UAE continues to position itself as a dynamic and attractive investment destination in the global economy.

Economic Diplomacy in International Organizations

The UAE actively engages in various international economic forums to promote its economic interests and bolster its global presence. The UAE showcases its commitment to international cooperation and economic development by participating in these organizations. These forums provide a platform for the UAE to interact with other countries, share best practices, and explore opportunities for collaboration. The UAE shapes global economic policies and fosters dialogue on key economic issues by participating in international economic organizations. The country's engagement in these forums helps enhance its reputation as a reliable and proactive player in the international economic arena. The UAE leverages its membership in international economic organizations to build strategic partnerships, attract foreign investments, and promote trade relations. By actively participating in these forums, the UAE is willing to abide by international norms and regulations, strengthening its credibility as a responsible global economic player. Moreover, the UAE's involvement in international economic organizations allows it to stay abreast of emerging trends and developments in the global economy. This enables the country to adapt its economic diplomacy strategies and policies to address evolving challenges and opportunities in the international economic landscape. Overall, the UAE's engagement in international economic organizations underscores its commitment to economic diplomacy as a key pillar of its foreign policy. By actively participating in these forums, the UAE positions itself as a proactive and influential player in the international economic arena, contributing to global economic stability and prosperity.

Participation in International Economic Forums

The UAE actively participates in various international economic forums to engage with global economic leaders, share insights, and shape emerging economic trends. The UAE seeks to showcase its economic achievements by participating in these forums, fostering partnerships, and contributing to the dialogue on pressing economic issues. One such important forum is the World Economic Forum (WEF), held annually in Davos, Switzerland. The UAE's presence at the WEF provides a platform to interact with world leaders, industry experts, and policymakers. It is an opportunity to highlight the UAE's economic successes, discuss key challenges, and explore global collaboration opportunities. Another significant forum is the G20 Summit, where the UAE has participated as a guest invitee. The G20 brings together the world's major economies to discuss and coordinate economic policies. The UAE's involvement in the G20 allows it to contribute to discussions on key economic issues, share its perspectives, and build relationships with key decision-makers. Additionally, the UAE actively participates in regional economic forums such as the World Economic Forum on the Middle East and North Africa. These regional forums provide a platform for the UAE to engage with its neighbors, exchange best practices, and explore opportunities for economic cooperation within the region. Overall, the UAE's participation in international economic forums enhances its global economic influence, facilitates knowledge-sharing, and allows it to stay abreast of emerging economic trends and developments. The UAE solidifies its position as a key player in the global economic landscape through active engagement in these forums.

Influence on Global Economic Policies

The UAE's active participation in international economic forums has positioned it as a key player in shaping global economic policies. Through engagement with organizations such as the World Trade Organization, International Monetary Fund, and World Bank, the UAE has influenced discussions and decisions on various economic issues. By leveraging its economic strength and strategic partnerships, the UAE has effectively advocated for policies that benefit its national interests and contribute to the stability of the global economy. Furthermore, the UAE's role in these forums has allowed it to showcase its economic achievements and share best practices with the international community, solidifying its position as a reputable player in the global economic arena. Through its participation in international economic forums, the UAE continues to play a significant role in shaping the future of global economic policies, ensuring that its voice is heard and its interests are represented on the world stage.

Economic Diplomacy and Economic Statecraft

Economic diplomacy and statecraft are essential for shaping the UAE's foreign policy objectives. By leveraging its economic power, the UAE has influenced global economic policies and strengthened diplomatic relations with other countries. The UAE has positioned itself as a key player in the global economy through strategic investments, trade agreements, and international partnerships. One of the key aspects of economic statecraft is the ability to use economic leverage to achieve diplomatic goals. By utilizing its economic resources effectively, the UAE can influence other countries and international organizations. This can range from offering financial incentives for cooperation to implementing economic sanctions as a form of pressure. Furthermore, economic statecraft is crucial in advancing the UAE's national interests and promoting its strategic objectives. By aligning economic interests with diplomatic initiatives, the UAE can effectively pursue its goals on the global stage. This integration of economic and diplomatic efforts allows the UAE to maximize its impact and ensure a favorable outcome in international negotiations. In conclusion, economic diplomacy and statecraft are integral to the UAE's foreign policy strategy. By harnessing its economic power and resources, the UAE can effectively shape global economic policies and advance its diplomatic agenda. The UAE continues to strengthen its position as a key player in the international arena through strategic investments, trade partnerships, and economic leverage.

Use of Economic Leverage in Diplomatic Relations

Using economic leverage in diplomatic relations is fundamental to the UAE's foreign policy strategy. Through strategic economic statecraft, the UAE leverages its economic power to achieve its foreign policy objectives and strengthen its position on the global stage. Economic leverage is crucial in shaping diplomatic conversations and negotiations, giving the UAE a powerful tool to influence decision-making processes and outcomes. By leveraging its economic resources, the UAE can incentivize cooperation, reward friendly nations, and discourage behavior contrary to its interests. This approach allows the UAE to assert its influence in international relations and advance its strategic goals with precision and impact. Through skillful economic leverage, the UAE can navigate complex geopolitical dynamics and secure outcomes that align with its national interests. As the UAE continues to expand its economic prowess and global footprint, economic leverage will remain a key instrument in its diplomatic toolkit, ensuring that it maintains a strategic advantage in the ever-evolving landscape of international politics.

Economic Statecraft in Achieving Foreign Policy Objectives

Economic statecraft plays a crucial role in the UAE's foreign policy endeavors, serving as a strategic tool to advance the nation's diplomatic objectives and further its interests on the global stage. The UAE effectively employs economic diplomacy to achieve its foreign policy goals by leveraging its economic resources. Economic statecraft encompasses a wide range of strategies and tactics the UAE utilizes to influence and shape international relations. Through skillful negotiations, strategic investments, and economic partnerships, the UAE strategically deploys its economic power to strengthen its position in the global arena and bolster its diplomatic initiatives. One key aspect of economic statecraft is using economic incentives and disincentives to incentivize cooperation and discourage actions contrary to the UAE's interests. The UAE can build strong relationships with other nations and foster mutual understanding by offering economic benefits such as trade agreements, investment opportunities, and economic aid. Moreover, the UAE strategically employs economic sanctions, trade restrictions, and other financial measures to pressure countries that threaten its security or engage in activities that counter international norms. By leveraging its economic leverage, the UAE can effectively signal its displeasure with certain actions and compel other nations to reconsider their behavior. In times of crisis or diplomatic tensions, economic statecraft becomes a vital tool for the UAE to navigate challenging situations and protect its national interests. By using its economic resources strategically, the UAE can influence the behavior of other actors, mitigate risks, and work towards resolving conflicts through economic means. Overall, economic statecraft is a potent instrument in the UAE's foreign policy toolkit. It allows the nation to wield its economic power to achieve its strategic objectives and promote stability and prosperity in the region and beyond.

Economic Diplomacy in Crisis Management

Economic Diplomacy in Crisis Management During times of crisis, economic diplomacy plays a crucial role in the UAE's foreign policy toolkit. The UAE leverages its economic resources and influence to mitigate conflicts, foster stability, and promote reconciliation in volatile regions. By employing various economic tools, the UAE has demonstrated its commitment to conflict resolution and peacebuilding efforts on the international stage. One key facet of economic diplomacy in crisis management is providing humanitarian aid and assistance to impoverished countries. The UAE has been actively involved in delivering humanitarian aid to conflict-affected regions, providing vital resources such as food, medical supplies, and shelter to alleviate the suffering of affected populations. This humanitarian assistance not only helps in addressing immediate needs but also contributes to building trust and goodwill among nations. Additionally, the UAE has utilized economic incentives and financial support as part of its crisis management strategy. By offering financial assistance, investment opportunities, and development aid to conflict-affected countries, the UAE aims to stimulate economic growth, create employment opportunities, and promote stability. These economic incentives catalyze peacebuilding initiatives and help in rebuilding war-torn regions. Furthermore, economic diplomacy in crisis management involves diplomatic negotiations and mediation efforts to resolve conflicts peacefully. The UAE has actively participated in diplomatic dialogues, peace negotiations, and mediation processes to facilitate dialogue between conflicting parties and promote peaceful resolution. The UAE has helped de-escalate tensions, facilitate ceasefire agreements, and lay the groundwork for sustainable peace through its diplomatic engagements. In conclusion, economic diplomacy plays a vital role in crisis management by offering a strategic approach to addressing conflicts and promoting peace. The UAE's proactive engagement in crises highlights its commitment to leveraging its economic resources for the greater good of humanity and advancing its foreign policy objectives through humanitarian assistance, economic incentives, and diplomatic interventions.

Economic Tools for Conflict Resolution

Economic Tools for Conflict Resolution Economic sanctions have long been utilized as a key tool in diplomatic efforts to address conflicts and promote peace. By imposing targeted restrictions on trade, investment, or financial transactions, countries can exert pressure on adversaries and incentivize changes in behavior. The effectiveness of economic sanctions lies in their ability to inflict economic pain on the targeted party, thereby compelling them to reconsider their actions. In addition to sanctions, economic incentives can also play a crucial role in conflict resolution. By offering economic assistance, trade opportunities, or investment incentives, parties involved in a conflict can be incentivized to resolve their differences peacefully. Economic incentives provide a tangible benefit for cooperation and help build trust between conflicting parties. Furthermore, economic diplomacy can involve the facilitation of economic agreements or trade deals as a means to foster peace and stability. Countries can create incentives for peaceful relations and discourage conflict escalation by promoting economic interdependence and mutual benefits. Economic cooperation can serve as a foundation for building positive diplomatic ties and promoting long-term stability in conflict-prone regions. Lastly, economic diplomacy can encompass economic leverage to encourage conflicting parties to negotiate. By leveraging economic resources or access to markets, countries can influence the behavior of conflicting parties and create conditions conducive to peace talks. The strategic use of economic power in conflict resolution can help de-escalate tensions and pave the way for diplomatic negotiations. In conclusion, economic tools play a vital role in conflict resolution by offering a range of mechanisms to influence the behavior of conflicting parties. Economic diplomacy can be a powerful force for promoting peace and stability in regions plagued by conflict, whether through sanctions, incentives, economic agreements, or leverage. By harnessing the economic dimension of diplomacy, countries like the UAE can contribute to global efforts to mitigate conflicts and build a more peaceful world.

Economic Diplomacy in Post-Conflict Reconstruction

After a conflict has ended, post-conflict reconstruction is crucial in rebuilding societies and restoring stability. Economic diplomacy plays a significant role in this phase by mobilizing resources, attracting investments, and promoting sustainable development. The UAE's approach to post-conflict reconstruction combines economic assistance, infrastructure development, and capacity-building initiatives to support countries in rebuilding their economies and fostering peace and stability. In post-conflict settings, the UAE leverages its economic resources and expertise to support reconstruction efforts. The UAE aims to create sustainable economic opportunities and improve the quality of life for communities affected by conflict through strategic investments in key sectors such as infrastructure, healthcare, education, and agriculture. By investing in infrastructure projects, the UAE contributes to rebuilding essential services and revitalizing local economies, laying the foundation for long-term growth and stability. Furthermore, the UAE's economic diplomacy efforts in post-conflict reconstruction extend beyond financial aid, including capacity-building programs and technical assistance. By providing training and skills development opportunities to local populations, the UAE empowers communities to participate in the reconstruction process and build resilient economies. The UAE fosters inclusive and sustainable growth in post-conflict environments through collaboration with local stakeholders, international organizations, and development partners. The UAE faces various challenges and opportunities in navigating the complexities of post-conflict reconstruction. From addressing security concerns and political instability to promoting economic diversification and social cohesion, the UAE's economic diplomacy strategy must be adaptable and responsive to the context of each post-conflict environment. By fostering partnerships with local governments, civil society organizations, and international donors, the UAE can maximize the impact of its reconstruction efforts and contribute to long-term peace and prosperity in conflict-affected regions. Looking ahead, the future of economic diplomacy in post-conflict reconstruction will likely be shaped by emerging trends such as digital transformation, climate change resilience, and sustainable development practices. By harnessing innovative technologies, promoting environmental sustainability, and embracing inclusive economic growth, the UAE can continue to lead in supporting post-conflict reconstruction efforts globally. As the UAE enhances its economic diplomacy toolkit and adapts to evolving challenges, it remains committed to building a more peaceful and prosperous world through effective post-conflict reconstruction initiatives.

Future Trends and Challenges in Economic Diplomacy

Future Trends and Challenges in Economic Diplomacy The future landscape of economic diplomacy presents many opportunities and challenges for the UAE. As the global geopolitical and economic dynamics continue to evolve, the UAE must remain agile and proactive in adapting its economic diplomacy strategies to stay ahead of the curve. One of the emerging trends in economic diplomacy is the increasing focus on digitalization and technology. In a world where digital connectivity is crucial to economic development, the UAE must leverage technology to enhance its economic diplomacy efforts. Embracing innovations such as blockchain, artificial intelligence, and fintech can open new avenues for economic cooperation and bolster the UAE's position as a forward-thinking economic powerhouse. Another key trend is the growing importance of sustainability and green economy in economic diplomacy. As the world grapples with environmental challenges, countries increasingly prioritize sustainable development and green initiatives. The UAE can capitalize on this trend by positioning itself as a leader in clean energy technology, eco-friendly infrastructure projects, and sustainable investment practices. By integrating sustainability into its economic diplomacy agenda, the UAE can enhance its reputation as a responsible global player committed to addressing pressing environmental issues. However, alongside these opportunities, the UAE also faces significant challenges in navigating the complex terrain of economic diplomacy. One of the major challenges is the rising protectionist sentiments and trade tensions among countries. In an era of increasing trade wars and nationalist policies, the UAE must carefully navigate the shifting global trade landscape to safeguard its economic interests and maintain open markets for its goods and services. Moreover, geopolitical uncertainties and regional conflicts pose another challenge to the UAE's economic diplomacy efforts. Instability in neighboring regions can disrupt trade routes, hinder investment opportunities, and create economic volatility. To mitigate these risks, the UAE must engage in proactive diplomatic initiatives to promote peace and stability in the region, safeguarding its economic interests and ensuring sustainable growth. In conclusion, the future of economic diplomacy for the UAE holds both promise and complexity. By embracing emerging trends, leveraging technology, and prioritizing sustainability, the UAE can position itself as a frontrunner in economic diplomacy on the global stage. However, navigating challenges such as protectionism and geopolitical instability will require strategic foresight, diplomatic finesse, and proactive engagement to secure the UAE's economic interests and advance its global prosperity.

Emerging Economic Diplomacy Strategies

The UAE is adopting new strategies to bolster its economic diplomacy efforts in the ever-changing global landscape. One such emerging strategy is diversifying its economic partnerships beyond traditional sectors. This includes increasing collaborations in emerging industries such as renewable energy, technology, and innovation. By investing in these sectors, the UAE aims to position itself as a leader in the global economy and stay ahead of future trends. Moreover, the UAE is enhancing its economic diplomacy through sustainable development initiatives. By prioritizing sustainable practices in trade and investment activities, the UAE promotes environmental stewardship and attracts like-minded partners who value sustainability. This strategic approach strengthens the UAE's international reputation and aligns with the global shift towards green economies. Additionally, the UAE is leveraging its position as a regional hub for business and finance to expand its economic diplomacy reach. By positioning itself as a gateway to the Middle East and beyond, the UAE attracts foreign investment and fosters economic partnerships with countries seeking access to the region's markets. This proactive stance reinforces the UAE's status as a key player in the global economic arena. By embracing these emerging economic diplomacy strategies, the UAE is poised to navigate the challenges and seize the opportunities that lie ahead in the dynamic world of international trade and investment.

Challenges and Opportunities for UAE's Economic Diplomacy Efforts

Challenges and Opportunities for UAE's Economic Diplomacy Efforts The UAE's economic diplomacy efforts face various challenges and opportunities as the country navigates the complex global economic landscape. One key challenge is the evolving dynamics of global trade and investment, which require the UAE to adapt its economic strategies to remain competitive. Additionally, geopolitical tensions and regional conflicts can impact the UAE's economic relations with certain countries, necessitating diplomatic finesse to mitigate potential risks. On the other hand, the UAE's strategic location as a gateway between East and West presents significant opportunities for expanding its economic reach and influence. By leveraging its position as a hub for trade and investment, the UAE can further solidify its role as a key player in the global economy. Moreover, the country's robust infrastructure and investment-friendly policies attract foreign businesses and investors, enhancing its economic diplomacy efforts. The UAE must continuously innovate and adapt its economic diplomacy strategies to capitalize on these opportunities and overcome challenges. This requires a keen understanding of emerging global trends and proactive engagement with key partners and stakeholders. By fostering strong economic relations and promoting a favorable business environment, the UAE can maximize the impact of its economic diplomacy efforts and reinforce its position as a leading economic player on the world stage.

The strategic use of economic tools plays a pivotal role in the UAE's foreign policy endeavors, shaping its diplomatic objectives and bolstering its global standing. By harnessing the power of economic diplomacy, the UAE seeks to forge robust international partnerships, promote economic growth, and secure its national interests on the global stage. The UAE strategically leverages its economic resources to advance its diplomatic agenda through a multifaceted approach encompassing trade relations, investment strategies, and participation in international economic forums. One key aspect of the UAE's economic diplomacy efforts lies in its pursuit of bilateral trade relations and economic partnerships with key global players. Through fostering strong trade ties and cultivating strategic alliances, the UAE aims to enhance its economic resilience, diversify its trading partners, and foster economic stability. By actively engaging in trade promotion initiatives and negotiating free trade agreements, the UAE positions itself as a strategic hub for international commerce, creating a conducive environment for business growth and investment. Moreover, the UAE's economic diplomacy extends beyond traditional trade relations to investments in infrastructure development and energy-related strategic sectors. The UAE enhances its economic competitiveness by investing in critical infrastructure projects and forging partnerships in the energy industry. It reinforces its role as a key player in the global economy. These investments drive economic growth and contribute to regional connectivity, bolstering the UAE's position as a hub for trade and investment in the Middle East. Furthermore, the UAE's active participation in international economic forums and organizations underscores its commitment to shaping global economic policies and fostering international cooperation. By engaging with multilateral institutions and advocating for inclusive economic development, the UAE leverages its economic diplomacy to influence decision-making processes and promote shared prosperity on the global stage. The UAE demonstrates its willingness to collaborate with the international community and contribute to advancing global economic governance through its involvement in international economic discussions. In navigating the complexities of economic diplomacy, the UAE faces many challenges and opportunities. As economic dynamics evolve and geopolitical landscapes shift, the UAE must adapt its economic diplomacy strategies to address emerging challenges and capitalize on new opportunities. By proactively addressing issues such as trade barriers, economic sanctions, and geopolitical tensions, the UAE can safeguard its economic interests and mitigate potential risks to its economic stability. Moreover, by harnessing emerging trends in economic diplomacy, such as digital trade and green investments, the UAE can position itself at the forefront of global economic innovation, enhancing its competitiveness and influence on the world stage. In conclusion, the intricate relationship between economic diplomacy and foreign policy underscores the importance of economic tools in advancing the UAE's diplomatic objectives and enhancing its global standing. By strategically utilizing its economic resources, the UAE can navigate the complexities of the global economy, forge strong international partnerships, and promote sustainable economic growth. Through proactive engagement in economic diplomacy, the UAE reaffirms its commitment to fostering economic prosperity, driving innovation, and shaping the future of global economic governance.

In a Nutshell

INTRODUCTION TO ECONOMIC DIPLOMACY
Economic diplomacy refers to the use of economic tools, including trade, investment, and financial relations, to advance a country's foreign policy goals. It involves leveraging economic resources to achieve diplomatic objectives, enhance national security, and promote national economic interests abroad[1][3].

DEFINITION AND IMPORTANCE
Economic diplomacy is defined as the process by which countries negotiate and implement economic policies and agreements that are mutually beneficial, aiming to promote national economic interests, enhance geopolitical standing, and secure long-term economic development[1][3]. It is crucial for managing international relations and ensuring a country's position in the global economy.

ROLE IN SHAPING FOREIGN POLICY GOALS
Economic diplomacy is instrumental in shaping a country's foreign policy. By fostering trade relations, securing energy supplies, or investing in foreign infrastructure, nations can strengthen alliances, deter adversaries, and increase their influence globally[1][3][12].

HISTORICAL FOUNDATIONS OF UAE'S ECONOMIC DIPLOMACY

The UAE's economic diplomacy has roots in its early trade routes and the pearling industry, which established the region as a critical player in international trade long before oil discovery[6]. This historical context set the stage for the UAE's modern economic diplomacy strategies.

EARLY TRADE ROUTES AND ECONOMIC NETWORKS

Historically, the UAE was a central hub in the maritime silk routes, facilitating trade between the East and the West. These early trade networks laid the groundwork for the UAE's expansive economic diplomacy[6].

EVOLUTION TOWARDS MODERN ECONOMIC DIPLOMACY

With the discovery of oil, the UAE's economic diplomacy evolved significantly, focusing on energy exports and later diversifying into sectors like finance, tourism, and technology. This shift has been crucial in transforming its economic landscape and diplomatic reach[12].

KEY ECONOMIC PARTNERSHIPS AND AGREEMENTS

The UAE has established key economic partnerships and agreements globally, including with major economies such as the United States, China, and India. These partnerships are crucial for its economic diplomacy, enhancing trade, investment, and technological cooperation[8][10][15].

BILATERAL TRADE RELATIONS

The UAE maintains robust bilateral trade relations with numerous countries, leveraging these relationships to bolster its economic and political objectives. These relations are supported by a network of trade agreements that facilitate economic exchange[8][14].

FREE TRADE AGREEMENTS AND ECONOMIC ALLIANCES

The UAE is part of several free trade agreements and economic alliances, including the Gulf Cooperation Council (GCC) and agreements with countries outside the Middle East. These alliances reduce trade barriers and promote economic integration[14].

INVESTMENT PARTNERSHIPS

Investment partnerships are a cornerstone of the UAE's economic diplomacy, with significant investments in global markets through sovereign wealth funds and private sector ventures. These investments help the UAE to exert economic influence and secure strategic interests abroad[3][4].

ECONOMIC DIPLOMACY IN THE ENERGY SECTOR

The UAE's economic diplomacy in the energy sector is pivotal, focusing on both hydrocarbon exports and investments in renewable energy. These efforts ensure energy security and position the UAE as a leader in global energy markets[12][18].

ENERGY RESOURCES AND GLOBAL ENERGY MARKETS

The UAE leverages its substantial energy resources to influence global energy markets, using its oil and gas supplies as diplomatic tools while also leading initiatives in renewable energy[12][18].

STRATEGIC PARTNERSHIPS IN ENERGY INDUSTRY

Strategic partnerships in the energy industry, such as with other oil-producing nations and renewable energy investments, are key to the UAE's economic diplomacy, helping to stabilize global energy supplies and promote sustainable energy[12][18].

ECONOMIC DIPLOMACY IN INFRASTRUCTURE DEVELOPMENT

The UAE's economic diplomacy extends to infrastructure development, where it invests in building ports, roads, and airports in other countries. These projects enhance the UAE's strategic ties and foster regional connectivity[4][18].

INVESTMENTS IN INFRASTRUCTURE PROJECTS

Investments in global infrastructure projects are a critical element of the UAE's economic diplomacy, facilitating trade and opening new markets for UAE businesses while also strengthening bilateral relations[4][18].

IMPACT ON ECONOMIC GROWTH AND REGIONAL CONNECTIVITY

The UAE's economic diplomacy significantly impacts economic growth and regional connectivity, promoting development both within the UAE and in its partner countries[4][18].

TRADE PROMOTION AND INVESTMENT ATTRACTION

Trade promotion and investment attraction are vital components of the UAE's economic diplomacy. Initiatives aimed at enhancing the UAE's trade relations and attracting foreign investment are central to its economic strategy[12][18].

TRADE PROMOTION INITIATIVES

The UAE implements various trade promotion initiatives, such as participating in global trade fairs and establishing trade agreements, to enhance its export capabilities and attract foreign investors[8][14].

INVESTMENT PROMOTION STRATEGIES

Investment promotion strategies involve creating favorable business environments, offering incentives, and providing support services to attract and retain foreign investors[4][12].

ECONOMIC DIPLOMACY IN INTERNATIONAL ORGANIZATIONS

The UAE's active participation in international economic forums and organizations allows it to influence global economic policies and advocate for its interests on the international stage[12][20].

PARTICIPATION IN INTERNATIONAL ECONOMIC FORUMS

The UAE frequently participates in international economic forums, such as the World Economic Forum and the United Nations, to discuss and shape global economic policies[12][20].

INFLUENCE ON GLOBAL ECONOMIC POLICIES

Through its active engagement in international organizations, the UAE influences global economic policies, promoting open trade and investment policies that benefit its economic interests[12][20].

ECONOMIC DIPLOMACY AND ECONOMIC STATECRAFT

Economic statecraft, where the UAE uses its economic resources as tools in diplomatic engagements, is an integral part of its foreign policy. This approach includes leveraging trade and investment to build alliances and resolve conflicts[1][3].

USE OF ECONOMIC LEVERAGE IN DIPLOMATIC RELATIONS

The UAE uses its economic leverage to achieve foreign policy objectives, influencing other nations through economic means rather than military force[1][3].

ECONOMIC STATECRAFT IN ACHIEVING FOREIGN POLICY OBJECTIVES

Economic statecraft is effectively used by the UAE to achieve its foreign policy objectives, ensuring national security and economic prosperity through strategic economic actions[1][3].

ECONOMIC DIPLOMACY IN CRISIS MANAGEMENT
In times of crisis, the UAE employs economic diplomacy to manage and resolve conflicts, using economic incentives or sanctions to influence outcomes[1][3].

ECONOMIC TOOLS FOR CONFLICT RESOLUTION
Economic tools, such as development aid and investment, are used by the UAE to facilitate conflict resolution and support post-conflict reconstruction in affected regions[5][20].

ECONOMIC DIPLOMACY IN POST-CONFLICT RECONSTRUCTION
The UAE's economic diplomacy plays a crucial role in post-conflict reconstruction, investing in rebuilding infrastructure and restoring economic stability in war-torn regions[5][20].

FUTURE TRENDS AND CHALLENGES IN ECONOMIC DIPLOMACY
Emerging trends in economic diplomacy include digital diplomacy, sustainable development, and the increasing importance of multilateralism. The UAE must navigate these trends while addressing challenges such as global economic shifts and regional instabilities[1][3].

References

[1] https://scholarworks.uaeu.ac.ae/cgi/viewcontent.cgi?article=1018&context=business_dissertations
[2] https://insightss.co/testing/uaes-foreign-policy-and-its-impact-on-the-region/
[3] https://www.khaleejtimes.com/world/the-six-pillars-of-the-uae-economic-diplomacy
[4] https://www.mofaic.gov.ae/en/mediahub/news/2022/12/6/06-12-2022-uae-speech
[5] https://www.cmi.no/publications/file/7169-the-uaes-humanitarian-diplomacy-claiming-state-sovereignty.pdf
[6] https://www.uae-embassy.org/business-trade/uae-economic-overview
[7] https://scholarworks.uaeu.ac.ae/business_dissertations/17/
[8] https://www.uae-embassy.org/uae-us-cooperation/economic
[9] https://www.cmi.no/publications/7169-the-uaes-humanitarian-diplomacy-claiming-state-sovereignty
[10] https://added.gov.ae/Media-Center/Business-News/UAEs-Comprehensive-Economic-Partnership-Agreements
[11] https://www.fpri.org/article/2023/04/big-changes-in-united-arab-emirates-foreign-policy/
[12] https://www.mofa.gov.ae/en/The-Ministry/The-Foreign-Policy/Economic-Diplomacy
[13] https://carnegieendowment.org/sada/86130
[14] https://www.trade.gov/country-commercial-guides/united-arab-emirates-trade-agreements
[15] https://commerce.gov.in/international-trade/trade-agreements/comprehensive-economic-partnership-agreement-between-the-government-of-the-republic-of-india-and-the-government-of-the-united-arab-emirates-uae/
[16] https://www.stimson.org/2023/uae-entry-into-brics-increases-its-diplo-

matic-and-economic-options/
[17] https://www.iranintl.com/en/202309115082
[18] https://www.reuters.com/world/middle-east/abu-dhabi-fund-adq-wields-economic-diplomacy-forge-regional-ties-2022-10-16/
[19] https://foreignpolicy.com/2024/01/25/the-hidden-rivalry-of-saudi-arabia-and-the-uae/
[20] https://www.mofa.gov.ae/en/The-Ministry/UAE-International-Development-Cooperation

IV

Soft Power and Cultural Diplomacy

Introduction to Soft Power and Cultural Diplomacy

Soft power and cultural diplomacy play essential roles in shaping a country's image and influence on the global stage. Soft power refers to the ability of a nation to attract and persuade others through its culture, values, and policies rather than through coercion or force. It is a crucial tool in modern diplomacy, allowing countries to exercise influence and achieve their foreign policy goals through non-military means. On the other hand, cultural diplomacy involves using cultural assets, such as art, music, literature, and language, to enhance understanding and build relationships between nations. A country can strengthen its international partnerships and foster mutual respect by showcasing its cultural heritage and engaging in cultural exchange programs. The concept of soft power was popularized by political scientist Joseph Nye, who argued that a nation's influence is not solely based on its military or economic strength but also on its ability to appeal to others through its culture, values, and policies. In an interconnected world where information flows freely, and perceptions matter, soft power has become increasingly important in shaping international relations. Cultural diplomacy enables countries to connect with people personally and emotionally, transcending language barriers and political differences. By promoting their cultural heritage and engaging in cultural exchange programs, nations can build trust, foster goodwill, and open doors for dialogue and cooperation. In an era marked by global challenges and complex geopolitical dynamics, soft power and cultural diplomacy offer valuable tools for building bridges, promoting understanding, and advancing mutual interests. By investing in their cultural assets and engaging with the world through cultural exchange and public diplomacy initiatives, countries can enhance their influence, build lasting relationships, and contribute to a more peaceful and prosperous world.

Understanding Soft Power: Definition and Significance in Diplomacy

Soft power is a concept coined by Joseph Nye, referring to a nation's ability to influence others through attraction and persuasion rather than coercion. Soft power is crucial in shaping international relations and achieving foreign policy goals in diplomacy. Unlike hard power, which relies on military force or economic sanctions, soft power relies on a country's cultural attractiveness, values, and policies to influence the global stage. Soft power operates on the principle of winning hearts and minds, appealing to the shared values and aspirations of people worldwide. It involves using cultural assets, such as music, art, literature, language, and traditions, to create a positive image of the country and enhance its reputation. By projecting a compelling narrative about its history, values, and achievements, a nation can build trust and credibility with other countries, paving the way for cooperation and collaboration. In diplomacy, soft power is especially valuable for fostering long-term relationships and addressing complex global challenges. It can help build bridges between different cultures, promote mutual understanding, and create opportunities for dialogue and partnership. Soft power also enables countries to shape perceptions, influence public opinion, and generate support for their policies and initiatives. The significance of soft power in diplomacy lies in its ability to transcend borders and connect people on a deeper emotional level. It allows countries to build strategic alliances, attract investment, and enhance their influence in international institutions. By leveraging their cultural assets and values, nations can increase their soft power resources and strengthen their position in the global arena. In summary, understanding soft power is essential for modern diplomacy, as it offers a unique and effective tool for advancing national interests, building relationships, and promoting global peace and prosperity. By harnessing the power of attraction and persuasion, countries can create a positive image on the world stage and achieve their foreign policy objectives with greater success.

The Role of Culture in Diplomacy: Promoting National Identity and Values

Cultural diplomacy is crucial in promoting a nation's identity and values on the global stage. Countries can showcase their unique heritage, traditions, and beliefs through cultural exchanges and initiatives to foster mutual understanding and respect. By sharing aspects of their culture with the world, countries can strengthen relationships, build trust, and cultivate long-lasting connections with other nations. Cultural diplomacy is a powerful tool in shaping perceptions and promoting positive engagement between countries. It allows for communicating complex ideas and emotions that transcend language barriers, fostering a deeper connection between people from different backgrounds. By highlighting the richness and diversity of their culture, nations can create a favorable image that resonates with global audiences. Furthermore, cultural diplomacy helps to bridge differences and promote dialogue in a non-confrontational manner. Countries can find common ground and build bridges of understanding by emphasizing commonalities and shared values through cultural expressions such as art, music, literature, and cuisine. This shared appreciation for cultural heritage can serve as a platform for meaningful conversations and collaborations that transcend political or economic interests. In today's interconnected world, the role of culture in diplomacy is more important than ever. As countries seek to engage with one another globally, cultural diplomacy offers a unique opportunity to connect at a human level and forge genuine relationships based on mutual respect and appreciation. By promoting their national identity and values through cultural initiatives, countries can establish themselves as global leaders in promoting peace, understanding, and cooperation among diverse communities.

Cultural Exchange Programs: Building Bridges and Fostering Understanding

Cultural exchange programs are crucial in international diplomacy as they facilitate interactions between different cultures and promote mutual understanding. These programs serve as a platform for people from different backgrounds to come together, share their experiences, and learn from each other. By participating in cultural exchange programs, individuals can gain valuable insights into other societies' customs, traditions, and values, which can help bridge cultural divides and foster cross-cultural understanding. The UAE has been actively organizing and participating in various cultural exchange programs to promote its national identity and values on the global stage. Through initiatives such as artist residencies, cultural festivals, and exchange programs for students and professionals, the UAE has been able to showcase its rich cultural heritage to a global audience. These programs not only highlight the diversity and creativity of Emirati culture but also serve as a means of building bridges with people from other countries. Cultural exchange programs also allow individuals to develop personal connections and form lasting friendships across borders. Participates can build trust, empathy, and respect for each other's traditions and values by engaging in cultural exchanges. This personal connection forms the foundation for stronger diplomatic relations between nations, as it fosters a sense of goodwill and cooperation that transcends political differences. Moreover, cultural exchange programs help challenge stereotypes and misconceptions about different cultures. By experiencing firsthand the richness and complexity of other cultural traditions, participants in these programs can break down barriers and promote a more inclusive and harmonious global community. This enhanced cultural understanding benefits individuals on a personal level and contributes to building a more peaceful and tolerant world. In conclusion, cultural exchange programs are vital in building bridges and fostering understanding between nations. By promoting cultural dialogue and collaboration, these initiatives contribute to the development of strong and vibrant diplomatic relations that are rooted in mutual respect and appreciation for diversity. The UAE's active engagement in cultural exchange programs underscores its commitment to promoting intercultural dialogue and building a more connected and inclusive global society.

Public Diplomacy Initiatives: Showcasing the UAE's Cultural Heritage

Public Diplomacy Initiatives: Showcasing the UAE's Cultural Heritage Public diplomacy initiatives play a vital role in promoting the UAE's rich cultural heritage globally. The UAE showcases its traditions, arts, and values to worldwide audiences through various events, exhibitions, and programs. These initiatives not only foster greater understanding and appreciation of the UAE's culture but also help to strengthen relations with other nations. By organizing cultural festivals, art exhibitions, and performances, the UAE highlights the diversity and uniqueness of its cultural heritage. These events provide a platform for artists, musicians, and performers to share their talents and traditions with international audiences, fostering a sense of unity and mutual respect. Furthermore, the UAE utilizes public diplomacy initiatives to promote cultural exchange and dialogue. Collaborative projects with international partners, such as joint art exhibitions or cultural exchange programs, serve as opportunities to engage in meaningful cross-cultural interactions and promote intercultural understanding. Traditional and social media platforms are valuable tools in showcasing the UAE's cultural heritage to a global audience. Through strategic communication efforts, the UAE leverages these channels to highlight the beauty and richness of its traditions, arts, and cultural practices, reaching diverse audiences and shaping positive perceptions of the country. Overall, public diplomacy initiatives focused on showcasing the UAE's cultural heritage play a key role in enhancing the country's reputation, fostering goodwill, and building enduring relationships with countries worldwide. Through these efforts, the UAE continues to be a beacon of cultural diplomacy, promoting tolerance, cultural exchange, and mutual understanding on the world stage.

Utilizing Traditional and Social Media for Cultural Diplomacy

Utilizing Traditional and Social Media for Cultural Diplomacy
The UAE has recognized the power of traditional and social media in advancing its cultural diplomacy efforts on the global stage. Through strategic communication channels, the country has been able to showcase its rich heritage, values, and modern achievements to audiences worldwide. Traditional media outlets such as television, radio, and print publications have significantly promoted Emirati culture and traditions to a global audience. Additionally, social media platforms such as Instagram, Twitter, and Facebook have provided the UAE with a direct and immediate way to engage with diverse audiences and share its cultural narrative. By leveraging influencers, content creators, and official government accounts, the UAE has successfully amplified its cultural diplomacy initiatives and reached a wider demographic of individuals who may not have been exposed to Emirati culture otherwise. Furthermore, the UAE has utilized innovative digital campaigns, virtual exhibitions, and online events to connect with international audiences and foster cultural exchange. By creating engaging and interactive digital content, the country has been able to break down barriers and stereotypes while highlighting the diversity and vibrancy of Emirati culture. In an increasingly interconnected world, the UAE recognizes the importance of utilizing both traditional and social media platforms to strengthen cultural ties, promote intercultural dialogue, and enhance its global reputation as a hub of creativity, innovation, and tolerance. Through strategic communication efforts, the UAE continues to engage with the international community and build lasting relationships based on mutual understanding and respect.

Educational and Scholarly Exchanges: Investing in Future Relations

Educational and scholarly exchanges play a crucial role in fostering mutual understanding and building lasting relationships between nations. By investing in educational programs and opportunities for academic collaboration, the UAE is actively paving the way for future generations to engage with diverse perspectives and ideas. Scholarly exchanges facilitate the exchange of knowledge and expertise in various fields of study, enriching research and academic discourse. Through partnerships with universities and research institutions around the world, the UAE is creating a vibrant intellectual community that transcends borders and promotes cross-cultural dialogue. Furthermore, educational exchanges provide students and scholars with valuable opportunities to immerse themselves in different academic environments, expanding their horizons and nurturing a global mindset. By studying abroad or hosting international students, the UAE is nurturing a new generation of global citizens who are equipped to address complex challenges and contribute to a more interconnected world. These educational initiatives also enhance the UAE's soft power by showcasing the country's commitment to education, innovation, and intellectual exchange. By investing in the future through educational and scholarly exchanges, the UAE lays the foundation for long-term diplomatic relationships and bridges of understanding that transcend cultural differences.

Art and Cultural Exhibitions: Enhancing Global Visibility and Influence

Art and cultural exhibitions enhance a country's global visibility and influence. These exhibitions serve as a platform to showcase a nation's rich cultural heritage, artistic talent, and creativity to an international audience. Through art and cultural exhibitions, the UAE can connect with people from diverse backgrounds, fostering a better understanding and appreciation of its traditions and values. The UAE can position itself as a hub for creativity and innovation by hosting or participating in international art and cultural exhibitions. These events allow artists, curators, and cultural experts to exchange ideas, collaborate on projects, and create new partnerships that transcend geographical boundaries. Moreover, the UAE can highlight its commitment to promoting cultural diversity and fostering intercultural dialogue through these exhibitions. The UAE can attract global attention and draw visitors to its vibrant arts scene through strategic participation in major art fairs, biennales, and cultural festivals worldwide. By showcasing the work of Emirati and international artists, the country can enhance its reputation as a center for artistic excellence and cultural exchange. Additionally, these exhibitions can serve as a platform for promoting cross-cultural understanding and building bridges between different communities. The UAE's investment in art and cultural exhibitions boosts its soft power and contributes to its economic development. By supporting the growth of the creative industries, the country can create new opportunities for job creation, innovation, and economic growth. Furthermore, by promoting cultural tourism through art and cultural exhibitions, the UAE can attract visitors worldwide, diversifying its economy and promoting sustainable development. In conclusion, art and cultural exhibitions enhance the UAE's global visibility and influence. By leveraging its rich cultural heritage and artistic talent, the country can strengthen its soft power and establish itself as a global cultural hub. Through strategic participation in international art events, the UAE can showcase its creativity, foster intercultural dialogue, and contribute to economic growth and development.

Sports Diplomacy: Harnessing the Power of Athletic Competitions and Events

Sports diplomacy harnesses the power of athletics to strengthen international relations and promote cooperation among nations. Countries can foster connections, build trust, and enhance their global influence through sports competitions and events. The UAE has actively utilized sports diplomacy as a tool to engage with other nations and showcase its values and capabilities on the world stage. By hosting international sporting events, participating in tournaments, and supporting sports initiatives, the UAE has successfully leveraged the universal appeal of sports to enhance its diplomatic efforts and promote goodwill across borders.

Measuring the Impact of Soft Power and Cultural Diplomacy Efforts

Understanding the impact of soft power and cultural diplomacy efforts is crucial for assessing the effectiveness of these strategies in achieving foreign policy objectives. One key aspect of measuring impact is analyzing the reception and perception of cultural initiatives in target countries. By conducting surveys, focus groups, and interviews, diplomats can gather valuable feedback on how their cultural programs are received and whether they contribute to a positive image of the UAE. Another way to measure impact is through quantitative data analysis. This can involve tracking metrics such as website traffic, social media engagement, attendance numbers at cultural events, and media coverage. By analyzing these data points, policymakers can gauge the reach and influence of their cultural diplomacy efforts and make informed decisions about resource allocation and strategy adjustments. Furthermore, partnerships and collaborations with local academic institutions and cultural organizations can provide valuable insights into the long-term impact of cultural initiatives. By engaging in joint research projects and longitudinal studies, diplomats can assess the lasting effects of cultural exchanges on perceptions of the UAE and on bilateral relations. Ultimately, the impact of soft power and cultural diplomacy efforts is often measured in terms of shifts in public opinion, increased trust and goodwill towards the UAE, and enhanced cultural understanding between nations. By continuously evaluating the effectiveness of these initiatives and adapting strategies based on feedback and data analysis, the UAE can further strengthen its influence and reputation on the global stage.

In a Nutshell

UNDERSTANDING SOFT POWER: DEFINITION AND SIGNIFICANCE IN DIPLOMACY

Soft power, a term coined by Joseph Nye, refers to the ability of a country to influence others through attraction and persuasion rather than coercion or payment. It relies on cultural, ideological, and institutional appeal to shape the preferences and behaviors of other nations[1][2][8]. In diplomacy, soft power is significant because it enhances a country's ability to achieve its foreign policy objectives without the use of force, fostering a positive image and credibility internationally.

THE ROLE OF CULTURE IN DIPLOMACY: PROMOTING NATIONAL IDENTITY AND VALUES

Culture plays a pivotal role in diplomacy by promoting a nation's identity and values on the global stage. The UAE, for instance, leverages its rich cultural heritage to strengthen diplomatic ties and enhance its soft power. Initiatives like the Louvre Abu Dhabi not only showcase the UAE's commitment to cultural diversity but also position it as a bridge between Eastern and Western cultures[4][19].

CULTURAL EXCHANGE PROGRAMS: BUILDING BRIDGES AND FOSTERING UNDERSTANDING

Cultural exchange programs are essential tools for building bridges and fostering mutual understanding between countries. These programs, which can include student exchanges, cultural tours, and art exhibitions, allow people from different nations to experience and appreciate each other's cultures firsthand, thereby reducing cultural barriers and enhancing diplomatic relations[5][12].

PUBLIC DIPLOMACY INITIATIVES: SHOWCASING THE UAE'S CULTURAL HERITAGE

The UAE's public diplomacy initiatives are designed to showcase its cultural heritage and modern achievements globally. Events like Expo 2020 Dubai serve as platforms for the UAE to present its innovations and cultural richness to the world, enhancing its soft power and international reputation[14][15].

UTILIZING TRADITIONAL AND SOCIAL MEDIA FOR CULTURAL DIPLOMACY

Traditional and social media are powerful tools in cultural diplomacy, used to reach a global audience effectively. The UAE employs these platforms to promote its cultural events, national achievements, and key diplomatic messages, thus broadening its influence and engaging with international publics[7][20].

EDUCATIONAL AND SCHOLARLY EXCHANGES: INVESTING IN FUTURE RELATIONS

Educational and scholarly exchanges are critical components of the UAE's cultural diplomacy, fostering long-term relationships with future leaders and intellectuals worldwide. These programs, which include scholarships and research collaborations, help inculcate a positive view of the UAE among international students and academics, thereby investing in future bilateral relations[5][20].

ART AND CULTURAL EXHIBITIONS: ENHANCING GLOBAL VISIBILITY AND INFLUENCE

Art and cultural exhibitions are vital for enhancing a country's global visibility and influence. By hosting and participating in international art fairs and cultural exhibitions, the UAE showcases its artistic and cultural vibrancy, attracting global attention and appreciation, which in turn supports its diplomatic objectives[4][5].

SPORTS DIPLOMACY: HARNESSING THE POWER OF ATHLETIC COMPETITIONS AND EVENTS

Sports diplomacy is another effective avenue of cultural diplomacy, where hosting and performing in international sports events can enhance a country's soft power. The UAE's hosting of events like the FIFA Club World Cup and the Formula 1 Grand Prix in Abu Dhabi positions it as a hub for international sports, improving its global stature and fostering international goodwill[12][14].

MEASURING THE IMPACT OF SOFT POWER AND CULTURAL DIPLOMACY EFFORTS

Measuring the impact of soft power and cultural diplomacy is challenging but essential for assessing effectiveness and guiding future strategies. Metrics can include changes in international public opinion, increased foreign direct investment, tourism, and enhanced bilateral relations. The UAE monitors these indicators to evaluate the success of its cultural diplomacy and adjust its strategies accordingly[9][10].

In summary, the UAE's strategic use of cultural diplomacy and soft power significantly enhances its diplomatic reach and global standing. By investing in cultural, educational, and sports initiatives, and effectively utilizing media, the UAE not only promotes its national identity and values but also fosters international relationships that are crucial for its broader foreign policy objectives.

References

[1] https://www.hks.harvard.edu/publications/soft-power-and-public-diplomacy-revisited
[2] https://bestdiplomats.org/soft-power-in-ir/
[3] https://www.diplomacy.edu/resource/soft-power-the-means-to-success-in-world-politics/
[4] https://ae.insightss.co/uaes-cultural-mosaic-embracing-diversity/
[5] https://www.linkedin.com/pulse/cultural-diplomacy-uae-zaki-nusseibeh
[6] https://journalse.com/pliki/pw/4-2020-Golebiowski.pdf
[7] https://ijoc.org/index.php/ijoc/article/download/16150/3583
[8] https://education.cfr.org/learn/reading/what-soft-power
[9] https://softpower30.com/what-is-soft-power/
[10] https://brandfinance.com/insights/soft-power-why-it-matters
[11] https://onlinelibrary.wiley.com/doi/full/10.1111/dome.12282
[12] https://www.linkedin.com/pulse/cultural-diplomacy-showcasing-national-identity-stage-igor-podzigun
[13] https://www.humanitarianstudies.no/resource/recent-trends-in-the-international-humanitarian-regime-and-the-rise-of-the-uae/
[14] https://dash.harvard.edu/bitstream/handle/1/37375015/Engelland-Gay_Final%20v2.pdf?sequence=1
[15] https://www.unesco.org/en/articles/cutting-edge-standing-out-reaching-out-cultural-diplomacy-sustainable-development
[16] https://bestdiplomats.org/cultural-diplomacy/
[17] https://uscpublicdiplomacy.org/blog/nation-branding-and-public-diplomacy-united-arab-emirates-0
[18] https://carijournals.org/journals/index.php/JIRP/article/download/1425/1731/4508

[19] https://scholarworks.uaeu.ac.ae/cgi/viewcontent.cgi?article=1854&context=all_theses

[20] https://www.gsineducation.com/blog/bridging-cultures-and-communities-the-vital-role-of-international-education

V

Security and Defense in UAE Foreign Policy

Introduction to Security Challenges

The United Arab Emirates faces diverse security challenges in today's complex global landscape. These challenges stem from both regional and international sources, requiring a comprehensive and strategic approach to safeguarding the nation's interests. The UAE's security environment is dynamic and constantly evolving, from traditional security threats to emerging non-traditional risks. Historically, the UAE has navigated a precarious security landscape marked by regional conflicts, terrorism, and geopolitical tensions. These factors have shaped the nation's approach to security and defense, influencing its strategic outlook and policy decisions. As a young nation with ambitious development goals, the UAE has invested significant resources in building robust defense capabilities to protect its sovereignty and national interests. In recent years, the UAE's security challenges have become increasingly complex and multifaceted. The proliferation of non-state actors, cyber threats, and hybrid warfare tactics pose new challenges that require innovative and agile responses. Additionally, the evolving regional dynamics and shifting geopolitical alliances have added layers of complexity to the UAE's security environment. In light of these challenges, the UAE has adopted a proactive and forward-looking security posture, enhancing its military capabilities, bolstering defense cooperation with allies, and investing in cutting-edge technology to address emerging threats. The UAE aims to mitigate risks and safeguard its stability and prosperity in an uncertain world by staying vigilant and adaptive. As the UAE continues navigating the complexities of the modern security landscape, it remains committed to upholding its peace, stability, and cooperation principles. The UAE endeavors to address security challenges effectively and ensure a secure future for its people and the region through strategic planning, robust defense capabilities, and collaboration with partners.

Historical Context of UAE's Security and Defense Policy

The historical foundations of the UAE's security and defense policy can be traced back to the formation of the federation in 1971. The UAE faced numerous security challenges during this period, including territorial disputes, border conflicts, and internal security threats. In response to these challenges, the country began to prioritize the development of its defense capabilities and the establishment of a robust national security framework. The UAE's security and defense policy evolved significantly over the years, guided by the country's visionary leadership. The late Sheikh Zayed bin Sultan Al Nahyan, the founding father of the UAE, played a crucial role in shaping the country's security strategy. Under his leadership, the UAE adopted a policy of non-alignment and sought to build strong defense capabilities to ensure the security and stability of the federation. In the early years of the federation, the UAE focused on building its military forces and establishing defense partnerships with key allies. The country invested heavily in defense infrastructure, training programs, and technological advancements to enhance its defense capabilities. The UAE also actively participated in regional security initiatives and peacekeeping missions to demonstrate its commitment to regional stability. The strategic location of the UAE in the volatile Middle East region further underscored the importance of a robust security and defense policy. The country faced threats from regional conflicts, terrorism, and maritime piracy, requiring a proactive approach to safeguard its national security interests. As a result, the UAE developed a comprehensive security strategy that combined military, diplomatic, and economic measures to address emerging security challenges. The historical context of the UAE's security and defense policy reflects a pragmatic and forward-thinking approach to security issues. The country's commitment to building strong defense capabilities, forging strategic partnerships, and promoting regional stability has been instrumental in ensuring the security and prosperity of the federation.

National Security Strategy and Objectives

The UAE's national security strategy is guided by a comprehensive approach that seeks to safeguard the country's territorial integrity, protect its citizens and residents, and uphold regional stability. The overarching objective of the UAE's national security strategy is to ensure the safety and prosperity of the nation in a rapidly changing geopolitical environment. Central to the UAE's national security strategy is the principle of deterrence, which aims to dissuade potential aggressors from threatening the country's security interests. This strategy is underpinned by a strong and modern military capability and strategic alliances and partnerships with like-minded nations. In addition to deterrence, the UAE's national security strategy emphasizes the importance of proactive measures to address emerging threats and vulnerabilities. This includes investment in advanced technology and cybersecurity measures to protect critical infrastructure and secure sensitive information. The UAE's national security objectives also extend beyond traditional military concerns to encompass economic security, energy security, and resilience against non-traditional security threats such as terrorism, cyber-attacks, and pandemics. The country's security strategy is thus holistic in nature, considering a wide range of factors that could impact the nation's stability and well-being. Moreover, the UAE is committed to promoting regional security and stability through active engagement in international fora and diplomatic initiatives. The country's participation in peacekeeping operations, counterterrorism efforts, and humanitarian missions reflects its dedication to upholding global security norms and contributing to international peace and security. Overall, the UAE's national security strategy is founded on foresight, agility, and cooperation principles. By remaining vigilant, adaptive, and collaborative in its approach to security challenges, the UAE is well-positioned to navigate the complexities of the modern security environment and protect its interests at home and abroad.

UAE's Military Capabilities and Modernization Efforts

The UAE has significantly invested in developing its military capabilities and modernizing its armed forces. With a focus on enhancing readiness and effectiveness, the country has implemented various initiatives to strengthen its defense capabilities. One key aspect of the UAE's military modernization efforts is acquiring advanced military technology and equipment. The country has procured state-of-the-art aircraft, maritime vessels, and armored vehicles to enhance its operational capabilities. These acquisitions have allowed the UAE to maintain a technologically advanced and well-equipped military force. In addition to equipment upgrades, the UAE has also prioritized the professional training and development of its military personnel. Through comprehensive training programs and joint exercises with allied countries, the UAE's armed forces have enhanced their skills and readiness for a range of operational scenarios. Furthermore, the UAE has focused on developing its defense industry capabilities to reduce its dependence on foreign suppliers. The country aims to enhance its self-sufficiency and strengthen its defense industrial base by investing in domestic defense production and technology development. Overall, the UAE's military capabilities and modernization efforts demonstrate its commitment to maintaining a strong defense posture and ensuring the nation's security and interests.

Alliances and Security Partnerships

The UAE has bolstered its national security and defense capabilities through strategic partnerships and alliances. These partnerships are a cornerstone of the country's security strategy, enhancing interoperability and information sharing with key allies. The UAE's military engagements with various nations deter potential threats and demonstrate its commitment to regional stability. One of the UAE's key security partnerships is with the United States, which dates back several decades and encompasses defense cooperation, intelligence sharing, and joint military exercises. This alliance has been crucial in enhancing the UAE's defense capabilities and strengthening its regional position. Additionally, the UAE is a member of the Saudi-led coalition in Yemen, where it plays a significant role in counterterrorism operations and maritime security efforts. The UAE's security partnerships extend beyond traditional allies to include regional and international organizations such as the Gulf Cooperation Council (GCC), the Arab League, and the United Nations. These collaborative efforts enable the UAE to address security challenges on a broader scale and promote dialogue and cooperation among nations. Furthermore, the UAE has developed strong relationships with European and Asian countries, engaging in defense cooperation agreements and joint training exercises. These partnerships not only enhance the UAE's military capabilities but also foster diplomatic ties and promote peace and security on a global scale. In conclusion, the UAE's alliances and security partnerships are crucial in safeguarding the country's national interests and maintaining regional stability. By collaborating with a diverse range of partners, the UAE can address evolving security threats effectively and contribute to regional and international peace and security.

Counterterrorism and Counter-Piracy Efforts

The UAE prioritizes combating terrorism and piracy, acknowledging the significant threats they pose to regional and global security. In combating terrorism, the UAE has implemented robust measures to prevent and counter extremist ideologies within its borders. The country has also engaged in international efforts to disrupt terrorist networks and financing, cooperating closely with partner nations and organizations. Additionally, the UAE has been actively involved in counter-piracy efforts, especially in the Gulf of Aden and the Arabian Sea. The UAE Navy has participated in multinational naval operations to combat piracy and ensure the safety of maritime trade routes. Through coordination with international partners, the UAE has contributed to deterring and suppressing piracy activities in the region. By addressing these dual threats of terrorism and piracy, the UAE demonstrates its commitment to maintaining regional stability and safeguarding global security. Through proactive measures and collaboration with allies, the UAE continues to play a vital role in countering these challenges and promoting regional peace and security.

Defense Cooperation Agreements

Defense cooperation agreements are vital in enhancing the UAE's security capabilities and ensuring regional stability. These agreements are formal arrangements between the UAE and other countries to promote mutual defense interests and cooperation. By entering into these agreements, the UAE strengthens its defense capabilities, enhances interoperability with partner countries, and contributes to broader regional security initiatives. Additionally, these agreements facilitate information sharing, joint training exercises, and technology transfers, further bolstering the UAE's defense capabilities. Furthermore, defense cooperation agreements also serve as a tangible demonstration of the UAE's commitment to regional security and cooperation, fostering stronger diplomatic ties with partner countries. The UAE can effectively address common security challenges, collaborate on peacekeeping operations, and promote regional stability through these agreements.

Maritime Security and Protection of Strategic Sea Lanes

The UAE places great emphasis on ensuring the security of its maritime domain and safeguarding the vital sea lanes that pass through its waters. As a strategically located maritime hub connecting the East and the West, the UAE recognizes the importance of maritime security in maintaining global trade and economic stability. The UAE works diligently to enhance maritime security measures through strategic partnerships and cooperative agreements with regional and international actors. The UAE Navy is critical in conducting patrols, surveillance missions, and anti-piracy operations to safeguard its coastal waters and beyond. Furthermore, the UAE actively participates in multilateral efforts to combat maritime threats like piracy and illegal trafficking. By engaging in joint exercises and information-sharing initiatives with other navies, the UAE strengthens its maritime security capabilities and contributes to maintaining stability in the region. In addition to protecting its own maritime interests, the UAE also plays a key role in securing strategic sea lanes, such as the Strait of Hormuz, through which a significant portion of the world's oil shipments pass. By ensuring the safety and security of these crucial maritime routes, the UAE contributes to global energy security and economic prosperity. In an increasingly interconnected world where maritime trade plays a vital role in the global economy, the UAE's commitment to maritime security and the protection of strategic sea lanes underscores its role as a responsible maritime stakeholder and a reliable partner in promoting regional stability and prosperity.

Cybersecurity and Information Security

The UAE recognizes the critical importance of cybersecurity and information security in today's interconnected world. As digital technology advances, so do the threats posed by malicious actors seeking to exploit vulnerabilities in cyberspace. The UAE has developed a comprehensive cybersecurity strategy encompassing defensive and offensive capabilities to address these challenges. Cyber threats come in various forms, including cybercrime, espionage, and cyber warfare. The UAE has established specialized agencies and units to combat these threats and secure its information infrastructure. These efforts include enhancing cybersecurity awareness among the public, promoting best practices in cybersecurity, and investing in cutting-edge technologies to detect and respond to cyber incidents swiftly. In addition to safeguarding its own networks and systems, the UAE is actively engaged in international cybersecurity cooperation. The country participates in regional and global cybersecurity initiatives, collaborates with like-minded partners, and contributes expertise to strengthen the collective cybersecurity resilience of the international community. The future trends in UAE's security and defense policy will undoubtedly include a greater emphasis on cybersecurity and information security. As digitalization continues to transform the geopolitical landscape, the UAE will prioritize cybersecurity investments, capacity-building, and international cooperation to stay ahead of evolving cyber threats and protect its national interests in the digital realm.

Future Trends in UAE's Security and Defense Policy

With the rapid technological advancements and the evolving nature of security threats, the UAE is expected to continue enhancing its security and defense policy to adapt to these changing realities.

One key future trend in the UAE's security and defense policy is further integrating artificial intelligence and predictive analytics into military operations. By leveraging cutting-edge technology, the UAE aims to enhance its situational awareness, decision-making capabilities, and overall defense posture. The UAE will likely focus on developing and strengthening its strategic partnerships with key regional and global allies to enhance its security cooperation and information sharing. Collaborative initiatives such as joint exercises, training programs, and intelligence sharing will be crucial for the UAE to address emerging security challenges more effectively. Furthermore, the UAE is expected to continue investing in its defense capabilities and modernization efforts to maintain a technologically advanced and capable military force. This includes acquiring advanced weapon systems, enhancing its cybersecurity defenses, and investing in research and development to stay ahead of potential threats. As the UAE looks towards the future, it must prioritize cybersecurity measures to safeguard its critical infrastructure and information systems from cyber threats. Developing robust cybersecurity strategies, implementing best practices, and increasing cyber resilience will be essential components of the UAE's security and defense policy in the future. Overall, the UAE's security and defense policy in the future will be shaped by a combination of technological advancements, strategic partnerships, military modernization efforts, and a strong focus on cybersecurity. By staying proactive, adaptive, and forward-thinking, the UAE is poised to meet tomorrow's security challenges effectively.

In a Nutshell

HISTORICAL CONTEXT OF UAE'S SECURITY AND DEFENSE POLICY

The UAE's security and defense policy has evolved significantly since its formation in 1971. Initially, the federation faced regional threats and internal discord among the emirates, which shaped its early security strategies. The Iran-Iraq War and subsequent regional conflicts underscored the UAE's vulnerability and the need for a robust defense mechanism. Over the years, the UAE has shifted from relying primarily on Western security guarantees to developing its own sophisticated military capabilities[1][2].

NATIONAL SECURITY STRATEGY AND OBJECTIVES

The UAE's national security strategy focuses on protecting national sovereignty, ensuring economic security, and maintaining internal stability. This strategy is supported by a comprehensive approach that includes political, economic, and military dimensions. The UAE aims to deter regional threats, particularly from Iran, and to manage its complex relationships with neighboring countries through diplomacy and strategic partnerships[1][2][3].

UAE'S MILITARY CAPABILITIES AND MODERNIZATION EFFORTS

The UAE has invested heavily in modernizing its military, making it one of the most technologically advanced in the region. This includes acquiring sophisticated weapons such as the THAAD missile defense system and F-16 fighter jets. The UAE has also focused on developing domestic defense industries to reduce reliance on foreign suppliers. These efforts reflect the UAE's strategic goal to build a capable, ready, and technologically advanced military force[5][9].

ALLIANCES AND SECURITY PARTNERSHIPS

The UAE has established strong security partnerships, notably with the United States and France. More recently, it has expanded its alliances to include other global powers such as Russia and China. These partnerships are crucial for the UAE's strategy to balance regional threats and enhance its strategic autonomy. The UAE is also an active participant in regional coalitions, such as the Saudi-led coalition in Yemen and the Global Coalition against Daesh[5][8][20].

COUNTERTERRORISM AND COUNTER-PIRACY EFFORTS

The UAE prioritizes counterterrorism, participating in international efforts to combat extremist groups. This includes military operations and funding counterterrorism initiatives. Additionally, the UAE has been involved in counter-piracy operations in the Gulf of Aden and off the Somali coast, reflecting its strategic interest in securing maritime trade routes vital for its economy[13][20].

DEFENSE COOPERATION AGREEMENTS

The UAE has signed several defense cooperation agreements with countries around the world. These agreements include arms sales, joint military exercises, and training programs.

Such agreements enhance the UAE's defense capabilities and foster strategic ties with key global and regional powers, reinforcing its position in international security affairs[8][20].

MARITIME SECURITY AND PROTECTION OF STRATEGIC SEA LANES

Maritime security is critical to the UAE's defense strategy, given its strategic location near the Strait of Hormuz and its reliance on maritime trade. The UAE has invested in naval capabilities and cooperates with international partners to secure maritime routes against threats such as piracy, smuggling, and territorial disputes[5][20].

CYBERSECURITY AND INFORMATION SECURITY

Recognizing the importance of cybersecurity, the UAE has developed a comprehensive national cybersecurity strategy. This includes establishing regulatory frameworks, enhancing critical infrastructure security, and fostering international cooperation on cyber threats. The strategy aims to protect the nation from cyber threats that could impact its security, economy, and social stability[4].

FUTURE TRENDS IN UAE'S SECURITY AND DEFENSE POLICY

The UAE is likely to continue enhancing its military capabilities and expanding its network of international alliances. The focus will likely be on technological advancements, including artificial intelligence and unmanned systems, which are becoming integral to modern warfare. Additionally, the UAE will continue to navigate complex regional dynamics, particularly concerning Iran and its role in broader Middle Eastern security[5][9].

In summary, the UAE's security and defense policy is characterized by a proactive approach to building military capabilities, forming strategic alliances, and engaging in global security efforts. This multifaceted strategy enhances the UAE's defense posture and contributes to regional and international security stability.

References

[1] https://www.chathamhouse.org/2020/07/risk-perception-and-appetite-uae-foreign-and-national-security-policy-0/2-uaes-foreign-and
[2] https://ivypanda.com/essays/homeland-security-strategy-in-the-uae/
[3] https://www.cfc.forces.gc.ca/259/290/301/305/alnaqbi.pdf
[4] https://tdra.gov.ae/userfiles/assets/vzjmlB3CM34.pdf
[5] https://www.emerald.com/insight/content/doi/10.1108/REPS-09-2019-0124/full/html
[6] https://www.insightturkey.com/articles/military-bases-in-the-foreign-policy-of-the-united-arab-emirates
[7] https://www.academia.edu/40491223/The_UAEs_Evolving_National_Security_Strategy
[8] https://www.uae-embassy.org/uae-us-cooperation
[9] https://www.army-technology.com/news/uae-defence-investment/
[10] https://ciaotest.cc.columbia.edu/olj/meria/meria99_foley01.html
[11] https://www.stimson.org/2023/uae-entry-into-brics-increases-its-diplomatic-and-economic-options/
[12] https://www.washingtoninstitute.org/policy-analysis/regional-security-cooperation-partnerships-middle-east
[13] https://uaeun.org/uae-in-the-world/regional-stability/
[14] https://www.desc.gov.ae
[15] https://www.linkedin.com/pulse/uaes-national-food-security-strategy-2051-setting-global-sajwani
[16] https://www.tandfonline.com/doi/full/10.1080/14650045.2023.2268542
[17] https://www.csis.org/analysis/changing-trends-gulf-military-and-security-forces-net-assessment
[18] https://www.washingtoninstitute.org/policy-analysis/emirati-military-support-making-difference-somalia

[19] https://carnegieendowment.org/sada/86130
[20] https://www.uae-embassy.org/uae-us-cooperation/security

VI

Regional Dynamics: The UAE and the Middle East

Introduction to Regional Dynamics

The Middle East is a region of immense complexity and rich history, marked by a tapestry of cultures, traditions, and geopolitical dynamics. Positioned at the crossroads of three continents, the Middle East has long been a focal point of global affairs, shaped by a myriad of influences ranging from ancient civilizations to modern power struggles. The United Arab Emirates (UAE) is uniquely positioned within this diverse landscape, characterized by its strategic location, economic prosperity, and forward-thinking leadership. As a relatively young nation, the UAE has rapidly emerged as a key player in regional dynamics, navigating a complex web of alliances, rivalries, and conflicts. Historically, the UAE's position in the Middle East has been shaped by a combination of factors, including its geographical proximity to key players in the region, such as Saudi Arabia and Iran, as well as its historical ties to neighboring countries like Oman and Qatar. The UAE's founding fathers recognized the importance of regional stability and cooperation, laying the groundwork for a foreign policy prioritizing dialogue, diplomacy, and mutual respect. Today, the UAE's engagement in regional dynamics is multifaceted, encompassing economic partnerships, security cooperation, cultural exchanges, and humanitarian initiatives. By actively participating in regional organizations and forums, such as the Gulf Cooperation Council (GCC) and the Arab League, the UAE has demonstrated its commitment to promoting peace, prosperity, and unity across the Middle East. Furthermore, the UAE's strategic alliances with countries like the United States, France, and India have bolstered its position on the global stage, enabling it to play a more influential role in shaping regional dynamics. Through a combination of soft power initiatives, economic investments, and diplomatic efforts, the UAE has sought to balance its regional interests with its broader vision of stability and progress for the Middle East. As the UAE continues to navigate the complexities of regional dynamics, its leadership remains committed to fostering positive relations with its neighbors, addressing key challenges, and seizing opportunities for collaboration and mutual benefit. The future of the UAE in the Middle East is one of proactive engagement, constructive dialogue, and a shared pursuit of a brighter tomorrow for all nations in the region.

Historical Context: The UAE's Position in the Middle East

The United Arab Emirates (UAE) has a rich history that is deeply intertwined with its position in the Middle East. From its formation in 1971 to the present day, the UAE has played a significant role in regional dynamics and has emerged as a key player in the broader Middle Eastern landscape. The UAE's strategic location along the Arabian Gulf has long been a focal point for trade and commerce, dating back centuries to its origins as a hub for pearl diving and maritime trade. The region's historical connections to the Indian subcontinent, East Africa, and the Arabian Peninsula have shaped the UAE's cultural identity and economic prosperity. The UAE's modern history is marked by rapid development and diversification driven by visionary leadership and a commitment to innovation. The discovery of oil in the 1950s transformed the UAE's economy and positioned it as a major player in the global energy market. This newfound wealth laid the foundation for the country's ambitious development projects and infrastructure investments. A commitment to stability, cooperation, and economic growth in the Middle East has guided the UAE's foreign policy. As a member of the Gulf Cooperation Council (GCC) and the Arab League, the UAE has actively engaged with its regional neighbors to address common challenges and promote dialogue and mutual understanding. Over the years, the UAE has emerged as a key mediator in regional conflicts and has played a constructive role in promoting peace and stability in the Middle East. Its approach to diplomacy is characterized by pragmatism, flexibility, and a willingness to engage with all parties to find peaceful solutions to complex issues. In summary, the UAE's historical context in the Middle East positions it as a dynamic and influential player in regional affairs. Its strategic location, economic diversification, and commitment to peace and stability have helped shape its role as a key player in the region and a valued partner on the global stage.

Geopolitical Landscape: Key Players and Challenges

The Middle East is characterized by complex geopolitical dynamics, with numerous key players shaping the political landscape. Among the prominent actors are countries like Saudi Arabia, Iran, Israel, and Turkey, each exerting significant influence in the region. These countries often compete for power and influence, leading to tensions and rivalries that impact regional stability. One of the key challenges in the Middle East is the ongoing conflicts and civil wars that have resulted in humanitarian crises and mass displacement of populations. These conflicts involve many actors, including state and non-state actors, making it difficult to achieve lasting peace and stability in the region. The presence of extremist groups like ISIS and Al-Qaeda further compounds the security challenges in the Middle East, posing a threat not only to regional stability but also to global security. The fight against terrorism remains a top priority for many countries in the region and requires close cooperation and coordination among international partners. Another significant challenge in the Middle East is the competition for regional dominance between Sunni and Shia powers, particularly Saudi Arabia and Iran. This power struggle manifests in proxy conflicts across the region, exacerbating existing tensions and hindering efforts for diplomatic resolution of conflicts. Furthermore, the Middle East is a region rich in natural resources, particularly oil and gas, which adds another layer of complexity to the geopolitical landscape. Competition over energy resources and access to key strategic locations further complicates relationships between countries in the region. Overall, the geopolitical landscape of the Middle East is marked by a delicate balance of power, rivalries, and challenges that have far-reaching implications for regional stability and global security. In navigating these complexities, the UAE strategically promotes dialogue, cooperation, and peaceful resolution of conflicts in the region.

Economic Interactions: Trade and Investment in the Region

The Middle East region serves as a dynamic hub for economic interactions, fostering trade and investment opportunities among its key players. The United Arab Emirates, with its strategic location and vibrant economy, plays a pivotal role in shaping the region's economic landscape. The UAE's commitment to economic diversification and innovation has propelled its position as a key economic player in the Middle East. Trade relations within the region are characterized by diverse products and services, reflecting each country's unique strengths and capabilities. The UAE's robust trade network spans the Middle East, facilitating the flow of goods and services contributing to the region's economic growth. With its world-class infrastructure and business-friendly environment, the UAE is a gateway for trade between East and West, connecting markets and facilitating cross-border commerce. Strategic partnerships and economic initiatives that aim to enhance growth and collaboration drive investment flows in the region. The UAE's investment footprint in the Middle East is marked by a focus on key sectors such as energy, infrastructure, and technology, reflecting its commitment to sustainable development and economic empowerment. By investing in strategic projects and fostering partnerships with regional stakeholders, the UAE aims to drive economic prosperity and foster long-term growth. The UAE's role in facilitating economic interactions in the Middle East is underpinned by its commitment to promoting a conducive business environment and fostering innovation. The UAE has attracted diverse businesses and industries through initiatives such as free trade zones and investment incentives, contributing to the region's economic dynamism. By leveraging its strategic advantages and promoting collaboration, the UAE seeks to enhance economic interactions further and drive sustainable growth across the Middle East. In conclusion, economic interactions in the Middle East are shaped by a dynamic interplay of trade, investment, and collaboration among key regional players. The UAE's strategic initiatives and commitment to innovation position it as a key driver of economic growth and prosperity in the Middle East, fostering a vibrant and resilient economic landscape for the future.

Security Cooperation: Alliances and Partnerships

Security Cooperation: Alliances and Partnerships Security cooperation is a cornerstone of the UAE's foreign policy in the Middle East region. The UAE has strategically formed alliances and partnerships with various countries and organizations to address common security challenges and promote regional stability. One key partnership for the UAE is its alliance with the Gulf Cooperation

Council (GCC) members, including Saudi Arabia, Bahrain, Kuwait, Oman, and Qatar. The GCC serves as a platform for coordination on security matters, focusing on countering terrorism, maritime security, and defense cooperation. The UAE also maintains strong defense ties with Western countries, particularly the United States and European nations. These alliances include defense agreements, joint military exercises, and intelligence sharing to enhance regional security and combat shared threats. In addition to formal alliances, the UAE engages in security cooperation with countries in the Middle East through bilateral agreements and multilateral forums. This collaboration extends to border security, counter-terrorism efforts, and defense capacity-building. Furthermore, the UAE has played a significant role in regional security initiatives, such as the Middle East Strategic Alliance (MESA) and the Arab Coalition in Yemen. These collective security efforts demonstrate the UAE's commitment to promoting regional peace and stability through collaborative security mechanisms. Overall, the UAE's security cooperation with its allies and partners in the Middle East reflects its proactive approach to addressing security challenges and advancing shared interests for regional peace and security.

Cultural and Social Ties: Shared Heritage and Influence

The cultural and social ties between the United Arab Emirates (UAE) and other countries in the region are deeply rooted in a shared heritage that has influenced relationships and interactions for centuries. The UAE's strategic location at the crossroads of the Middle East has facilitated cultural exchanges and social connections that have strengthened bonds and fostered mutual understanding among nations. The UAE's rich history and diverse cultural landscape have contributed to its influence in the region, as its traditions, values, and customs resonate with many neighboring countries. From traditional art forms and culinary delights to shared religious practices and language similarities, the cultural ties between the UAE and other countries in the Middle East serve as a foundation for closer relations and collaborative efforts. Moreover, the UAE's commitment to promoting cultural diplomacy and preserving its heritage has enabled it to showcase its unique identity and customs on the world stage. Through initiatives such as hosting international cultural events, supporting artistic endeavors, and preserving historical landmarks, the UAE has reinforced its cultural influence and promoted cross-cultural dialogue with countries in the region. Additionally, social connections play a significant role in shaping the UAE's relationships with neighboring nations, as people-to-people interactions help build trust and facilitate cooperation in various areas. The UAE's welcoming and inclusive society, coupled with its hospitality and openness to other cultures, has created an environment where individuals from different backgrounds can come together to exchange ideas, build friendships, and work towards common goals. Overall, the cultural and social ties between the UAE and countries in the region reflect a shared heritage that continues to influence interactions and collaborations in various spheres. By embracing its cultural diversity and promoting social connections, the UAE has solidified its position as a key player in the Middle East, fostering lasting relationships and contributing to regional stability and prosperity.

Regional Conflicts and Crisis Management

Regional conflicts and crisis management are critical aspects of the UAE's foreign policy in the Middle East. The region has been plagued by numerous conflicts and humanitarian crises, requiring swift and effective diplomatic responses from the UAE. The UAE's approach to regional conflicts is guided by a commitment to promoting peace, stability, and security in the Middle East. One notable conflict in the region is the ongoing Yemen crisis, where the UAE has played a significant role in supporting efforts to resolve the conflict and alleviate the humanitarian suffering of the Yemeni people. The UAE has been involved in humanitarian aid delivery, reconstruction projects, and diplomatic initiatives to foster dialogue and negotiations between conflicting parties. Another key regional conflict is the Syrian civil war, which has resulted in immense human suffering and displacement. The UAE has supported international efforts to end the conflict and provide humanitarian assistance to those affected by the crisis. The UAE has also supported reconstruction efforts and promoted stability in post-conflict Syria. In addition to these conflicts, the UAE has been engaged in crisis management efforts in other parts of the region, such as Libya and Iraq, where instability and conflict have posed significant challenges to peace and security. The UAE has employed a multi-faceted approach to crisis management, including diplomatic engagement, humanitarian aid, capacity-building initiatives, and support for peacekeeping efforts. Overall, the UAE's approach to regional conflicts and crisis management underscores its commitment to promoting peace, stability, and prosperity in the Middle East. Through active diplomatic engagement, humanitarian assistance, and support for conflict resolution initiatives, the UAE continues to play a constructive role in addressing the region's complex challenges.

Humanitarian Diplomacy: UAE's Role in the Middle East

The United Arab Emirates has demonstrated a strong commitment to humanitarian diplomacy in the Middle East, playing a pivotal role in providing aid and support to those affected by conflict and crisis. Through its proactive and strategic approach, the UAE has become a key player in humanitarian efforts, leveraging its resources and expertise to impact the ground positively. The UAE's humanitarian diplomacy initiatives encompass various activities, including emergency response, healthcare, education, and infrastructure development. The country has responded quickly to humanitarian crises in the region, providing critical aid such as food, water, shelter, and medical supplies to those in need. In addition, the UAE has invested in long-term projects to address the root causes of poverty and instability, contributing to sustainable development and resilience in conflict-affected areas. One of the key pillars of the UAE's humanitarian diplomacy is its partnership with international organizations and NGOs. The country works closely with organizations such as the United Nations, the Red Cross and Red Crescent Movement, and various humanitarian agencies to coordinate and deliver assistance effectively. By collaborating with these entities, the UAE can maximize the impact of its humanitarian efforts and ensure that aid reaches those most in need. Furthermore, the UAE's humanitarian diplomacy extends beyond providing immediate relief to those affected by crises. The country has also been actively involved in promoting peacebuilding, reconciliation, and conflict resolution initiatives in the region. The UAE fosters stability and security by engaging in diplomatic efforts and dialogue, ultimately paving the way for sustainable development and prosperity in the Middle East. Overall, the UAE's role in humanitarian diplomacy in the Middle East exemplifies its commitment to upholding the principles of humanity, solidarity, and compassion on the global stage. Through its proactive and impactful initiatives, the UAE continues to make a significant difference in millions of people affected by conflict and crisis, embodying the spirit of generosity and goodwill that defines its foreign policy approach.

Regional Organizations: UAE's Participation and Impact

The UAE actively participates in various regional organizations, significantly shaping policies and initiatives that impact the Middle East. One key organization the UAE is a member of is the Gulf Cooperation Council (GCC), a political and economic alliance of six Gulf countries. The UAE's involvement in the GCC highlights its commitment to regional cooperation and solidarity. The country works closely with other GCC members to address common challenges and promote regional stability. Another important regional organization that the UAE is part of is the Arab League. As a member of this pan-Arab organization, the UAE collaborates with other Arab states on political, economic, cultural, and social development issues. Through its membership in the Arab League, the UAE seeks to strengthen ties with neighboring Arab countries further and contribute to advancing the Arab world. Additionally, the UAE is a key member of the Organization of Islamic Cooperation (OIC). This multilateral organization aims to promote solidarity among Muslim countries and address issues of common concern. The UAE's participation in the OIC reflects its commitment to promoting Islamic values and principles internationally. Furthermore, the UAE plays an active role in the Gulf Region and the broader Middle East by participating in organizations such as the Organization of Arab Petroleum Exporting Countries (OAPEC) and the Arab Monetary Fund. These organizations focus on regional economic cooperation and development, aligning with the UAE's vision for stability and prosperity in the Middle East. Overall, the UAE's participation in regional organizations underscores its proactive approach to regional diplomacy and its commitment to fostering collaboration and unity among countries in the Middle East. Through its engagement in these forums, the UAE shapes the regional agenda and promotes mutual understanding and cooperation among regional nations.

Future Prospects: The UAE's Vision for Stability and Prosperity in the Middle East

The UAE's vision for stability and prosperity in the Middle East is deeply rooted in the country's commitment to regional collaboration and sustainable development. As a key player in the region, the UAE recognizes the importance of fostering peace, security, and economic growth to ensure a prosperous future for all nations in the Middle East. Through active participation in regional organizations such as the Gulf Cooperation Council (GCC), the Arab League, and the Organization of Islamic Cooperation (OIC), the UAE has worked tirelessly to promote dialogue, cooperation, and mutual respect among countries in the region. The UAE has sought to address shared challenges and promote common interests for the region's greater good by engaging in multilateral initiatives and partnerships. Looking ahead, the UAE is dedicated to playing a proactive role in shaping the future of the Middle East by promoting stability, mutual understanding, and economic prosperity. Through initiatives such as the UAE Vision 2021 and the UAE Centennial 2071, the country aims to create a sustainable and inclusive future for all citizens in the region. By investing in education, innovation, and technology, the UAE is working to build a knowledge-based economy that will drive growth and create opportunities for future generations. By supporting entrepreneurship, fostering creativity, and embracing diversity, the UAE is positioning itself as a hub for innovation and progress in the Middle East. In conclusion, the UAE's vision for stability and prosperity in the Middle East is characterized by a commitment to collaboration, innovation, and sustainable development. By working with regional partners and engaging in constructive dialogue, the UAE is paving the way for a brighter and more prosperous future for all nations in the region.

In a Nutshell

HISTORICAL CONTEXT: THE UAE'S POSITION IN THE MIDDLE EAST

Established in 1971, the UAE has rapidly transformed from a collection of small sheikhdoms into a significant regional power. Its strategic location along key maritime routes and oil wealth have positioned it as a central player in Middle Eastern politics and economics. The UAE's historical ties with both Western and regional powers, coupled with its economic transformation, have enabled it to mediate regional conflicts and extend its influence across the Middle East[2][11].

GEOPOLITICAL LANDSCAPE: KEY PLAYERS AND CHALLENGES

The Middle East is a complex geopolitical arena with key players, including Saudi Arabia, Iran, Israel, and Turkey, each with distinct strategic interests. The UAE navigates this landscape by balancing relationships, such as strengthening ties with Saudi Arabia and Israel, while managing its historically complicated relations with Iran. The region faces challenges such as sectarian conflicts, the threat of terrorism, and the influence of external powers like the US and Russia[1][3].

ECONOMIC INTERACTIONS: TRADE AND INVESTMENT IN THE REGION

The UAE's highly diversified economy, with significant investments in trade, real estate, tourism, and finance. It serves as a major trade hub connecting the East and West. The UAE's ports and airlines facilitate extensive trade flows within and beyond, enhancing its role as a central economic player in the Middle East. Substantial UAE investments in neighboring countries further bolster economic ties [8][19].

SECURITY COOPERATION: ALLIANCES AND PARTNERSHIPS

The UAE participates actively in regional security initiatives, including the Gulf Cooperation Council (GCC) and military coalitions. It has developed strong defense ties with the US and other Western nations, and more recently, it has engaged in security dialogues with Russia and China. The UAE's involvement in security matters reflects its broader strategy to maintain stability and counter threats, particularly from Iran and extremist groups[1][4].

CULTURAL AND SOCIAL TIES: SHARED HERITAGE AND INFLUENCE

Culturally, the UAE shares a rich Arab heritage with its neighbors, characterized by language, religion, and customs. It has leveraged this shared cultural identity to enhance its regional soft power through initiatives like the Louvre Abu Dhabi and international cultural festivals. These efforts strengthen social ties and position the UAE as a cultural leader in the Arab world[9][18].

REGIONAL CONFLICTS AND CRISIS MANAGEMENT

The UAE has been involved in several regional conflicts, including military operations in Yemen and Libya. It has also played a role in mediating disputes, such as hosting peace talks and offering humanitarian aid. The UAE's approach to crisis management often involves a combination of diplomatic, military, and humanitarian strategies to stabilize the region and protect its interests[5][13].

HUMANITARIAN DIPLOMACY: UAE'S ROLE IN THE MIDDLE EAST

The UAE's humanitarian diplomacy is a critical aspect of its foreign policy. It provides substantial aid to war-torn areas and supports refugee populations. This humanitarian engagement addresses immediate crises and enhances the UAE's international standing and soft power in the Middle East and globally[10].

REGIONAL ORGANIZATIONS: UAE'S PARTICIPATION AND IMPACT

The UAE is active in regional organizations such as the GCC and the Arab League. Its participation fosters regional cooperation on economic, political, and security issues. The UAE often plays a pivotal role in these organizations, pushing for integration and cooperation to address common challenges[3][12].

FUTURE PROSPECTS: THE UAE'S VISION FOR STABILITY AND PROSPERITY IN THE MIDDLE EAST

The UAE envisions a stable and prosperous Middle East where economic integration, political stability, and social cohesion are enhanced. It aims to continue its leadership role in promoting regional development, peace, and security. The

UAE's strategic investments in renewable energy, technology, and infrastructure are part of this vision to ensure long-term stability and prosperity in the region[2][11].

In summary, the UAE's multifaceted approach to its role in the Middle East involves leveraging its economic power, participating in security alliances, promoting cultural diplomacy, and engaging in humanitarian efforts. These actions are guided by a vision to foster a stable, prosperous, and integrated region, reflecting the UAE's growing influence and strategic ambitions in the Middle East.

References

[1] https://www.washingtoninstitute.org/policy-analysis/regional-security-cooperation-partnerships-middle-east
[2] https://www.chathamhouse.org/2020/07/risk-perception-and-appetite-uae-foreign-and-national-security-policy-0/2-uaes-foreign-and
[3] https://www.tandfonline.com/doi/full/10.1080/14650045.2023.2268542
[4] https://carnegieendowment.org/2019/02/08/middle-east-strategic-alliance-has-long-way-to-go-pub-78317
[5] https://www.chathamhouse.org/2020/07/risk-perception-and-appetite-uae-foreign-and-national-security-policy-0/8-case-study-uae
[6] https://www.bbc.com/news/world-middle-east-14703998
[7] https://www.iiss.org/globalassets/media-library---content--migration/files/research-papers/2022/hanns-seidel-paper---regional-security-and-alliances.pdf
[8] https://www.imf.org/en/Blogs/Articles/2024/05/13/more-diversified-trade-can-make-middle-east-and-central-asia-more-resilient
[9] https://www.ispionline.it/en/publication/geopolitics-tolerance-inside-uaes-cultural-rush-22155
[10] https://www.cmi.no/publications/7169-the-uaes-humanitarian-diplomacy-claiming-state-sovereignty
[11] https://en.wikipedia.org/wiki/History_of_the_United_Arab_Emirates
[12] https://www.whitehouse.gov/briefing-room/statements-releases/2022/07/16/fact-sheet-the-united-states-strengthens-cooperation-with-middle-east-partners-to-address-21st-century-challenges/
[13] https://www.geopoliticalmonitor.com/the-middle-easts-shifting-political-landscape/
[14] https://www.uae-embassy.org/abraham-accords-sustainable-inclusive-growth
[15] https://www.nato.int/cps/en/natohq/topics_84336.htm

[16] https://www.csis.org/analysis/changing-trends-gulf-military-and-security-forces-net-assessment

[17] https://theconversation.com/israel-gaza-conflict-how-could-it-change-the-middle-easts-political-landscape-expert-qanda-215473

[18] https://www.unesco.org/en/articles/cutting-edge-standing-out-reaching-out-cultural-diplomacy-sustainable-development

[19] https://www.imf.org/external/pubs/ft/mena/04econ.htm

VII

Global Partnerships: The UAE on the Global Stage

Global Partnerships

The UAE's global partnerships play a pivotal role in shaping the country's foreign policy and advancing its interests on the international stage. These partnerships are built on mutual respect, shared goals, and strategic alignment. By engaging with countries and organizations worldwide, the UAE has enhanced its diplomatic influence, promoted economic growth, and contributed to global development efforts. As a nation with a rich history and a dynamic economy, the UAE has proactively forged partnerships with key global players. From its formation to the present, the UAE has cultivated relationships with various countries and international organizations. This historical overview provides valuable insights into the UAE's foreign policy's evolution and engagement with the global community. The UAE has actively participated in international organizations through multilateral engagement to address global challenges and advocate for its interests. By contributing to initiatives within the United Nations, the World Trade Organization, and other forums, the UAE has positioned itself as a responsible global citizen and a valuable partner in promoting peace, security, and sustainable development. On a bilateral level, the UAE has established strategic partnerships with countries with common values and objectives. By forging strong relationships with key allies such as the United States, China, and India, the UAE has been able to deepen cooperation in areas such as trade, security, and technology. These partnerships have strengthened the UAE's position in the international community and facilitated mutual benefits for all parties involved. The UAE's global partnerships extend beyond traditional diplomatic channels to encompass economic cooperation, cultural exchange, and security collaboration. The UAE has significantly contributed to global development and humanitarian efforts by leveraging its resources and expertise in various fields. Through initiatives such as the Year of Giving and the UAE's commitment to the Sustainable Development Goals, the country has demonstrated its commitment to positively impacting the world stage. The UAE's global partnerships will continue to play a crucial role in shaping its foreign policy agenda and advancing its strategic objectives. By leveraging its diverse network of relationships, the UAE is well-positioned to navigate the complexities of the global landscape and seize opportunities for collaboration and growth. As the UAE strengthens its partnerships with existing allies and explores new avenues for cooperation, it is poised to make meaningful contributions to the international community and secure its status as a global player to be reckoned with.

Historical Overview of UAE's Global Partnerships

The UAE's engagement with the global community can be traced back to its early days as a nation. From its inception in 1971, the UAE sought to establish diplomatic relations with countries worldwide to foster cooperation and mutual understanding. In the early years, the UAE focused on building alliances with neighboring Arab states and advancing the cause of Arab unity. As the UAE's foreign policy evolved, so did its global partnerships. The country embarked on a diversification strategy to expand its diplomatic reach beyond the Arab world. The UAE established diplomatic relations with various countries in Asia, Europe, Africa, and the Americas, forging alliances based on shared interests and mutual respect. One of the key milestones in the UAE's global engagement was its accession to the United Nations in 1971. Since then, the UAE has actively participated in various UN bodies and initiatives, advocating for international cooperation and peace. The country has also played a prominent role in multilateral organizations such as the World Trade Organization, the International Monetary Fund, and the World Bank. In addition to its multilateral engagements, the UAE has cultivated solid bilateral relationships with key global players. The country has strategic partnerships with countries such as the United States, China, and India, based on shared economic interests, security cooperation, and cultural exchange. These partnerships have helped the UAE elevate its profile on the global stage and position itself as a key player in international affairs. Overall, the historical overview of the UAE's global partnerships demonstrates its commitment to diplomacy, cooperation, and mutual respect in its relations with the international community. As the UAE continues to navigate the complex landscape of global politics, its historical partnerships serve as a solid foundation for building a more interconnected and peaceful world.

Multilateral Engagement: The UAE in International Organizations

The UAE is prominent in various international organizations, shaping global policies and initiatives. With a commitment to multilateralism, the UAE has sought to build partnerships and promote cooperation on a global scale. One of the key organizations in which the UAE has been actively involved is the United Nations (UN). As a member of the UN since its inception in 1971, the UAE has contributed to peacekeeping missions, humanitarian efforts, and sustainable development programs. The country has consistently advocated for peaceful resolution of conflicts and has supported initiatives to promote stability and security worldwide. In addition to the UN, the UAE is also a member of the World Trade Organization (WTO), playing a vital role in international trade and economic issues. The country has actively participated in trade negotiations and discussions, advocating for fair trade practices and market access for developing nations. Furthermore, the UAE's membership in the International Monetary Fund (IMF) and the World Bank reflects its commitment to global economic stability and development. The UAE has engaged with these organizations and contributed to policy discussions on financial reforms, debt relief, and poverty reduction strategies. The UAE's involvement in regional organizations such as the Gulf Cooperation Council (GCC) and the Arab League further solidifies its commitment to multilateral engagement. By collaborating with neighboring countries and Arab states, the UAE seeks to address regional challenges, enhance security cooperation, and promote economic integration. The country's active participation in these regional forums highlights its role as a key player in the Middle East's political landscape. Moreover, the UAE has strongly advocated for environmental protection and sustainable development on the global stage. The country's membership in the United Nations Environment Programme (UNEP) and other environmental organizations underscores its dedication to addressing climate change, biodiversity conservation, and sustainable resource management. The UAE showcases its commitment to a greener and more sustainable future for all nations by engaging in multilateral efforts to combat environmental challenges. The UAE's engagement in international organizations reflects its vision for a more interconnected and prosperous world. Through active participation in multilateral forums, the country demonstrates its willingness to collaborate with the international community to address complex global issues and advance common goals.

Bilateral Relations: Key Partnerships and Alliances

The UAE has cultivated solid bilateral relationships with key countries and alliances worldwide, recognizing the strategic importance of forging partnerships to advance its national interests. One of the UAE's closest partners is the United States, with whom it maintains a robust strategic alliance encompassing various areas of cooperation, including security, defense, trade, and investment. The UAE and the US are committed to regional stability and combating terrorism, making them natural allies in the volatile Middle East region. In recent years, the UAE has deepened its ties with China, recognizing the economic opportunities presented by China's rapid growth and development. The UAE-China partnership has expanded beyond trade and investment to include collaboration in infrastructure development, technology transfer, and cultural exchange. The UAE's strategic location as a gateway between East and West positions it as a vital partner for China's ambitious Belt and Road Initiative. India is another key partner for the UAE, with strong historical and cultural ties between the two countries dating back centuries. The UAE-India relationship has flourished recently, driven by mutual trade, energy, and security cooperation interests. The UAE is home to a large Indian expatriate community, significantly strengthening people-to-people ties between the two nations. The UAE's partnership with Saudi Arabia is characterized by shared strategic interests in the Gulf region and beyond. The two countries have collaborated closely on regional issues, including the Yemen crisis and efforts to counter Iranian influence in the Middle East. The UAE-Saudi alliance is a cornerstone of stability in the Gulf Cooperation Council (GCC) and has been instrumental in promoting peace and security in the region. Looking to the future, the UAE seeks new partnerships and alliances to enhance its global influence and promote mutual prosperity. By fostering strong bilateral relationships with key countries and alliances, the UAE can leverage its strategic position and resources to address complex challenges and seize opportunities for growth and development on the global stage.

Economic Cooperation: Trade and Investment Partnerships

The UAE has strategically forged strong trade and investment partnerships with countries and regions worldwide, contributing to its position as a global economic hub. The UAE's economic cooperation efforts encompass various sectors, including finance, energy, technology, and infrastructure. The UAE has become a crucial player in the global economy through proactive engagement and investment in key markets. In the realm of trade, the UAE has prioritized diversification and expansion of its export markets. With a strategic location at the crossroads of Asia, Africa, and Europe, the UAE is a vital trade hub connecting emerging markets and established economies. The country has negotiated numerous trade agreements to facilitate the flow of goods and services, fostering economic growth and development on both regional and international scales. Regarding investment partnerships, the UAE has proactively leveraged its substantial financial resources to invest in key sectors globally. The UAE's sovereign wealth funds have significantly invested in diverse industries, ranging from real estate and hospitality to technology and renewable energy. These investments generate returns for the UAE and contribute to the economic development of partner countries and regions. The UAE's emphasis on economic cooperation extends beyond traditional sectors, including emerging industries such as fintech and artificial intelligence. The country aims to position itself as a global leader in technology and innovation through initiatives like Dubai's Blockchain Strategy and the UAE AI Strategy. By fostering partnerships with international tech companies and supporting local startups, the UAE is catalyzing the growth of a dynamic digital economy. Furthermore, the UAE's focus on sustainable development aligns with its economic cooperation efforts. The country has prioritized investments in renewable energy projects and green technologies, underscoring its commitment to environmental stewardship and climate action. By partnering with countries and organizations that share these sustainability goals, the UAE is advancing global efforts to combat climate change and promote a more sustainable future for all. In conclusion, the UAE's economic cooperation initiatives highlight its proactive approach to engaging with the global economy. Through strategic trade agreements, investment partnerships, and a focus on innovation and sustainability, the UAE is forging a path towards long-term economic growth and prosperity, both domestically and internationally.

Humanitarian Initiatives: UAE's Contribution to Global Development

The UAE is committed to global development and humanitarian initiatives, significantly addressing various challenges communities worldwide face. Through humanitarian efforts, the UAE has provided vital support in disaster relief, healthcare, education, and infrastructure development. One notable aspect of the UAE's humanitarian initiatives is its response to global crises. The UAE has quickly mobilized aid and resources to assist countries affected by natural disasters, conflicts, and other emergencies. This rapid response reflects the UAE's dedication to alleviating suffering and promoting stability in regions facing humanitarian challenges. In addition to emergency response efforts, the UAE has also focused on long-term development projects to improve the quality of life for vulnerable populations. This includes healthcare, education, water and sanitation initiatives, and sustainable economic development. By investing in these critical areas, the UAE aims to create lasting positive impact and support the well-being of communities in need. Furthermore, the UAE has established partnerships with a wide range of international organizations and non-governmental organizations to maximize the impact of its humanitarian initiatives. By collaborating with other stakeholders, the UAE can leverage resources, expertise, and networks to address complex global challenges more effectively. The UAE's commitment to global development and humanitarian initiatives aligns with its broader foreign policy objectives. By actively supporting vulnerable populations and promoting sustainable development, the UAE demonstrates its values and principles on the world stage. It builds a more stable, prosperous, and interconnected global community.

Cultural Diplomacy: Promoting UAE's Image and Values Globally

Cultural diplomacy plays a crucial role in shaping the image of the UAE on the global stage. The UAE showcases its rich heritage, values, and traditions through various initiatives and programs. Embracing diversity and promoting intercultural dialogue, the UAE is committed to building bridges with people from different backgrounds. Cultural exchanges, art exhibitions, and heritage festivals are platforms through which the UAE shares its cultural treasures with the international community. The UAE's investment in cultural diplomacy highlights its belief in the power of soft power to influence perceptions and foster mutual understanding. By promoting cultural exchange programs, the UAE creates opportunities for cultural dialogue and collaboration, fostering connections that transcend boundaries and promote shared values. Through initiatives like the Sheikh Zayed Book Award and the Louvre Abu Dhabi, the UAE has established itself as a hub for cultural dialogue and exchange, engaging with global audiences and showcasing its commitment to promoting cultural diversity and creativity. Furthermore, the UAE's support for cultural institutions, artistic ventures, and heritage preservation projects reflects its dedication to preserving and promoting cultural heritage at home and abroad. By celebrating cultural diversity and promoting artistic expression, the UAE is committed to fostering creativity, dialogue, and mutual respect on the global stage. Through initiatives that promote cultural understanding and appreciation, the UAE continues to build long-lasting relationships and enhance its reputation as a global cultural hub.

Innovation and Technology Partnerships

The UAE has been at the forefront of leveraging innovation and technology partnerships to enhance its global standing. Through strategic collaborations with leading tech companies and research institutions, the UAE has positioned itself as a hub of innovation in the Middle East. These partnerships have driven economic growth and facilitated advancements in various sectors such as healthcare, transportation, and sustainability. One key area of focus for the

UAE is digital transformation. The country has prioritized adopting cutting-edge technologies such as artificial intelligence, blockchain, and the Internet of Things to drive efficiency and innovation across industries. Through partnerships with global tech giants, the UAE has gained access to expertise and resources that have accelerated its digital transformation agenda. Moreover, the UAE's commitment to innovation extends to sustainability. The country has partnered with international organizations and tech companies to develop renewable energy projects, smart cities, and green initiatives. The UAE aims to address environmental challenges by harnessing technological advancements and building a more sustainable future for its citizens and the global community. The UAE has established partnerships with top-tier universities and research centers in research and development to drive innovation and knowledge creation. These collaborations have led to breakthroughs in healthcare, aerospace, and advanced manufacturing sectors, bolstering the UAE's reputation as a center of innovation and excellence. The UAE's innovation and technology partnerships are crucial in shaping its future trajectory. By embracing cutting-edge technologies and fostering collaboration with global partners, the UAE is well-positioned to drive growth, enhance competitiveness, and address complex global challenges in the digital age.

Security Cooperation: Counterterrorism and Peacekeeping Efforts

The UAE is crucial in global security cooperation, particularly in counterterrorism and peacekeeping efforts. With a strategic geographic location and a commitment to maintaining regional stability, the UAE has actively engaged in international efforts to combat terrorism and promote peace. The UAE has strongly supported multilateral initiatives to counter terrorism, including the Global Counterterrorism Forum and the UN Counter-Terrorism Committee. The UAE has contributed resources, intelligence sharing, and expertise through these partnerships to enhance global efforts to combat terrorist threats. In addition to its counterterrorism efforts, the UAE has been actively involved in peacekeeping missions worldwide. The UAE Armed Forces have participated in UN peacekeeping missions in countries such as Afghanistan, Somalia, and Yemen, providing crucial support to help stabilize conflict-affected areas and facilitate the delivery of humanitarian aid. Furthermore, the UAE has established strategic partnerships with key countries and organizations to strengthen security cooperation. The UAE has worked collaboratively with its partners to enhance security measures and respond effectively to emerging security challenges through joint military exercises, intelligence sharing, and capacity-building programs. Looking ahead, the UAE remains committed to expanding its security cooperation initiatives to address evolving threats to global security. By leveraging its expertise, resources, and partnerships, the UAE aims to promote peace and security at both regional and international levels.

Future Prospects: Challenges and Opportunities in Strengthening Global Partnerships

As the UAE continues to navigate the complex global landscape, there are challenges and opportunities to strengthen its global partnerships. One key challenge is balancing its alliances and partnerships while maintaining its independent foreign policy stance. The UAE must carefully navigate geopolitical rivalries and regional conflicts to ensure its partnerships do not compromise its national interests. Furthermore, the rise of non-traditional security threats, such as cyberattacks and disinformation campaigns, poses new challenges to global security cooperation. The UAE must collaborate closely with its partners to address these emerging threats and strengthen cybersecurity measures globally. On the other hand, there are also significant opportunities for the UAE to enhance its global partnerships. The country's strategic location, stable economy, and forward-thinking leadership position it as a key player in the international arena. By leveraging its strengths and expertise in various sectors, such as energy, technology, and innovation, the UAE can foster deeper collaboration with its global partners and contribute meaningfully to global challenges. In addition, the UAE's commitment to humanitarian initiatives and sustainable development provides a solid foundation for building stronger relationships with countries and organizations worldwide. By prioritizing these values in its foreign policy agenda, the UAE can further enhance its reputation as a responsible global actor and a valuable partner in addressing pressing global issues. Looking ahead, the UAE must seize the opportunities presented by increasing connectivity and globalization to expand its network of global partnerships. By proactively engaging with new and existing partners, the UAE can forge mutually beneficial relationships that enhance its influence and contribute to global peace, stability, and prosperity.

In a Nutshell

The UAE on the Global Stage

The United Arab Emirates (UAE) has established itself as a significant player on the global stage through strategic partnerships, multilateral engagement, cultural diplomacy, and contributions to global development. Here's an in-depth look at the various aspects of the UAE's global presence:

Global Partnerships

Key Partnerships and Alliances

The UAE has forged strong alliances with major global powers, including the United States, the United Kingdom, China, and India. These partnerships span various sectors, including defense, trade, technology, and energy. For instance, the UAE-UK Strategic Investment Partnership emphasizes investments in life sciences, technology, and green energy, aiming for a £10 billion investment over five years[9]. Similarly, the UAE's strategic partnership with China has bolstered economic and technological cooperation, making the UAE a key partner in China's global expansion[15].

Multilateral Engagement

The UAE is actively involved in multilateral organizations and initiatives, leading in global efforts to address climate change, sustainable development, and humanitarian aid. The UAE hosted COP28 in 2023, leading diplomatic efforts to reach significant agreements on climate action[1]. Additionally, the UAE is home to the International Renewable Energy Agency (IRENA), underscoring its commitment to global sustainability[1].

Contribution to Global Development

The UAE has a long history of providing foreign assistance to reduce poverty, promote peace, and foster economic development. The Abu Dhabi Development Fund and other UAE institutions have financed numerous projects worldwide, including renewable energy initiatives in the Caribbean and Pacific islands and infrastructure projects in Africa and Asia[2]. The UAE's foreign aid policy is rooted in its Arab and Islamic heritage, emphasizing unconditional support for humanity[2].

Cultural Diplomacy

Cultural diplomacy is a cornerstone of the UAE's soft power strategy. The country has invested in cultural exchange programs, art exhibitions, and educational initiatives to promote its cultural heritage and values globally. Events like Expo 2020 Dubai showcased the UAE's cultural and technological achievements, fostering international collaboration and understanding[16]. The UAE also engages in sports diplomacy, hosting major international sports events to enhance its global visibility and influence[13].

Innovation and Technology Partnerships

The UAE has positioned itself as a global hub for innovation and technology. Initiatives like Smart Dubai and the National AI Strategy 2031 aim to integrate advanced technologies across various sectors, driving socio-economic growth[17]. The UAE has established partnerships with global tech hubs, fostering collaboration and knowledge exchange to stay at the forefront of technological advancements[14].

Security Cooperation

Defense Cooperation Agreements

The UAE has signed numerous international defense cooperation agreements, enhancing its military capabilities and strategic alliances. These agreements often include joint military exercises, arms sales, and training programs, reinforcing the UAE's defense posture[4].

Counterterrorism and Counter-Piracy Efforts

The UAE plays a significant role in counterterrorism and counter-piracy operations regionally and globally. It participates in international coalitions and provides substantial support for initiatives to combat extremism and ensure maritime security[4].

Cybersecurity and Information Security

Recognizing the growing importance of cybersecurity, the UAE has developed a comprehensive national cybersecurity strategy. This strategy includes regulatory frameworks, critical infrastructure protection, and international cooperation to address cyber threats and ensure information security[18].

Future Trends in UAE's Security and Defense Policy

The UAE is expected to continue enhancing its military capabilities and expanding its network of international alliances. The focus will likely be on technological advancements, including artificial intelligence and unmanned systems, which are becoming integral to modern warfare. Additionally, the UAE will continue to navigate complex regional dynamics, particularly concerning Iran and its role in broader Middle Eastern security[10].

Conclusion

The UAE's proactive approach on the global stage encompasses a blend of economic, cultural, and security strategies. The UAE has significantly enhanced its international standing through robust global partnerships, active multilateral engagement, and a commitment to innovation and development. Its efforts in cultural diplomacy, technological advancement, and security cooperation reflect a comprehensive strategy to foster global stability, prosperity, and influence.

References

[1] https://www.uae-embassy.org/discover-uae/climate-and-energy/international-engagement
[2] https://www.mofa.gov.ae/en/The-Ministry/UAE-International-Development-Cooperation
[3] https://www.firststep.ae/strategic-alliances-key-points-to-consider-when-entering-a-business-partnership/
[4] https://mof.gov.ae/strategic-regional-and-global-partners/
[5] https://www.linkedin.com/pulse/uaes-rise-soft-power-building-bridges-through-culture-%D8%B9%D9%85%D8%B1-%D8%A7%D9%84%D8%A8%D9%88%D8%B3%D8%B9%D9%8A%D8%AF%D9%8A-sccnf
[6] https://www.uaeusaunited.com/stories/uae-global-hub-innovation
[7] https://wam.ae/en/article/b42pjtr-uae-identifies-priorities-for-achieving
[8] https://sustainabledevelopment.un.org/content/documents/20161UAE_SDGs_Report_Full_English.pdf
[9] https://investopia.ae/summaries/uae-uk-strategic-partnership-for-the-future-in-supporting-economic-growth/
[10] https://www.orfonline.org/research/uae-s-evolving-role-as-a-key-actor-in-the-middle-east-and-beyond
[11] https://robustagroup.com/insights/uae-business-leaders-forecast-the-next-wave-of-tech-partnership-evolution/
[12] https://www.firstpost.com/opinion/shaping-the-21st-century-world-order-india-uae-and-saudi-arabias-strategic-alliance-13141872.html
[13] https://www.wam.ae/en/article/b0xl6yk-uae-enters-2024-with-unwavering-determination
[14] https://candergroup.com/fostering-innovation-and-collaboration-within-uaes-tech-and-digital-teams/
[15] https://wam.ae/en/article/b36k5ni-uae-key-partner-chinas-global-

expansion-says

[16] https://www.unesco.org/en/articles/cutting-edge-standing-out-reaching-out-cultural-diplomacy-sustainable-development

[17] https://www.cio.com/article/2514745/the-uae-emerges-as-a-global-leader-in-ai-driving-innovation-and-future-technology.html

[18] https://moiat.gov.ae/en/about-us/sustainability-development-goals

VIII

Energy Diplomacy: A Core Component of UAE Foreign Policy

Energy Diplomacy in the UAE

Energy diplomacy in the UAE is critical to the country's foreign policy strategy. The UAE's strategic geographic location and abundant energy resources have positioned it as a key player in the global energy landscape. As one of the largest oil producers in the world and a growing player in renewable energy, the UAE has leveraged its energy wealth to build solid diplomatic relationships and promote its national interests on the international stage. Energy resources have long been a cornerstone of the UAE's foreign policy, shaping its relationships with key partners and driving economic growth and development. The country's significant oil reserves have allowed it to play a central role in global energy markets and establish itself as a reliable supplier of energy resources to countries worldwide. In recent years, the UAE has also made significant investments in renewable energy, particularly solar power. This shift towards clean energy sources aligns with global efforts to combat climate change and enhances the UAE's standing as a leader in sustainable development and innovation. Energy security is a top priority for the UAE, given its reliance on oil and gas exports for economic prosperity. The country has implemented various strategies to diversify its energy sources and reduce its dependence on fossil fuels, including investing in nuclear power and promoting energy efficiency measures. Overall, energy diplomacy plays a crucial role in shaping the UAE's foreign policy objectives and enhancing its influence on the global stage. By leveraging its energy resources and expertise, the UAE continues strengthening its relationships with key partners, promoting sustainable energy solutions, and addressing pressing energy challenges regionally and internationally.

The Significance of Energy Resources in UAE Foreign Policy

Energy resources play a pivotal role in shaping the foreign policy of the United Arab Emirates (UAE). With its significant oil and natural gas reserves, the UAE has emerged as a key player in the global energy landscape. The abundance of energy resources has propelled the UAE's economic development and elevated its status as a strategic energy hub in the region. As a significant producer and exporter of oil, the UAE holds considerable influence in global energy markets, enabling it to forge diplomatic solid ties with energy-consuming nations. The UAE's energy resources are the cornerstone of its foreign policy, providing the foundation for its engagement with the international community. Energy diplomacy has become a key tool for the UAE to project its influence on the global stage and advance its national interests. By leveraging its energy wealth, the UAE has cultivated strong partnerships with countries worldwide, enabling it to pursue a proactive and dynamic foreign policy agenda. Moreover, the significance of energy resources in UAE foreign policy extends beyond economic considerations. Energy security remains a top priority for the UAE, given its critical role in sustaining its economy and ensuring its national security. By strategically managing its energy resources and diversifying its energy mix, the UAE aims to enhance its energy security and safeguard its long-term interests. In conclusion, energy resources are paramount to the UAE's foreign policy objectives. The country's abundant energy reserves drive its economic growth and underpin its diplomatic efforts on the global stage. As the UAE continues to navigate the complexities of the international energy landscape, its energy resources will remain a cornerstone of its foreign policy strategy, shaping its engagement with the world and reinforcing its position as a key player in the global energy arena.

Energy Security and Diversification Efforts

Given the country's significant dependence on energy resources for economic growth and development, energy security is a critical aspect of the UAE's foreign policy strategy. Recognizing the importance of ensuring a stable and reliable energy supply, the UAE has implemented various initiatives to enhance its energy security and diversification efforts. One key focus has been reducing reliance on traditional fossil fuels and increasing investment in renewable energy sources. The UAE's ambitious goal to generate 50% of its energy from clean sources by 2050 reflects its commitment to enhancing energy security through diversification. In addition to promoting renewable energy, the UAE has also pursued strategic partnerships with key global energy players to secure its energy supply. These partnerships involve bilateral agreements that ensure a stable flow of energy resources and technology transfer to the UAE. By forging strong ties with energy-rich countries and international energy companies, the UAE strengthens its position in the global energy market and mitigates potential risks to its energy security. Furthermore, the UAE has invested heavily in infrastructure development to enhance its energy security capabilities. Upgrading and expanding existing infrastructure, such as pipelines, refineries, and storage facilities, allows the UAE to manage its energy resources more efficiently and respond effectively to fluctuations in global energy markets. By adopting a multi-faceted approach to energy security and diversification, the UAE demonstrates its proactive stance in addressing potential challenges and vulnerabilities in the energy sector. These efforts strengthen the country's resilience to external shocks and contribute to its long-term sustainability and competitiveness in the global energy landscape.

Bilateral Energy Agreements with Key Partners

The UAE has strategically engaged in bilateral energy agreements with key partners to ensure reliable energy supply and strengthen diplomatic relations. These agreements are crucial in enhancing energy security and fostering economic cooperation between the UAE and its partners. By establishing mutually beneficial relationships, the UAE has diversified its energy resources and expanded its presence in the global energy market. One of the key partners for the UAE in the energy sector is Saudi Arabia. The two countries have a history of collaboration in the energy field, with joint ventures and agreements strengthening their ties. The strategic partnership between the UAE and Saudi Arabia has not only enhanced energy security. Still, it has paved the way for greater cooperation in other areas, such as trade and investment. Another significant partner for the UAE is Japan. The UAE has long-standing energy partnerships with Japan, particularly in liquefied natural gas (LNG). These agreements have enabled the UAE to export its energy resources to Japan, a major energy importer, and secure a stable market for its products. The vital energy ties between the UAE and Japan have contributed to enhancing bilateral relations and promoting economic cooperation. The UAE has also forged essential energy agreements with European countries like the United Kingdom and Italy. These agreements have facilitated energy trade between the UAE and European nations, promoting energy security and diversification for both parties. Through these bilateral energy agreements, the UAE has leveraged its energy resources to build strategic alliances and strengthen its position in the global energy market. In conclusion, bilateral energy agreements with key partners have played a pivotal role in shaping the UAE's energy diplomacy strategy. By establishing solid and collaborative relationships with energy-importing countries, the UAE has ensured a stable supply of energy resources, promoted economic cooperation, and enhanced its global energy presence. These agreements contribute to the UAE's energy security and reinforce its position as a key player in the international energy arena.

The Role of Renewable Energy in UAE Diplomacy

The UAE has strategically positioned itself as a global leader in renewable energy, recognizing the importance of transitioning towards a more sustainable future. Environmental concerns drive the country's proactive approach to renewable energy and play a significant role in its diplomatic efforts. By investing in renewable energy sources such as solar and wind power, the UAE has enhanced its international standing and strengthened its relationships with key partners on the global stage. Renewable energy projects are a cornerstone of the UAE's diplomatic agenda, showcasing the country's commitment to reducing its carbon footprint and embracing clean energy solutions. These initiatives have positioned the UAE as a pioneer in the renewable energy field and opened up new avenues for collaboration with other countries that share similar sustainability goals. The UAE has fostered partnerships with various nations by promoting renewable energy projects from developed economies to emerging markets. This cooperation extends beyond bilateral agreements and includes participation in international initiatives to advance renewable energy technologies and practices worldwide. Furthermore, the UAE's investment in renewable energy infrastructure has bolstered its domestic energy security and enabled the country to export its expertise and technology to other regions. By sharing its knowledge and resources, the UAE has proactively supported the global transition to sustainable energy sources. In conclusion, the role of renewable energy in UAE diplomacy cannot be overstated. By championing renewable energy initiatives, the UAE has not only positioned itself as a responsible global actor. Still, it has also strengthened its diplomatic ties and paved the way for a more sustainable and prosperous future.

Energy Infrastructure Development and Investment

Energy infrastructure development and investment are crucial in shaping the UAE's energy diplomacy strategy. The country has invested heavily in building a sustainable and robust energy infrastructure to support its growing energy needs and further solidify its position as a global energy player. The UAE has undertaken significant projects to enhance its energy infrastructure, including constructing energy-efficient buildings, smart grids, and renewable energy facilities. Investment in energy infrastructure is a key priority for the UAE government, as it seeks to diversify its energy sources and reduce its reliance on traditional fossil fuels. The country has implemented ambitious initiatives to modernize its energy infrastructure and promote using clean and renewable energy sources. These efforts have helped meet domestic energy demands and positioned the UAE as a leader in sustainable energy development. The UAE's strategic location as a central transit hub for energy resources has attracted significant foreign investment in its infrastructure projects. International partnerships and collaborations have played a vital role in facilitating the country's energy infrastructure development. The UAE has leveraged its energy diplomacy to attract foreign investment and expertise in building state-of-the-art energy facilities and infrastructure. Developing energy infrastructure in the UAE has also contributed to job creation and economic growth. Investments in energy projects have led to the creation of new employment opportunities and have stimulated economic development in the country. The focus on energy infrastructure development has enhanced the UAE's energy security and has been a driving force behind its economic diversification efforts. Energy infrastructure development and investment are central pillars of the UAE's energy diplomacy strategy. By investing in cutting-edge energy technologies and fostering international partnerships, the UAE continues strengthening its position as a global energy hub and a leader in sustainable energy development.

Leveraging Energy Diplomacy for Economic Growth

The UAE's energy diplomacy plays a crucial role in ensuring energy security and driving economic growth. By leveraging its position as a key player in the global energy market, the UAE has strengthened its economic ties with other nations and attracted foreign investment. Through strategic partnerships and investments in energy infrastructure projects, the UAE has diversified its economy and created new growth opportunities. One of the key ways the UAE has leveraged energy diplomacy for economic growth is through its emphasis on clean energy and sustainability. By investing in renewable energy sources such as solar and wind power, the UAE has reduced its carbon footprint and positioned itself as a leader in the clean energy sector. This has not only attracted international investment but has also created new job opportunities and stimulated economic growth. Furthermore, the UAE's energy diplomacy efforts have also focused on enhancing energy efficiency and innovation. By investing in research and development in the energy sector, the UAE has developed cutting-edge technologies that benefit its economy and can be exported to other nations. This focus on innovation has helped the UAE build a reputation as a hub for technological advancement in the energy sector, further driving economic growth and development. In conclusion, the UAE's strategic approach to energy diplomacy has ensured energy security and sustainability and has driven the country's economic growth. By leveraging its position as a key player in the global energy market and investing in clean energy technologies and innovation, the UAE has created new opportunities for economic development and strengthened its position as a leading player in the global economy.

Addressing Energy Challenges in the Region

Energy challenges in the region are multifaceted, ranging from political instability and security threats to fluctuating oil prices and the need for sustainable energy solutions. The UAE recognizes the importance of proactively addressing these challenges to ensure a stable and resilient energy sector. One key challenge is the geopolitical dynamics in the Middle East, which can impact energy production, transportation, and distribution. By engaging in diplomatic initiatives and cooperation with regional partners, the UAE aims to mitigate these risks and promote stability in the energy market. Moreover, the global shift towards renewable energy sources presents opportunities and challenges for the UAE's traditional oil-based economy. The country has been investing heavily in renewable energy projects, such as solar power plants and wind farms, to diversify its energy mix and reduce reliance on fossil fuels. However, transitioning to a more sustainable energy landscape requires significant investment, infrastructure development, and technological innovation. Additionally, the UAE faces domestic challenges related to energy efficiency and conservation. With a fast-growing population and rising energy consumption, there is a pressing need to implement policies and initiatives that promote energy efficiency and reduce waste. Investing in smart grid technology, promoting energy conservation practices, and raising awareness about sustainable energy practices are ways the UAE addresses these challenges at the local level. In conclusion, addressing energy challenges in the region requires a comprehensive and strategic approach that leverages diplomacy, innovation, and cooperation. By diversifying its energy sources, promoting renewable energy initiatives, and investing in energy efficiency measures, the UAE is positioning itself as a leader in addressing the evolving energy landscape regionally and globally.

Multilateral Energy Cooperation and Partnerships

Multilateral energy cooperation and partnerships are crucial in the UAE's foreign policy strategy. The UAE recognizes the importance of collaboration with international partners to address global energy challenges and achieve common goals. The UAE actively engages with countries worldwide to promote sustainable energy practices and ensure energy security through multilateral frameworks such as the International Renewable Energy Agency (IRENA) and the Organization of the Petroleum Exporting Countries (OPEC). Partnerships with key energy-producing and consuming nations are essential for the UAE to maintain its position as a leading energy player on the global stage. By fostering alliances and agreements with diverse countries, the UAE can enhance energy security, promote technological innovation, and drive economic development. These partnerships also facilitate knowledge sharing and capacity building, ensuring the UAE remains at the forefront of energy diplomacy. Furthermore, multilateral energy cooperation allows the UAE to contribute to the global energy sustainability and climate change dialogue. By working with other nations to develop renewable energy solutions and reduce carbon emissions, the UAE demonstrates its commitment to environmental stewardship and sustainable development. These partnerships help the UAE to build a positive reputation as a responsible and forward-thinking energy player in the international community. Looking ahead, the UAE will continue prioritizing multilateral energy cooperation and partnerships as a cornerstone of its foreign policy. By collaborating with a diverse network of countries and organizations, the UAE can leverage its energy resources and expertise to address emerging challenges and seize new opportunities in the global energy landscape. Through strategic alliances and shared initiatives, the UAE is poised to shape the future of energy diplomacy and contribute to a more sustainable and secure energy future for all.

Future Trends and Prospects for Energy Diplomacy in the UAE

As the UAE continues to assert its position as a global player in the energy sector, future trends and prospects for energy diplomacy are poised to shape the country's foreign policy landscape. One key trend on the horizon is the increasing focus on sustainability and renewable energy sources. The UAE's ambitious clean energy goals, such as the target to generate 50% of its energy from renewables by 2050, will drive its energy diplomacy agenda in the future. Another critical aspect of future energy diplomacy for the UAE is the emphasis on technology and innovation. As advancements in energy technology continue to reshape the global energy market, the UAE must stay at the forefront of these developments to maintain its competitive edge. Collaborating with international partners on research and development initiatives and investing in cutting-edge energy solutions will be crucial for the country's success in the future energy landscape. Moreover, diversifying energy sources and partners will be a key focus for the UAE. The UAE can enhance its energy security and global influence by expanding its energy portfolio to include a mix of conventional and renewable sources and cultivating partnerships with a diverse range of countries. Furthermore, the UAE's strategic location as a hub for energy trade and transit will play a significant role in shaping the future of its energy diplomacy. Leveraging its position as a gateway between East and West, the UAE has the potential to strengthen its role as a key player in the global energy market and secure its status as a pivotal energy hub in the region. In conclusion, the future of energy diplomacy in the UAE holds great promise, with opportunities for the country to lead in sustainable energy practices, technological innovation, and diversification strategies. By capitalizing on these trends and prospects, the UAE can position itself as a key player in the evolving energy landscape and make a lasting impact on the global energy sector.

In a Nutshell

Energy Diplomacy in the UAE
The UAE has strategically positioned itself as a key player in global energy diplomacy, leveraging its vast energy resources and commitment to renewable energy to enhance its international influence and economic growth. Here's an in-depth look at the various aspects of the UAE's energy diplomacy:

Energy Resources in UAE Foreign Policy
Its vast oil and natural gas reserves have significantly shaped the UAE's foreign policy. These resources have provided the country with substantial economic power, enabling it to effectively pursue regional and international interests. The wealth generated from energy exports has allowed the UAE to invest in various sectors globally, enhancing its diplomatic leverage and security[4].

Energy Security and Diversification Efforts
Recognizing the need to diversify its energy sources and reduce dependency on oil, the UAE has implemented aggressive strategies to incorporate renewable energy into its energy mix. The UAE Energy Strategy 2050 aims to achieve a mix of 44% clean energy, 38% gas, 12% clean coal, and 6% nuclear

energy[2]. This diversification not only ensures energy security but also aligns with global sustainability goals.

Bilateral Energy Agreements with Key Partners

The UAE has established numerous bilateral energy agreements with key global partners. For instance, it has signed significant deals with Germany to supply natural gas, enhancing energy security for both nations[12]. Additionally, partnerships with countries like France have focused on nuclear energy cooperation, further diversifying the UAE's energy portfolio[14].

Renewable Energy in UAE Diplomacy

The UAE is a pioneer in renewable energy within the Middle East, with substantial investments in solar, wind, and hydrogen energy. The country plans to triple its renewable energy capacity by 2030, aiming to reach 14.2 GW[1]. Initiatives like the Mohammed bin Rashid Al Maktoum Solar Park and the Noor Abu Dhabi solar park are key projects that highlight the UAE's commitment to renewable energy[2].

Energy Infrastructure Development and Investment

The UAE has invested heavily in developing energy infrastructure both domestically and internationally. Projects like the Barakah Nuclear Power Plant and the extensive solar parks demonstrate the UAE's commitment to building a robust and diversified energy infrastructure. Internationally, the UAE has invested in renewable energy projects across Africa and other regions, promoting sustainable development and energy access[6].

Leveraging Energy Diplomacy for Economic Growth

The UAE leverages its energy diplomacy to foster economic growth by securing investments and opening new markets. The country's strategic investments in renewable energy and critical minerals are designed to ensure long-term economic stability and growth, even as the global energy landscape shifts towards sustainability[3].

Addressing Energy Challenges in the Region

The UAE proactively addresses regional energy challenges, including securing maritime routes and ensuring stable energy supplies. The country's strategic location near the Strait of Hormuz, a critical chokepoint for global oil shipments, underscores its importance in regional energy security[10].

Multilateral Energy Cooperation and Partnerships

The UAE actively participates in multilateral energy forums and organizations, such as the International Renewable Energy Agency (IRENA), which is headquartered in Abu Dhabi. These platforms allow the UAE to influence global energy policies and promote international cooperation on renewable energy and sustainability[1].

Conclusion

The UAE's energy diplomacy is a multifaceted strategy encompassing energy source diversification, strategic bilateral and multilateral partnerships, and significant investments in renewable energy. By leveraging its energy resources and committing to sustainable development, the UAE not only enhances its own energy security and economic growth but also positions itself as a global leader in the energy transition.

IX

References

[1] https://energy.ec.europa.eu/news/energy-diplomacy-eu-and-uae-boost-cooperation-ahead-cop28-2023-09-08_en

[2] https://www.uae-embassy.org/discover-uae/climate-and-energy/uae-energy-diversification

[3] https://foreignpolicy.com/2024/03/21/saudi-arabia-uae-critical-mineral-energy-transition/

[4] https://ivypanda.com/essays/uae-foreign-policy-and-association-of-energy-sources/

[5] https://www.fpri.org/article/2023/04/big-changes-in-united-arab-emirates-foreign-policy/

[6] https://ecfr.eu/publication/beyond-competition-how-europe-can-harness-the-uaes-energy-ambitions-in-africa/

[7] https://www.securityoutlines.cz/security-dressed-in-green-what-motivates-uaes-push-for-sustainable-energy/

[8] https://www.arabnews.com/node/2497936/business-economyhttps:/www.arabnews.com/node/2532786/business-economy

[9] https://www.stimson.org/2018/uae-energy-diplomacy/

[10] https://www.strausscenter.org/energy-and-security-project/united-arab-emirates/

[11] https://demoessays.com/uae-foreign-policy-and-association-of-energy-sources/

[12] https://www.bloomberg.com/tosv2.html?url=L25ld3MvYXJ0aWNsZXMvMjAyNC0wMy0xOC91YWUtYWdyZWVzLTE1LXllYXItZ2FzLWRlYWwtaW4tYm9vc3QtdG8tZ2VybWFuLWVuZXJneS1zZWN1cml0eQ%3D%3D&uuid=2a088c73-3e7f-11ef-aba1-a641df16184e

[13] https://www.weforum.org/publications/fostering-effective-energy-transition-2023/in-full/united-arab-emirates/

[14] https://ae.ambafrance.org/16th-UAE-France-Strategic-Dialogue-affirms-the-two-nations-commitment-to

X

The UAE's Diplomatic Approach to Regional Conflict Resolution

Regional Conflict Resolution

Resolving regional conflicts in the Middle East has long been complex and challenging. With a history marked by territorial disputes, ethnic and religious tensions, and geopolitical rivalries, the region has been a hotspot for conflict for decades. These conflicts have had far-reaching implications, not only for the countries directly involved but also for the stability and security of the wider region. The historical context of regional conflicts in the Middle East provides essential insights into the root causes of these disputes and the dynamics that have fueled them over the years. From the Arab-Israeli conflict to the wars in Iraq and Syria, the region has been plagued by a series of protracted conflicts that have had devastating humanitarian consequences. Against this backdrop of conflict and instability, the UAE has emerged as a key player in efforts to promote regional conflict resolution. Drawing on its diplomatic expertise, strategic alliances, and commitment to peace and security, the UAE has actively engaged in mediating and resolving regional conflicts. By understanding the historical context of regional conflicts in the Middle East, we can better appreciate the challenges and opportunities in achieving lasting peace and stability. The UAE's approach to regional conflict resolution is shaped by this historical context and its commitment to fostering dialogue, cooperation, and reconciliation among all parties involved.

Historical Context of Regional Conflicts in the Middle East

The Middle East has been marked by centuries of complex and deeply rooted conflicts. Many factors, including colonial interventions, religious rivalries, ethnic tensions, and geopolitical power struggles characterize its history. From the Arab-Israeli conflict to the Iran-Iraq war, the region has seen numerous conflicts that have had far-reaching implications for regional stability and global security. The historical context of regional conflicts in the Middle East can be traced back to dismantling the Ottoman Empire after World War I, which led to artificial borders and the establishment of nation-states that often failed to reflect the region's diverse ethnic and religious compositions. This gave rise to internal tensions and external interventions that continue to shape the geopolitical landscape of the Middle East. The Arab-Israeli conflict, in particular, stands out as one of the most enduring and contentious conflicts in the region. The struggle for land and national identity between Israelis and Palestinians has resulted in multiple wars, uprisings, and peace negotiations, with the conflict remaining unresolved to this day. The ongoing conflict has had profound humanitarian consequences, displacing millions of people and fueling deep-seated animosities that have proven challenging to overcome. Moreover, regional rivalries between Sunni and Shia powers, such as Saudi Arabia and Iran, have further exacerbated tensions in the Middle East. Proxy wars and support for opposing factions have intensified conflicts in countries like Syria, Yemen, and Iraq, leading to devastating humanitarian crises and widespread suffering among civilian populations. The legacy of colonialism, the proliferation of extremist ideologies, and the pursuit of national interests by external powers have all contributed to the perpetuation of regional conflicts in the Middle East. The complexity and interconnectedness of these conflicts make them difficult to resolve through traditional diplomatic means, requiring innovative approaches and sustained efforts to promote lasting peace and stability in the region.

The UAE's Role as a Mediator and Peacemaker

The UAE has emerged as a significant player in regional conflict resolution, leveraging its diplomatic insight and strategic positioning to facilitate peace talks and negotiations in various conflict zones. With a history of neutrality and diplomacy, the UAE has actively mediated conflicts and promoted dialogue among conflicting parties. Through its Mediation for Peace initiative, the UAE has utilized its diplomatic channels to bring together warring factions and facilitate dialogue to resolve conflicts. The country's leadership has demonstrated a commitment to finding peaceful solutions to regional disputes, working closely with international partners and organizations to build consensus and promote stability. The UAE's approach to mediation and peacemaking is underpinned by a commitment to upholding the principles of sovereignty, non-interference, and respect for international law. By fostering open lines of communication and promoting dialogue, the UAE has played a key role in de-escalating tensions and fostering reconciliation in conflict-affected regions. Moreover, the UAE has actively supported peacebuilding efforts through humanitarian aid, reconstruction projects, and capacity-building initiatives. By addressing the root causes of conflict and supporting sustainable development in post-conflict societies, the UAE has contributed to long-term stability and peace in the region. The UAE's role as a mediator and peacemaker reflects its commitment to promoting peace, stability, and prosperity in the Middle East and beyond. Through its diplomatic efforts and strategic partnerships, the UAE continues to play a vital role in resolving regional conflicts and advancing the cause of peace and security.

Strategic Partnerships in Regional Conflict Resolution

The UAE has strategically cultivated partnerships with key regional and international actors to enhance its role in regional conflict resolution. These partnerships are crucial in promoting stability, security, and peace in conflict-ridden areas within the

Middle East and beyond. By collaborating with various stakeholders, the UAE has effectively leveraged its diplomatic influence and resources to address complex regional challenges. One of the key strategic partnerships that the UAE has fostered is with the Gulf Cooperation Council (GCC) member states. Through the GCC, the UAE has coordinated efforts with neighboring countries to address shared security threats and mediate regional conflicts. The collective diplomatic clout of the GCC has amplified the UAE's voice on regional issues and enabled it to play a more assertive role in conflict resolution initiatives. Additionally, the UAE has forged strategic alliances with global powers such as the United States and the United Kingdom. These partnerships have enabled the UAE to access advanced military capabilities, intelligence-sharing networks, and political support to mitigate regional conflicts. Collaborating with these significant powers has enhanced the UAE's diplomatic standing and provided valuable resources to contribute to peacekeeping and stabilization efforts in conflict zones. Furthermore, the UAE has actively engaged with regional organizations such as the Arab League and the Organization of Islamic Cooperation (OIC) to promote dialogue, build consensus, and facilitate peace talks among member states. By working within these multilateral frameworks, the UAE has strengthened its diplomatic ties with other Arab and Muslim-majority nations, fostering cooperation and solidarity in addressing regional conflicts. Moreover, the UAE has partnered with international organizations like the United Nations and non-governmental organizations (NGOs) to deliver humanitarian assistance, provide relief, and support reconstruction efforts in conflict-affected areas. These partnerships have enabled the UAE to demonstrate its commitment to alleviating the suffering of civilian populations caught in the crossfire of regional conflicts and to promote sustainable peacebuilding initiatives. Overall, the UAE's strategic partnerships in regional conflict resolution underscore its multifaceted approach to diplomacy and its proactive stance in addressing complex security challenges. By leveraging its alliances with key stakeholders, the UAE has positioned itself as a reliable mediator and peacemaker in the Middle East, contributing to maintaining peace and stability in the region.

Multilateral Diplomacy and Coalition Building

Multilateral diplomacy and coalition building are essential components of the UAE's approach to regional conflict resolution. By working with various countries and international organizations, the UAE aims to leverage collective efforts and resources to address complex challenges and foster peace in conflict-affected regions. The UAE recognizes the importance of building strong partnerships and alliances to promote stability and security in the Middle East and beyond. Through multilateral diplomacy, the UAE actively participates in international forums, such as the United Nations, Arab League, and Gulf Cooperation Council, to engage in constructive dialogue and negotiations with other nations. By collaborating with a diverse range of stakeholders, including regional and global actors, the UAE seeks to build consensus and support for diplomatic initiatives to resolve conflicts and promote sustainable peace. Furthermore, coalition building is significant in the UAE's efforts to address regional conflicts. The UAE has established strategic partnerships with key allies and like-minded countries to address shared security concerns and regional challenges collectively. The UAE and its partners can pool their expertise, resources, and influence to implement effective peacebuilding and conflict resolution strategies by working together within coalitions. Moreover, the UAE actively supports multilateral initiatives focused on humanitarian assistance and development in conflict zones. By collaborating with international humanitarian organizations and donor countries, the UAE provides crucial aid and support to alleviate the suffering of civilians affected by conflict. Through these collective efforts, the UAE is committed to promoting human security and protecting the most vulnerable populations in conflict-affected areas. In conclusion, multilateral diplomacy and coalition building are key elements of the UAE's diplomatic approach to regional conflict resolution. By fostering partnerships, engaging in dialogue, and promoting collaborative initiatives, the UAE strives to contribute to lasting peace and stability in the Middle East and beyond.

Humanitarian Initiatives and Aid in Conflict Zones

The UAE is committed to providing humanitarian aid and support in conflict zones worldwide. This commitment is rooted in the country's values of compassion, empathy, and a desire to alleviate the suffering of those in need. The UAE has delivered humanitarian assistance to conflict-affected areas, working with international organizations and local partners to ensure that aid reaches those most in need. The UAE has provided essential support through its humanitarian initiatives, such as food, shelter, medical supplies, and education to vulnerable populations in conflict zones. The country has also played a key role in promoting peace and stability in these regions, recognizing that sustainable peace can only be achieved by addressing the root causes of conflict and supporting communities to rebuild their lives. In addition to providing direct humanitarian aid, the UAE has been at the forefront of advocating for respect for international humanitarian law and protecting civilians in conflict zones. The country has consistently called for the rights of all individuals, regardless of their nationality or background, to be respected and protected during times of conflict. Furthermore, the UAE has proactively partnered with other countries and organizations to coordinate humanitarian responses in conflict zones. By working together with like-minded partners, the UAE has been able to maximize the impact of its humanitarian efforts and reach a larger number of people in need. This collaborative approach underscores the UAE's belief in the importance of multilateralism and collective action in addressing complex humanitarian challenges. Overall, the UAE's humanitarian initiatives and aid efforts in conflict zones demonstrate the country's commitment to promoting peace, stability, and human dignity worldwide. By providing essential support to those affected by conflict and advocating for the protection of civilians, the UAE is playing a vital role in mitigating the impact of conflicts and working towards a more peaceful and prosperous future for all.

Military and Security Contributions to Regional Stability

The UAE is crucial in enhancing regional stability through its military and security contributions. As a responsible regional actor, the UAE has actively participated in various peacekeeping operations and counterterrorism efforts, demonstrating its commitment to promoting security and stability. The UAE Armed Forces are well-trained and equipped to handle various security challenges, including counterterrorism operations, maritime security, and peacekeeping missions. UAE forces have been deployed to conflict zones such as Yemen and Syria, where they have worked alongside international partners to combat terrorist groups and restore peace. In addition to direct military interventions, the UAE provides support and training to regional partners to enhance their security capabilities. Through initiatives like the Emirates Defense Companies Council (EDCC) and joint military exercises, the UAE strengthens the capacity of its allies in the region to address security threats effectively. Furthermore, the UAE strongly emphasizes cybersecurity and countering cyber threats, recognizing the importance of safeguarding critical infrastructure and information networks in an increasingly digital world. By investing in cybersecurity measures and collaborating with international partners, the UAE aims to mitigate the risks posed by cyber-attacks and ensure the stability of the region's digital ecosystem. Overall, the UAE's military and security contributions are vital in maintaining regional stability and countering threats to peace and security. By actively engaging in security operations, supporting regional partners, and prioritizing cybersecurity measures, the UAE demonstrates its commitment to safeguarding the stability and prosperity of the Middle East.

Economic Development and Post-Conflict Reconstruction Efforts

The UAE's commitment to economic development and post-conflict reconstruction efforts in the region is evident in its comprehensive approach to rebuilding societies affected by conflict. By investing in infrastructure, supporting entrepreneurship, and promoting job creation, the UAE aims to foster long-term stability and prosperity in conflict-affected areas. Through partnerships with international organizations and local stakeholders, the UAE has implemented programs that address the root causes of conflict and promote sustainable development. Additionally, the UAE provides humanitarian aid and support to displaced populations, helping to alleviate the suffering caused by conflict and create conditions for a more peaceful and prosperous future. Through its focus on economic development and post-conflict reconstruction, the UAE demonstrates its commitment to building a more stable and prosperous region for all.

Challenges and Obstacles Faced in Regional Conflict Resolution

Navigating the complexities of regional conflict resolution presents many challenges for the UAE. One key challenge is the deep-rooted and multifaceted nature of conflicts in the Middle East, compounded by historical grievances and sectarian divisions. Additionally, the involvement of multiple state and non-state actors further complicates efforts to find sustainable solutions. Another significant challenge is the lack of trust and confidence among conflicting parties, making it difficult to effectively facilitate dialogue and negotiation processes. Furthermore, external interventions and geopolitical rivalries in the region often hinder progress towards peaceful resolutions. Resource constraints pose a practical challenge in supporting post-conflict reconstruction efforts. Rebuilding infrastructure, providing humanitarian assistance, and promoting economic development require significant financial resources and long-term commitment. The dynamic nature of conflicts and the evolving geopolitical landscape present ongoing challenges in predicting and adapting to changing circumstances. The UAE must remain flexible and responsive to emerging threats and opportunities in its diplomatic initiatives. Cultural and linguistic barriers can impede effective communication and understanding between conflict parties. Overcoming these barriers requires a nuanced approach that considers all stakeholders' diverse perspectives and interests. Finally, the long-term sustainability of peace agreements and reconciliation processes remains a critical challenge in regional conflict resolution. Ensuring buy-in from all relevant actors and addressing the root causes of conflicts are essential for building durable peace in the region.

Future Prospects for the UAE's Diplomatic Approach to Regional Conflict Resolution

As the UAE continues to navigate the complex landscape of regional conflict resolution, its diplomatic approach remains crucial in shaping the future prospects of peace and stability in the Middle East. The UAE is poised to be increasingly influential in mediating and resolving regional conflicts by leveraging its unique position as a regional power with global partnerships. One key aspect of the UAE's future diplomatic approach to regional conflict resolution is its commitment to multilateralism and coalition building. The UAE can foster cooperation and coordination toward peaceful solutions to ongoing conflicts by engaging with international organizations, regional blocs, and like-minded partners. Furthermore, the UAE's investment in humanitarian initiatives and aid in conflict zones will continue to be a cornerstone of its diplomatic efforts. By addressing the root causes of conflict and prioritizing the needs of affected populations, the UAE can build trust and lay the groundwork for sustainable peace. In addition, the UAE's military and security contributions to regional stability will remain a vital component of its diplomatic approach. Through strategic partnerships and joint initiatives, the UAE can bolster security architecture in the region and deter potential threats to peace and stability. Economic development and post-conflict reconstruction efforts will also play a crucial role in shaping the future prospects of the UAE's diplomatic approach to regional conflict resolution. By investing in infrastructure, job creation, and sustainable development projects in conflict-affected areas, the UAE can help rebuild societies and create conditions for lasting peace. Despite these opportunities, challenges and obstacles in regional conflict resolution persist. The UAE must navigate political rivalries, resource constraints, and complex dynamics to advance its diplomatic agenda effectively. By staying agile, adaptive, and proactive, the UAE can overcome these challenges and contribute meaningfully to regional peace and stability. In conclusion, the future prospects for the UAE's diplomatic approach to regional conflict resolution are promising yet complex. By building on its strengths, leveraging its partnerships, and addressing key challenges, the UAE can continue to play a significant role in shaping a more peaceful and stable Middle East.

In a Nutshell

The United Arab Emirates (UAE) has emerged as a significant player in regional conflict resolution and stability efforts in the Middle East and beyond. Here's an overview of the UAE's diplomatic approach and contributions:

1. Role as Mediator and Peacemaker:
The UAE has increasingly taken on the role of mediator in regional conflicts, leveraging its economic strength and diplomatic relationships. Notable examples include:

- Mediating the largest prisoner exchange between Russia and Ukraine in January 2024.
- Facilitating agreements on humanitarian aid delivery to Gaza.
- Acting as a "bridge builder" between the Global North and South during its tenure on the UN Security Council (2022-2023).

The UAE's approach emphasizes discretion, consensus-building, and culturally sensitive diplomacy, often focusing on achieving broad objectives rather than maintaining rigid positions.

2. Strategic Partnerships in Regional Conflict Resolution:
The UAE has formed strategic partnerships with key global and regional powers to enhance its conflict resolution efforts:

- Close cooperation with the United States on counter-extremism initiatives.
- Partnerships with European nations for security and economic cooperation.
- Engagement with Russia and China to diversify its diplomatic portfolio.

3. Multilateral Diplomacy and Coalition Building:
The UAE actively participates in multilateral forums and builds coalitions to address regional challenges:

- Member of the Gulf Cooperation Council (GCC), advocating for regional integration and security.
- Participation in the Global Coalition against Da'esh.
- Engagement with international organizations like the UN and IAEA on issues such as nuclear non-proliferation.

4. Humanitarian Initiatives and Aid in Conflict Zones:
The UAE has institutionalized its humanitarian efforts as part of its foreign policy:

- Providing substantial aid to war-torn areas and supporting refugee populations.
- Establishing institutions like the UAE's National Committee for Combating Terrorism and the Sawab Center to counter extremist propaganda.
- Hosting international centers like Hedayah for combating violent extremism.

5. Military and Security Contributions to Regional Stability:

The UAE has taken an active role in regional security operations:

- Participation in the Coalition to Support Legitimacy in Yemen.
- Military cooperation and training initiatives with African nations to combat terrorism and piracy.
- Establishment of military outposts in strategic locations to secure maritime routes and counter threats.

6. Challenges and Obstacles in Regional Conflict Resolution:
Despite its efforts, the UAE faces several challenges in its conflict resolution endeavors:

- Balancing relationships with competing regional powers (e.g., Iran vs. Saudi Arabia).
- Navigating complex regional dynamics, particularly in areas like Yemen and Libya.
- Addressing criticism over its military involvement in certain conflicts.
- Maintaining credibility as a neutral mediator while pursuing its own strategic interests.

The UAE's approach to regional conflict resolution combines economic diplomacy, strategic partnerships, humanitarian aid, and military contributions. Its efforts are characterized by a focus on stability, economic development, and countering extremism. While facing challenges, the UAE has positioned itself as a key player in shaping regional dynamics and promoting peace through a multifaceted diplomatic strategy.

XI

References

[1] https://www.washingtoninstitute.org/policy-analysis/arab-approach-mediation-reshaping-diplomacy-multipolar-world

[2] https://futureuae.com/en-US/Mainpage/Item/8990/emirati-diplomacy-driving-efforts-to-eas-conflicts-in-ukrain-and-gaza

[3] https://www.khairallahlegal.com/uae-law/partnership-disputes-in-the-uae-legal-insights-and-resolutions/

[4] https://www.cmi.no/publications/7169-the-uaes-humanitarian-diplomacy-claiming-state-sovereignty

[5] https://www.ispionline.it/en/publication/the-uaes-rising-military-role-in-africa-defending-interests-advancing-influence-172825

[6] https://uaeun.org/uae-in-the-world/regional-stability/

[7] https://www.c-r.org/accord/still-time-talk/qatars-mediation-%E2%80%93-motivations-acceptance-and-modalities

[8] https://mediate.com/news/the-arab-approach-to-mediation-reshaping-diplomacy-in-a-multipolar-world/

[9] https://www.humanitarianstudies.no/resource/recent-trends-in-the-international-humanitarian-regime-and-the-rise-of-the-uae/

XII

Public Diplomacy: Shaping Perceptions of the UAE

Public diplomacy serves as a critical tool in shaping how a country is perceived on the global stage. It goes beyond traditional diplomacy by engaging with foreign publics directly to promote a positive image and build understanding. In the context of the United Arab Emirates (UAE), public diplomacy plays a pivotal role in enhancing the country's reputation and fostering relationships with other nations. The UAE's commitment to public diplomacy is rooted in recognizing the interconnected nature of today's world. In an era where information flows rapidly across borders, communicating effectively and influencing perceptions is paramount. The UAE aims to showcase its values, achievements, and contributions to the international community by proactively engaging in public diplomacy efforts. Moreover, public diplomacy is a multifaceted endeavor encompassing various channels and strategies. From cultural exchanges and educational programs to strategic communication campaigns and digital outreach, the UAE leverages diverse tools to shape how it is perceived globally. By harnessing these resources effectively, the UAE can build bridges, challenge stereotypes, and foster mutual respect and cooperation with other nations. As the UAE continues to assert its presence on the world stage, the significance of public diplomacy in managing its reputation and shaping perceptions cannot be overstated. By investing in strategic initiatives that promote dialogue, understanding, and goodwill, the UAE can position itself as a trusted partner and a respected member of the global community. In the following chapters, we will delve deeper into the various facets of the UAE's public diplomacy efforts and explore their impact on its standing in the international arena.

The importance of public diplomacy in national reputation and perception.

Public diplomacy is crucial in shaping national reputation and perception on the global stage. It is the gateway through which countries can convey their values, culture, and policies to the international community. The United Arab Emirates recognizes the significance of public diplomacy in cultivating positive relationships with other nations and promoting a favorable image of the country abroad. The UAE understands the importance of proactively managing its reputation in a world where instantaneous communication and information travels swiftly. Public diplomacy enables the country to engage with foreign audiences, dispel misconceptions, and showcase its achievements and global contributions. The UAE can communicate its vision, values, and aspirations to a global audience by strategically crafting its messaging and utilizing various communication channels. The practice of public diplomacy in the UAE is deeply rooted in its commitment to openness, transparency, and inclusivity. Through cultural exchanges, educational initiatives, and media campaigns, the country seeks to foster mutual understanding and build bridges of cooperation with nations around the world. By promoting cultural heritage, innovation, and sustainability, the UAE aims to position itself as a forward-thinking and progressive nation actively contributing to global development and peace. As the UAE continues to play an increasingly influential role in regional and international affairs, the importance of public diplomacy cannot be overstated. The country can shape perceptions, build trust, and advance its national interests worldwide through strategic communication and engagement. The UAE is enhancing its soft power by investing in public diplomacy efforts and reaffirming its commitment to building a more connected and harmonious global community.

Historical Context

The history of public diplomacy in the UAE is deeply intertwined with the nation's journey of development and growth on the global stage. From its early days as a young nation to its current status as a regional and international hub, the UAE's approach to public diplomacy has evolved significantly over the years. In the formative years of the UAE, public diplomacy was primarily focused on establishing the country's presence and identity in the eyes of the international community. The leadership recognized the importance of projecting a positive image of the nation to attract investment, trade opportunities, and strategic partnerships. This early emphasis on building a solid reputation laid the foundation for the country's future public diplomacy efforts. As the UAE gained prominence globally, public diplomacy became a key tool in shaping the country's image and influencing perceptions. The government invested in cultural initiatives, educational programs, and media campaigns to showcase the nation's rich heritage, modern development, and progressive values. By highlighting its achievements in various fields and promoting an open, tolerant society, the UAE aimed to position itself as a forward-thinking and welcoming destination for business and tourism. The evolution of public diplomacy in the UAE also reflects the country's strategic priorities and foreign policy objectives. Over the years, public diplomacy initiatives have been closely aligned with the government's efforts to diversify the economy, promote innovation, and enhance bilateral relationships with partners worldwide. By engaging with global audiences through cultural events, educational exchanges, and digital platforms, the UAE has sought to build bridges and foster mutual understanding. The historical context of public diplomacy in the UAE underscores the nation's commitment to proactive engagement with the international community. The UAE has established a strong and positive reputation on the world stage by leveraging its unique identity, values, and resources. This historical journey serves as a testament to the importance of public diplomacy in shaping the country's image and enhancing its standing in the global arena.

The evolution of public diplomacy in the UAE and its significance in shaping the country's image.

The evolution of public diplomacy in the UAE is a dynamic journey that reflects the country's commitment to actively shaping its international image. From its early days as a fledgling nation to its current status as a global player, the UAE has strategically utilized public diplomacy to communicate its values, achievements, and aspirations to the world. At the heart of this evolution is the UAE's recognition of soft power and cultural influence in shaping perceptions and building relationships. By investing in cultural diplomacy, the UAE has amplified its rich heritage, arts, and traditions on the global stage, captivating audiences and fostering appreciation and understanding. UAE government entities have been pivotal in driving public diplomacy initiatives forward. Through institutions such as the Ministry of Foreign Affairs and International Cooperation, the National Media Council, and various cultural agencies, the UAE has implemented strategic programs and campaigns to engage with global audiences and convey its messages effectively. The significance of public diplomacy in shaping the country's image cannot be understated. It connects the UAE's domestic tolerance, diversity, and innovation ethos with the international community, creating a narrative that resonates with people worldwide. This strategic communication approach has enabled the UAE to position itself as a forward-thinking, progressive nation that is open to collaboration and dialogue on a global scale. As the UAE continues to expand its global footprint and engage with diverse audiences, the evolution of public diplomacy remains a cornerstone of its foreign policy. By adapting to changing communication trends and investing in innovative strategies, the UAE is poised to enhance its image and reputation on the world stage.

The Role of Government Entities

Government entities in the UAE play a crucial role in implementing public diplomacy strategies that promote the country's image and reputation on the global stage. These entities act as key drivers in shaping perceptions of the UAE and projecting its values, goals, and achievements to the international community. Ministries such as the Ministry of Foreign Affairs and International Cooperation, Culture and Youth, and the Ministry of Education oversee various public diplomacy efforts. They work collaboratively to develop and execute initiatives that showcase the UAE's rich cultural heritage, promote educational exchange programs, and enhance its global standing. The UAE's diplomatic missions abroad also significantly engage with foreign governments, international organizations, and local communities. These missions are vital platforms for fostering positive relations and sharing the UAE's narrative with diverse audiences through cultural events, educational programs, and diplomatic outreach. UAE government entities leverage various communication channels, including traditional media, social media platforms, and official publications, to amplify their public diplomacy messages. These entities strive to build trust, credibility, and understanding with international stakeholders by effectively communicating the country's values, policies, and achievements.

Collaboration between government entities and private sector partners further enhances the impact of public diplomacy initiatives. By working together on cultural exchange programs, business forums, and other collaborative projects, these entities strengthen the UAE's soft power and contribute to advancing its strategic objectives on the global stage. Overall, the coordinated efforts of government entities in implementing public diplomacy strategies play a vital role in shaping the positive perception of the UAE internationally and positioning the country as a respected and influential player in the global community.

Government entities and institutions play a crucial role in implementing public diplomacy strategies in the UAE. The Ministry of Foreign Affairs and International Cooperation is at the forefront of these efforts, working to promote the country's image on the global stage. Through diplomatic missions abroad, the ministry engages with foreign governments and international organizations, showcasing the UAE's culture, values, and achievements. The National Media Council is another key player in shaping perceptions of the UAE internationally. By regulating and promoting the media sector, the council ensures that accurate and positive information about the country is disseminated. This includes supporting the production of documentaries, films, and television programs highlighting the UAE's cultural diversity and modern achievements. Additionally, government-sponsored cultural institutions such as the Abu Dhabi Tourism and Culture Authority and the Dubai Culture and Arts Authority are vital in promoting the UAE's rich heritage and contemporary art scene. These entities showcase the country's cultural assets and foster cross-cultural understanding through initiatives like art exhibitions, music festivals, and heritage events. Moreover, the Emirates Diplomatic Academy plays a significant role in training the next generation of diplomats and public diplomacy professionals. By providing education and professional development opportunities, the academy equips future leaders with the skills and knowledge needed to effectively promote the UAE's interests and values on the global stage. Overall, the coordinated efforts of government entities and institutions in implementing public diplomacy strategies contribute to enhancing the UAE's reputation and fostering positive relationships with the international community.

Cultural Diplomacy

Cultural diplomacy plays a pivotal role in shaping the international image of the UAE. The rich tapestry of culture, arts, and heritage is a powerful tool for fostering understanding and building connections with people across the globe. The UAE's diverse cultural landscape, influenced by its history and traditions, bridges borders and promotes mutual respect and appreciation. The UAE showcases its vibrant cultural heritage to the world through initiatives such as art exhibitions, cultural festivals, and heritage preservation projects. These efforts promote the country's unique identity and highlight the values of tolerance, diversity, and inclusivity deeply embedded in Emirati society. By engaging in cultural exchanges and collaborations with international partners, the UAE opens doors for cross-cultural dialogue and mutual learning. The UAE is committed to building relationships based on shared values and mutual respect through cultural diplomacy, fostering a sense of connection and goodwill among nations. Promoting Emirati arts and culture globally enhances the country's soft power. It creates a positive perception of the UAE as a hub of creativity and innovation. By leveraging its cultural assets, the UAE showcases its dynamism and forward-thinking approach, positioning itself as a leader in the global cultural arena. In a world where cultural exchange plays an increasingly important role in diplomatic relations, the UAE's emphasis on cultural diplomacy underscores its commitment to building bridges and fostering understanding across borders. Through cultural initiatives that celebrate diversity and promote dialogue, the UAE continues to enrich the global cultural landscape and strengthen its reputation as a beacon of cultural vibrancy and creativity.

Culture, arts, and heritage are central to shaping the UAE's international image. The rich tapestry of Emirati culture, infused with traditions, values, and expressions, is a powerful tool for increasing global understanding and appreciation. Through initiatives that celebrate music, dance, literature, art, and cuisine, the UAE showcases the depth and diversity of its cultural heritage, inviting the world to explore and engage with its unique identity. A key aspect of cultural diplomacy is promoting Emirati cultural events and exhibitions on the global stage. By hosting cultural festivals, art exhibitions, and heritage showcases in major international capitals, the UAE creates opportunities for cross-cultural dialogue and mutual appreciation. These initiatives not only serve to showcase the country's artistic talent and cultural richness but also foster connections and understanding between people from different backgrounds. Moreover, the UAE's investment in preserving and promoting its heritage sites and historical landmarks reflects its commitment to maintaining a strong cultural identity. The restoration and conservation of architectural treasures, such as traditional forts, mosques, and historic districts, not only preserve the country's past but also serve as symbols of cultural pride and showcase the UAE's dedication to preserving its legacy for future generations. Through art and creativity, the UAE communicates universal values of peace, tolerance, and unity to a global audience. Artistic expressions, whether in the form of visual arts, traditional crafts, or contemporary performances, serve as a medium for promoting cross-cultural dialogue and understanding. By supporting local artists and providing platforms for creative expression, the UAE reinforces its commitment to fostering a vibrant cultural ecosystem that contributes to a more interconnected world. In essence, cultural diplomacy plays a pivotal role in promoting a positive image of the UAE internationally. The country showcases its unique identity and values by leveraging its cultural heritage, artistic expressions, and creative endeavors, fostering goodwill, understanding, and respect on the global stage. The UAE builds bridges between nations and peoples through cultural exchange and dialogue, contributing to a more harmonious and interconnected world.

Educational Exchange Programs

Education exchange programs are vital in fostering goodwill and understanding between nations. In the context of the UAE's public diplomacy efforts, educational initiatives and scholarships are potent tools to enhance the country's international reputation and strengthen relationships with other countries. By providing opportunities for students and scholars to study and conduct research in the UAE, these programs contribute to knowledge exchange and promote cross-cultural understanding and mutual respect. The UAE showcases its commitment to investing in human capital and building a knowledge-based economy through educational exchange programs. By attracting top talent from around the world to study in the UAE, the country positions itself as a hub for learning and innovation. These programs offer participants the chance to immerse themselves in the UAE's rich cultural heritage, experience its modern infrastructure, and engage with its diverse society. In doing so, they gain a deeper appreciation for the UAE's values, traditions, and aspirations. Furthermore, educational exchange programs create lasting connections between individuals that extend beyond academic pursuits. Participants develop personal and professional networks that can lead to future collaborations and partnerships. By nurturing these relationships, the UAE strengthens its diplomatic ties and builds bridges of friendship with people from diverse backgrounds and nationalities. Moreover, educational exchange programs contribute to developing a global mindset among participants, fostering a sense of global citizenship and interconnectedness. Students and scholars expand their horizons and develop a greater appreciation for diversity and inclusivity through exposure to different perspectives and ideas. This cultural exchange enriches the individuals involved and contributes to building a more tolerant and peaceful world. In conclusion, educational exchange programs are a cornerstone of the UAE's public diplomacy efforts, enabling the country to share its knowledge, values, and vision with the international community. Investing in education and fostering cross-cultural dialogue, the UAE cultivates goodwill and understanding, paving the way for closer collaboration and mutual respect on the global stage.

Educational exchange programs and scholarships foster goodwill and understanding between nations. By offering opportunities for students to study abroad or participate in cultural exchanges, the UAE can showcase its values, traditions, and modern developments to the world. These programs enhance participants' skills and knowledge, creating lasting connections and friendships that transcend borders. Through international collaborations in education, the UAE demonstrates its commitment to global cooperation and mutual learning. By investing in educational initiatives, the UAE promotes its achievements and contributes to building a more interconnected and peaceful world.

Media and Communication Strategies

The UAE's media and communication strategies play a pivotal role in shaping the country's image on the global stage. With a strong emphasis on traditional and digital platforms, the UAE effectively communicates its message to diverse audiences worldwide. Through strategic partnerships with international media outlets, the UAE ensures that accurate and positive narratives about the country are disseminated. The UAE utilizes traditional media channels such as television, radio, and print publications to effectively reach a wide audience and convey key messages. The country's government-funded news outlets, including Emirates News Agency (WAM) and Dubai Media Incorporated, serve as vital platforms for sharing news and information about the UAE's accomplishments and initiatives. Moreover, the UAE has also embraced digital communication channels to engage with a younger, tech-savvy audience. Social media platforms such as Twitter, Instagram, and YouTube are leveraged to amplify the country's voice and showcase its vibrant culture and progressive achievements. Through engaging and visually appealing content, the UAE captures the attention of online users and fosters a positive perception of the country. In addition to proactive communication strategies, the UAE prioritizes transparency and accessibility in its media outreach efforts. Press conferences, interviews with government officials, and press releases regularly provide the public with timely and accurate information. By maintaining open lines of communication, the UAE aims to build trust and credibility with domestic and international audiences. The UAE's media and communication strategies are powerful tools for enhancing its global reputation and promoting a positive image. The country effectively communicates its key messages and values to diverse stakeholders through a combination of traditional and digital channels, contributing to a greater understanding and appreciation of the UAE's rich heritage and modern achievements.

Examining how the UAE utilizes traditional and digital media to communicate its message to global audiences.

The UAE effectively disseminates its message to global audiences using traditional and digital media platforms. Traditional media outlets such as newspapers, television, and radio play a crucial role in reaching a wide range of demographics, both within the country and internationally. Through strategic partnerships with major news organizations and media houses, the UAE ensures that its key messages and initiatives are featured prominently in news coverage. Digital media platforms, including social media, websites, and online publications, have revolutionized how the UAE communicates with its global audience. The UAE government leverages social media channels like Twitter, Instagram, and LinkedIn to share real-time updates, news stories, and engaging content with followers worldwide. These platforms provide a direct line of communication with the public, allowing for immediate engagement and feedback on important issues. In addition to broadcasting its message through traditional and digital media channels, the UAE employs targeted communication strategies to enhance its global reputation. Public diplomacy campaigns utilize multimedia content, including videos, infographics, and interactive tools, to showcase the country's achievements, cultural richness, and vision for the future. By crafting compelling narratives and storytelling, the UAE captures audiences' attention and fosters a deeper understanding of its values and aspirations. Furthermore, the UAE is active at international events, conferences, and exhibitions to showcase its achievements and engage with global stakeholders. By participating in key industry events and diplomatic forums, the UAE amplifies its voice on the world stage and builds valuable relationships with other nations. Through a strategic combination of media outreach, digital engagement, and in-person interactions, the UAE continues to effectively communicate its message and values to a diverse global audience.

Public Relations Campaigns

Public Relations Campaigns play a crucial role in shaping the perception of the UAE on the global stage. By strategically crafting and disseminating messages through various channels, the UAE has effectively conveyed its key values, achievements, and initiatives to a wide audience. These campaigns showcase the country's progress and development, build relationships, foster trust, and engage with stakeholders internationally. One notable example of a successful public relations campaign is the "Year of Tolerance" initiative launched in 2019. This campaign aimed to promote diversity, inclusivity, and understanding in the UAE. Through events, initiatives, and partnerships, the UAE government demonstrated its commitment to tolerance and acceptance, resonating with audiences worldwide and enhancing its reputation as a progressive and harmonious society. Another impactful public relations campaign is the "Hope Probe Mission to Mars." This ambitious project captured global attention and positioned the UAE as a space exploration and innovation leader. Through strategic communication efforts, the UAE highlighted its dedication to scientific progress and its vision for a brighter future. The successful launch of the Hope Probe showcased the country's technological prowess and inspired admiration and respect from the international community. Public Relations Campaigns are a powerful tool for the UAE to amplify its voice, share its achievements, and connect with audiences globally. By crafting compelling narratives, leveraging digital platforms, and engaging with influencers and media outlets, the UAE continues to enhance its reputation, build partnerships, and shape perceptions in alignment with its strategic goals and values.

Evaluating successful public relations campaigns that have enhanced the UAE's reputation.

Successful public relations campaigns have played a paramount role in bolstering the UAE's global reputation and fostering positive perceptions of the nation. From strategic initiatives highlighting the country's advancements in various sectors to campaigns showcasing its vibrant culture and tourism offerings, the UAE has effectively utilized public relations to amplify its voice on the international stage. By collaborating with media outlets, influencers, and key stakeholders, these campaigns have successfully positioned the UAE as a progressive and dynamic country with a rich heritage and a commitment to innovation. Through storytelling and compelling narratives, these campaigns have captured audiences' attention worldwide and helped shape a positive image of the UAE as a forward-thinking and inclusive nation. As the UAE continues to invest in public relations efforts, it will further enhance its global standing and reinforce its reputation as a key player in the international community.

People-to-People Diplomacy

People-to-People Diplomacy Building connections beyond borders, people-to-people diplomacy plays a crucial role in fostering relationships and nurturing trust between nations. In the context of the UAE's foreign policy, this form of diplomacy emphasizes the power of individual interactions in shaping perceptions and enhancing cultural understanding. Through various initiatives and programs, the UAE has actively engaged in people-to-people diplomacy to create channels for dialogue and exchange. By facilitating cultural exchanges, educational opportunities, and collaborative projects, the UAE encourages citizens to connect with individuals worldwide, promoting mutual respect and harmony. One prominent example of people-to-people diplomacy in the UAE is the Sheikh Zayed Grand Mosque, a symbol of openness and tolerance that welcomes visitors of all backgrounds. The mosque serves as a platform for intercultural dialogue and understanding by showcasing the country's commitment to diversity and inclusivity. The UAE's investment in educational exchange programs has also allowed students and academics to engage with international counterparts, fostering relationships beyond borders. The UAE nurtures a community of global citizens committed to advancing knowledge and understanding by promoting academic collaboration and research partnerships. Furthermore, the UAE's support for cultural initiatives and artistic endeavors has enabled artists and creatives to showcase their talents internationally. Through exhibitions, festivals, and cultural events, the UAE promotes cultural diplomacy to bridge divides and celebrate shared humanity. In a world where personal connections hold significant influence, people-to-people diplomacy is a powerful tool for building bridges and forging lasting bonds. By prioritizing interpersonal relationships and citizen diplomacy, the UAE cultivates a network of goodwill that transcends political differences and fosters a sense of global community.

> Emphasizing the importance of interpersonal connections and citizen diplomacy in building relationships and trust.

Building relationships and trust through people-to-people diplomacy is a cornerstone of the UAE's foreign policy strategy. Personal connections and grassroots interactions are vital in fostering understanding and cooperation between nations. By engaging with individuals from diverse backgrounds and cultures, the UAE seeks mutual respect and empathy, laying the foundation for long-term partnerships. Citizen diplomacy initiatives, such as cultural exchanges, youth programs, and community events, enable ordinary people to participate in diplomacy and bridge boundaries. These interactions promote the UAE's values and traditions and facilitate meaningful dialogue and collaboration on shared global challenges. Through people-to-people diplomacy, the UAE aims to empower individuals to become ambassadors of goodwill and cultural exchange. The country cultivates a positive reputation abroad and strengthens its ties with the international community by fostering genuine connections and a spirit of openness and dialogue. In a world where interpersonal relationships are increasingly valued, people-to-people diplomacy is a powerful tool for building bridges of understanding and trust between nations. Investing in grassroots connections and citizen-led initiatives, the UAE is committed to creating a more interconnected and harmonious world, one relationship at a time.

Crisis Communication

Effective communication is pivotal in shaping public perception and maintaining trust during crises. Crisis communication is a strategic effort aimed at managing and mitigating situations that have the potential to impact the UAE's image. In today's interconnected world, crises can arise suddenly and spread rapidly, making it crucial for the UAE to have a proactive and transparent communication strategy. One key aspect of crisis communication is the timely dissemination of accurate information. Keeping the public informed helps to prevent misinformation and speculation from spreading, which can further damage the UAE's reputation. Transparency and honesty are essential during a crisis, as they demonstrate a commitment to addressing the situation and rebuilding trust. In addition to providing information, communication channels must be carefully chosen to ensure the message reaches the intended audience. Utilizing a mix of traditional media, social media platforms, and official statements helps convey a consistent and coherent message to domestic and international audiences. The UAE's government entities and diplomatic missions are crucial in disseminating information and addressing concerns during a crisis. Furthermore, crisis communication involves active engagement with stakeholders, including the public, media, and international partners. By engaging in dialogue and addressing questions and concerns, the UAE can demonstrate transparency and a willingness to work towards resolution. Building solid relationships with key stakeholders is essential for managing crises effectively and maintaining credibility. Another important aspect of crisis communication is preparedness. Developing a comprehensive crisis communication plan that outlines roles and responsibilities, communication protocols, and escalation procedures ensures that the UAE is ready to respond swiftly and effectively in times of crisis. Regular training and simulations can help test the plan's effectiveness and identify areas for improvement. In conclusion, crisis communication is a critical component of public diplomacy that helps to safeguard the UAE's reputation and maintain trust during challenging times. By prioritizing transparency, timely communication, stakeholder engagement, and preparedness, the UAE can effectively manage crises and emerge stronger from adversity.

Addressing the role of public diplomacy in managing and mitigating crises that may impact the UAE's image

During times of crisis, public diplomacy becomes crucial in managing and mitigating any negative impacts on the UAE's image. It is imperative to communicate effectively with various domestic and international stakeholders to provide accurate information and promptly address concerns. Transparency, empathy, and a proactive approach are key components in handling crises effectively. Public diplomacy can help shape the crisis narrative, ensure accurate information is disseminated, and counter any misinformation. By engaging with the media, utilizing social media platforms, and leveraging diplomatic channels, the UAE can maintain control over the messaging and steer the conversation positively. Building trust with the public and other nations is essential in times of crisis, as it helps strengthen relationships and demonstrates the UAE's commitment to transparency and accountability. Engaging in dialogue, assisting those affected, and showcasing resilience in adversity all enhance the country's reputation and credibility. Looking to the future, the UAE can further enhance its crisis communication strategies by investing in advanced technology, training personnel in crisis management, and collaborating with international partners to develop best practices. By continuously evaluating and refining its approach to crisis communication, the UAE can effectively safeguard its image and navigate through turbulent times with confidence and credibility.

Future Outlook

As the landscape of global diplomacy continues to evolve rapidly, the United Arab Emirates must remain proactive in adapting to new trends and challenges in public diplomacy. One key aspect that will shape the future of the UAE's public diplomacy efforts is the increasing importance of digital communication channels. In an era where information travels instantaneously across borders, the UAE must leverage digital platforms to communicate its message to a global audience effectively. Embracing innovative technologies and digital tools will be crucial in maintaining a strong, engaging online presence that resonates with international audiences. Moreover, the UAE should continue prioritizing cultural diplomacy as a cornerstone of its public diplomacy strategy. With its rich heritage and vibrant arts scene, the UAE has a wealth of cultural assets that can be utilized to foster greater understanding and appreciation of the country's unique identity. By showcasing its cultural diversity through exhibitions, performances, and cultural exchanges, the UAE can deepen its connections with people worldwide and promote a positive image internationally. In addition, investing in educational exchange programs and partnerships will be instrumental in building long-lasting relationships and fostering goodwill with countries across the globe. By offering scholarships, internships, and study abroad opportunities, the UAE can attract top talent worldwide and nurture future leaders who deeply understand and appreciate the country. Looking ahead, the UAE must also remain vigilant in managing crises that may arise and impact its reputation. Establishing robust crisis communication protocols and swift response mechanisms will be essential in addressing challenges effectively and maintaining credibility in the eyes of the global community. In conclusion, the future outlook for the UAE's public diplomacy efforts is promising, with opportunities for growth and innovation on the horizon. By embracing digital technologies, prioritizing cultural diplomacy, investing in educational exchanges, and maintaining a proactive approach to crisis communication, the UAE can continue to enhance its reputation on the world stage and build strong, enduring relationships with nations around the globe.

Emerging trends and challenges in public diplomacy and proposing strategies for future success.

As the landscape of international relations continues to evolve rapidly in the digital age, the field of public diplomacy faces new challenges and opportunities. One emerging trend is the increasing importance of digital platforms and social media in shaping perceptions and influencing public opinion. In today's interconnected world, the UAE must strategically leverage these channels to communicate its message and engage with global audiences effectively. Furthermore, the rise of disinformation and fake news poses a significant threat to the credibility of public diplomacy efforts. To combat this challenge, the UAE must prioritize transparency, authenticity, and fact-based communication in its outreach strategies. The UAE can build trust and credibility with international stakeholders by consistently disseminating accurate information and countering misinformation. In addition, the growing emphasis on citizen diplomacy and grassroots movements calls for a more inclusive and participatory approach to public diplomacy. Engaging with diverse communities, fostering dialogue, and empowering individuals to act as ambassadors for the UAE can enhance the country's soft power and influence on the global stage. The UAE should also focus on sustainability and long-term impact in its public diplomacy initiatives. The UAE can build lasting relationships beyond short-term objectives by investing in partnerships, capacity-building programs, and cultural exchanges promoting mutual understanding and cooperation. By adapting to these emerging trends and challenges with innovative strategies and a forward-thinking approach, the UAE can strengthen its public diplomacy efforts and continue to shape positive perceptions of the country in the international community.

In a Nutshell

How Public Diplomacy Is Shaping Perceptions of the UAE

Public diplomacy has become a cornerstone of the UAE's strategy to shape its global image and influence. The UAE has effectively utilized public diplomacy to project a positive image and foster international relationships through cultural diplomacy, educational exchanges, media strategies, and humanitarian initiatives.

The Evolution of Public Diplomacy in the UAE

Public diplomacy in the UAE has evolved significantly over the past few decades. Initially focused on traditional diplomatic channels, the UAE has expanded its approach to include various soft power tools. This evolution is driven by the need to enhance the country's global standing and influence through non-coercive means. Establishing the UAE Soft Power Council in 2017 marked a significant step in institutionalizing public diplomacy efforts, aiming to consolidate the UAE's reputation as a modern, tolerant, and innovative nation[2].

The Role of Government Entities, Agencies, and Institutions

Several government entities and institutions play a crucial role in the UAE's public diplomacy:

- **Ministry of Foreign Affairs and International Cooperation (MOFAIC)**: Oversees public and cultural diplomacy initiatives, supporting UAE missions worldwide[1].
- **Office of Public and Cultural Diplomacy**: Coordinates cultural diplomacy efforts, promoting UAE culture, heritage, and values globally[4].
- **UAE Soft Power Council**: Develop strategies to enhance the UAE's soft power and international reputation[5].

Cultural Diplomacy and the Role of Culture, Arts, and Heritage

Cultural diplomacy is a key component of the UAE's public diplomacy strategy. The UAE leverages its rich cultural heritage and contemporary art scene to foster international understanding and goodwill. Initiatives such as the Louvre Abu

Dhabi, the Sheikh Zayed Grand Mosque, and various cultural festivals showcase the UAE's commitment to cultural exchange and dialogue[1][3].

Educational Exchange Programs

Educational exchange programs are vital for building long-term relationships and enhancing mutual understanding. The UAE offers scholarships and exchange opportunities for students to study abroad, fostering a new generation of leaders with a global perspective. These programs help to create a positive image of the UAE among international students and academics[6][13].

Media and Communication Strategies

The UAE employs sophisticated media and communication strategies to project its image globally. This includes traditional media, social media, and digital platforms to disseminate information and engage with international audiences. The UAE's media strategy promotes its achievements, values, and vision for the future[15].

Public Relations Campaigns and People-to-People Diplomacy

Public relations campaigns enhance the UAE's image and promote its values. These campaigns often coincide with significant national events, such as the Year of Tolerance and the Year of Zayed, highlighting the UAE's commitment to tolerance, innovation, and cultural heritage. People-to-people diplomacy, facilitated through cultural exchanges and international events, further strengthens these efforts[2][14].

Crisis Communication

Effective crisis communication is essential for maintaining the UAE's positive image during challenging times. The UAE has developed robust crisis communication strategies to manage its reputation and provide timely information during crises. This includes coordinated responses from government entities and proactive engagement with international media to ensure accurate and positive coverage[15].

Conclusion

Public diplomacy is critical for the UAE in shaping global perceptions and enhancing its international influence. The UAE has successfully projected an image of a modern, tolerant, and innovative nation through cultural diplomacy, educational exchanges, strategic media engagement, and humanitarian initiatives. These efforts foster international goodwill and support the UAE's broader foreign policy objectives.

XIII

References

[1] https://www.mofa.gov.ae/en/The-Ministry/The-Foreign-Policy/Cultural-and-Public-Diplomacy
[2] https://uscpublicdiplomacy.org/blog/nation-branding-and-public-diplomacy-united-arab-emirates-0
[3] https://globally.org/cultural-diplomacy-exchange
[4] https://www.youtube.com/channel/UChCCN-SUiy9Z1pCMKIGGaS1A
[5] https://wam.ae/en/details/1395302634954
[6] https://www.moe.gov.ae/En/EServices/ServiceCard/Scholarships/Pages/Conditions4.aspx
[7] https://www.prweek.com/middleeast
[8] https://journalse.com/pliki/pw/4-2020-Golebiowski.pdf
[9] https://www.cmi.no/publications/7169-the-uaes-humanitarian-diplomacy-claiming-state-sovereignty
[10] https://www.uae-embassy.org/culture-outreach
[11] https://www.uae-embassy.org/events/uae-diplomacy-history
[12] https://www.fahr.gov.ae/Portal/Userfiles/Assets/Documents/31733b00.pdf

[13] https://www.moe.gov.ae/En/EServices/ServiceCard/Scholarships/pages/exchange.aspx

[14] https://www.linkedin.com/pulse/how-run-successful-pr-campaign-guide-dubai-based-vwyhf?trk=organization_guest_main-feed-card_feed-article-content

[15] http://cscanada.net/index.php/css/article/view/9720

XIV

Climate Diplomacy: Addressing Global Environmental Challenges

Setting the Stage

The global environmental landscape faces unprecedented challenges requiring urgent attention and collective action. Climate change, deforestation, loss of biodiversity, and pollution threaten our planet's health and future generations' well-being. At the same time, these challenges present opportunities for innovation, collaboration, and sustainable development. As we delve into the complexities of the environmental issues facing our world today, it is essential to acknowledge the interconnected nature of these challenges. The impact of climate change knows no boundaries, affecting populations around the globe and jeopardizing the delicate balance of ecosystems. The loss of biodiversity not only diminishes the richness of our natural world but also undermines the resilience of our planet to withstand environmental pressures. In the face of these challenges, there is a growing recognition of the need for concerted efforts to address environmental issues at both the local and global levels. Governments, businesses, civil society organizations, and individuals all have a role to play in safeguarding the environment and promoting sustainable practices. Understanding the complex interplay between human activities and the natural world can pave the way for a more sustainable and resilient future. As we embark on this journey to explore the global environmental landscape, we must approach these issues with urgency, empathy, and determination. Our actions today will have far-reaching consequences for our planet's future and its inhabitants' well-being. Let us confront these challenges head-on and work towards a more sustainable and harmonious relationship with the natural world.

The Global Environmental Landscape: Challenges and Opportunities

The global environmental landscape presents a complex tapestry of challenges and opportunities that require urgent attention from the international community. Climate change, biodiversity loss, deforestation, and pollution are just a few pressing issues facing our planet today. These challenges threaten our ecosystems' health and have far-reaching socioeconomic impacts on communities worldwide. Climate change is perhaps the most significant environmental challenge of our time, with rising global temperatures leading to more frequent and severe natural disasters, shifts in weather patterns, and rising sea levels. Biodiversity loss is another critical issue, as the loss of species diversity can destabilize ecosystems and disrupt essential ecosystem services that support life on Earth. Deforestation contributes to climate change and biodiversity loss, as clearing forests for agriculture, mining, and urban development destroys vital habitats and releases carbon stored in trees into the atmosphere. Pollution, whether from plastic waste, industrial emissions, or agricultural runoff, threatens human health, wildlife, and ecosystems, leading to pollution of waterways, air quality degradation, and biodiversity decline. Despite these challenges, there are also opportunities to address them through innovation, cooperation, and sustainable practices. Advancements in renewable energy technologies offer a pathway to reduce greenhouse gas emissions and transition to a low-carbon economy. Conservation efforts, protected area management, and sustainable land use practices can help preserve biodiversity and restore degraded ecosystems. International cooperation and multilateral agreements, such as the Paris Agreement and the Convention on Biological Diversity, provide frameworks for countries to work together to address these global environmental challenges. By leveraging the latest scientific research, engaging stakeholders at all levels, and implementing holistic strategies, we can seize the opportunities presented by these challenges to create a more resilient and sustainable future for future generations.

UAE's Commitment to Climate Action: Policies and Initiatives

The UAE's Commitment to Climate Action: Policies and Initiatives The UAE has demonstrated a strong commitment to addressing climate change through a series of policies and initiatives to reduce greenhouse gas emissions and promote sustainable development. One of the key initiatives is the UAE Energy Strategy 2050, which aims to increase the share of clean energy in the country's energy mix to 50% by 2050. This includes significant investments in renewable energy sources such as solar and wind power. Furthermore, the UAE has implemented the National Climate Change Plan 2017-2050, which outlines a comprehensive set of actions to reduce carbon emissions across various sectors, including energy, transportation, and industry. The plan emphasizes the importance of transitioning to a low-carbon economy and adapting to the impacts of climate change. In addition to domestic policies, the UAE has also actively promoted climate action on the international stage. The country is a signatory to the Paris Agreement and has set ambitious targets for reducing greenhouse gas emissions. The UAE has also been a key player in initiatives such as the International Renewable Energy Agency (IRENA) and the Abu Dhabi Sustainability Week, which bring together global leaders to discuss renewable energy and sustainability. The UAE's commitment to climate action is reflected in its policies and initiatives to promote sustainable development and reduce carbon emissions. The UAE plays a significant role in combating climate change by investing in clean energy, implementing comprehensive climate change plans, and engaging in international partnerships.

International Partnerships in Climate Diplomacy

The UAE's commitment to climate action is reinforced through its strategic partnerships in climate diplomacy. These partnerships play a crucial role in advancing the global agenda on climate change and enhancing cooperation in addressing environmental challenges. The UAE has actively engaged with international organizations, governments, and non-governmental entities to foster collaboration and exchange best practices in mitigating the impacts of climate change. One key aspect of the UAE's international partnerships in climate diplomacy is its collaboration with other countries in the region and beyond. Through bilateral agreements and multilateral frameworks, the UAE works towards shared goals in reducing carbon emissions, promoting renewable energy sources, and building climate resilience. By exchanging knowledge and expertise with partner countries, the UAE contributes to the collective efforts in combating climate change and achieving sustainable development objectives. Furthermore, the UAE has been a driving force in promoting South-South cooperation on climate action. By leveraging its experience and resources, the UAE supports developing countries in enhancing their capacity to address climate change challenges. Through partnerships with countries in Africa, Asia, and Latin America, the UAE shares technical know-how, provides financial assistance and facilitates technology transfer to accelerate its transition towards a low-carbon economy. In addition to governmental partnerships, the UAE also collaborates with international organizations and initiatives dedicated to climate action. The UAE's involvement in platforms such as the United Nations Framework Convention on Climate Change (UNFCCC), the Intergovernmental Panel on Climate Change (IPCC), and the Global Climate Action Summit demonstrates its commitment to multilateral cooperation in addressing climate change. By participating in these forums, the UAE contributes to shaping global policies and advocating for ambitious climate goals on the international stage. Overall, the UAE's engagement in international partnerships in climate diplomacy underscores its proactive approach to addressing environmental challenges and fostering global cooperation. Through collaborative efforts with diverse stakeholders, the UAE aims to constructively drive the collective response to climate change and promote sustainable development worldwide.

UAE's Role in International Climate Change Negotiations

The United Arab Emirates has been actively engaged in international climate change negotiations, recognizing the critical importance of global cooperation in addressing this pressing issue. As a responsible member of the international community, the UAE has participated in various climate summits and conferences to contribute its expertise and perspectives to the discussions. The UAE has been a vocal advocate for ambitious climate action and has consistently supported efforts to strengthen the global response to climate change. Through active participation in negotiations under the United Nations Framework Convention on Climate Change (UNFCCC), the UAE has emphasized the need for collective action to reduce greenhouse gas emissions and mitigate the impacts of climate change. In international climate change negotiations, the UAE has sought to bridge differences and build consensus among countries with diverse interests and priorities. By fostering dialogue and cooperation, the UAE has played a constructive role in advancing the climate agenda and promoting a shared understanding of the challenges and opportunities that lie ahead. Furthermore, the

UAE has demonstrated leadership in promoting innovative solutions and technologies to address climate change. By showcasing its own initiatives and best practices, the UAE has inspired other countries to adopt sustainable practices and pursue climate-friendly policies. Overall, the UAE's role in international climate change negotiations reflects its commitment to being a responsible global citizen and a proactive partner in the fight against climate change. Through continued engagement and cooperation with the international community, the UAE is poised to significantly contribute to advancing climate action and delivering a sustainable future for future generations.

Climate Finance and Investment: UAE's Contribution

The United Arab Emirates (UAE) has made significant strides in contributing to climate finance and investment on the global stage. Recognizing the urgent need for action to combat climate change, the UAE has focused on mobilizing financial resources to support sustainable development and environmental initiatives. As a responsible global actor, the UAE has committed to investing in projects and programs that promote environmental sustainability and combat climate change. The UAE has actively promoted renewable energy projects both domestically and internationally. Through initiatives such as the UAE's renewable energy program, the country has been a pioneer in developing and deploying clean energy technologies. By investing in renewable energy sources such as solar and wind power, the UAE has reduced its carbon footprint and supported the global transition to a low-carbon economy. In addition to investing in renewable energy, the UAE has prioritized sustainable infrastructure development. By implementing green building practices and sustainable urban planning, the UAE has reduced its environmental impact and promoted eco-friendly living spaces. The country's focus on sustainable infrastructure has benefited the environment, created economic opportunities, and improved the quality of life for its citizens. Furthermore, the UAE has actively engaged in climate finance initiatives at the international level. By contributing to multilateral climate funds and participating in climate finance mechanisms, the UAE has shown a strong commitment to supporting developing countries in their efforts to address climate change. Through financial contributions and technical assistance, the UAE has played a key role in advancing global climate action and promoting environmental sustainability. Overall, the UAE's contribution to climate finance and investment demonstrates its leadership in addressing climate change and promoting sustainable development on a global scale. By investing in renewable energy, sustainable infrastructure, and international climate finance initiatives, the UAE has shown its dedication to building a more sustainable and environmentally conscious future for current and future generations.

Technology and Innovation in Climate Diplomacy

The UAE has emerged as a global leader in leveraging technology and innovation to address climate change. Through its forward-thinking approach, the country has deployed cutting-edge solutions to reduce carbon emissions, increase energy efficiency, and promote sustainability. One notable area where the UAE has excelled is developing renewable energy technologies. The country has invested heavily in solar and wind power projects, such as the Mohammed bin Rashid Al Maktoum Solar Park and the Sweihan Wind Farm. These initiatives contribute to reducing reliance on fossil fuels and drive innovation in the field of clean energy. Furthermore, the UAE has been at the forefront of promoting smart cities and sustainable urban development. By incorporating advanced technologies such as the Internet of Things (IoT), artificial intelligence, and data analytics, the country can optimize resource management, enhance infrastructure efficiency, and improve its residents' overall quality of life. In transportation, the UAE has been exploring innovative solutions to reduce carbon emissions and promote eco-friendly modes of mobility. Initiatives such as electric vehicle charging infrastructure, autonomous transportation systems, and sustainable aviation fuels are all part of the country's efforts to build a greener and more sustainable transportation sector. Through its focus on technology and innovation in climate diplomacy, the UAE is addressing domestic environmental challenges and positioning itself as a key player in the global fight against climate change. By harnessing the power of innovation, the country is paving the way for a more sustainable future for generations to come.

Environmental Sustainability in UAE's Foreign Policy Agenda

Environmental sustainability is a core pillar of the UAE's foreign policy agenda. Recognizing the urgent need for collective action to address environmental challenges, the UAE has integrated sustainability principles into its diplomatic endeavors. Through a multifaceted approach, the UAE seeks to promote sustainable practices, protect biodiversity, and mitigate the impact of climate change on a global scale. The UAE's commitment to environmental sustainability is evident in its support for international agreements and initiatives to tackle climate change and preserve natural resources. By ratifying key treaties such as the Paris Agreement and the Convention on Biological Diversity, the UAE has demonstrated its dedication to upholding global environmental standards. In addition to advocacy and policy initiatives, the UAE actively promotes sustainable development through investments in renewable energy and green technologies. The country's ambitious renewable energy targets and innovative projects, such as the Mohammed bin Rashid Al Maktoum Solar Park, showcase its leadership in transitioning to a low-carbon economy. Furthermore, the UAE recognizes the interconnectedness of environmental sustainability and socio-economic development. By championing sustainable practices in sectors such as agriculture, water management, and waste reduction, the country aims to create a more resilient and environmentally conscious society. Through collaboration with international partners, the UAE leverages its expertise in environmental sustainability to address global challenges such as desertification, water scarcity, and air pollution. By sharing best practices and promoting knowledge exchange, the UAE contributes to a more sustainable future for the planet. By embedding environmental sustainability into its foreign policy agenda, the UAE reaffirms its commitment to being a responsible global citizen and a proactive agent for positive change in environmental conservation and sustainable development.

Addressing Climate Migration and Adaptation

Climate migration and adaptation are pressing issues today, with rising sea levels, extreme weather events, and environmental degradation threatening communities worldwide. The UAE has recognized the importance of addressing these challenges and has incorporated climate migration and adaptation into its foreign policy agenda. In response to the increasing risks of climate-induced migration, the UAE has focused on enhancing resilience and preparedness in vulnerable regions. Through partnerships with international organizations and other countries, the UAE has supported initiatives to assist communities at risk of displacement due to climate change impacts. By providing resources and expertise, the UAE has demonstrated its commitment to addressing the humanitarian aspects of climate migration. In addition to addressing climate-induced migration, the UAE has also prioritized adaptation strategies to mitigate the impacts of climate change. Investing in sustainable infrastructure, promoting water conservation and efficient resource management, and implementing nature-based solutions are key measures the UAE has undertaken to adapt to a changing climate. By taking proactive steps to build resilience and reduce vulnerability, the UAE sets an example for effective climate adaptation strategies. Furthermore, the UAE has engaged in diplomatic efforts to foster collaboration on climate migration and adaptation at the international level. Through participation in multilateral forums and dialogues, the UAE has advocated for collective action to address the challenges posed by climate-induced migration and promote adaptive solutions. The UAE contributes to global efforts to build a more sustainable and resilient future by sharing knowledge, best practices, and innovative approaches. As climate change continues to threaten communities worldwide, the UAE's proactive stance on climate migration and adaptation underscores its leadership in addressing environmental challenges. By prioritizing sustainable development, resilience-building, and international cooperation, the UAE is playing a crucial role in shaping a more secure and sustainable world in the face of climate change.

Conclusion: The UAE's Leadership in Global Climate Diplomacy

The UAE's leadership in global climate diplomacy is both exemplary and forward-thinking. The country has positioned itself as a key player in shaping international responses to environmental challenges by addressing the pressing issues of climate migration and adaptation. Through its proactive policies and initiatives, the UAE has demonstrated a strong commitment to sustainable development and cooperation on a global scale. As a bridge between the developed and developing world, the UAE has sought to foster meaningful dialogue and collaboration to address the urgent need for climate action. By investing in technology and innovation, the country has shown that achieving economic growth is possible while prioritizing environmental sustainability. The UAE's role in international climate change negotiations has been instrumental in driving consensus and advancing solutions that benefit both people and the planet. The UAE has leveraged its resources and expertise through strategic alliances and partnerships to support climate finance and investment in vulnerable regions. As the world faces increasingly complex challenges related to climate change, the UAE's leadership in global climate diplomacy serves as a beacon of hope and inspiration for a more sustainable future.

In a Nutshell

Climate Diplomacy and How the UAE Addresses Global Environmental Challenges

The UAE has taken a proactive role in addressing global environmental challenges through its climate diplomacy. This approach encompasses a range of strategies, from international partnerships to investments in renewable energy and climate finance. Here's an in-depth look at how the UAE is tackling these issues:

Global Environmental Landscape

The global environmental landscape is characterized by pressing issues such as climate change, biodiversity loss, and pollution. These challenges are exacerbated by fossil fuel consumption, deforestation, and poor governance[1][3]. The UAE recognizes these global challenges and has positioned itself as a leader in climate action, particularly in the Middle East.

UAE's Commitment to Climate Action

The UAE has made significant commitments to climate action, including being the first country in the Gulf Cooperation Council (GCC) to ratify the Paris Agreement in 2016[5]. The UAE's Net Zero by 2050 strategy, announced in 2022, underscores its commitment to reducing carbon emissions and transitioning to a sustainable economy[4]. Hosting COP28 in 2023 demonstrated the UAE's dedication to leading global climate discussions[12].

International Partnerships in Climate Diplomacy

The UAE has established numerous international partnerships to advance its climate diplomacy. These include collaborations with the United States on renewable energy projects and the Agriculture Innovation Mission for Climate (AIM for Climate)[4]. The UAE also partners with the United Nations Climate Security Mechanism to address the interlinkages between climate change, peace, and security[8][20].

UAE's Role in International Climate Change Negotiations

The UAE plays a significant role in international climate change negotiations. As the host of COP28, the UAE led efforts to reach a historic agreement on transitioning away from fossil fuels and increasing renewable energy capacity[11][12]. The UAE's leadership in these negotiations reflects its strategic vision and commitment to global climate goals.

Climate Finance and Investment

The UAE is a major player in climate finance, investing heavily in domestic and international renewable energy projects. The UAE has provided over $1.5 billion in aid for renewable energy projects in more than 40 developing countries[11]. The UAE's financial institutions are also developing frameworks to support sustainable investments and green finance initiatives[13].

Technology and Innovation in Climate Diplomacy

Innovation and technology are central to the UAE's climate diplomacy. The country has invested in cutting-edge technologies such as AI and machine learning to address climate challenges. Initiatives like the ACT28 AI for Climate Hackathon highlight the UAE's commitment to leveraging technology for sustainable solutions[6]. Projects like Masdar City and the Mohammed bin Rashid Al Maktoum Solar Park are examples of the UAE's innovative approach to sustainability[4].

Environmental Sustainability in UAE's Foreign Policy Agenda

Environmental sustainability is a key component of the UAE's foreign policy. The UAE's efforts to promote renewable energy, reduce carbon emissions, and support sustainable development are integral to its international engagements. The UAE's participation in multilateral organizations like the International Renewable Energy Agency (IRENA) underscores its commitment to global sustainability[11].

Addressing Climate Migration and Adaptation

The UAE recognizes the importance of addressing climate migration and adaptation. The UAE supports initiatives to enhance climate resilience and adaptation in vulnerable regions through partnerships with international organizations. The UAE's contributions to the UN Climate Security Mechanism include funding for climate advisors in countries like Afghanistan to assess and mitigate climate-related security risks[20].

Conclusion

The UAE's climate diplomacy is characterized by a comprehensive approach that includes international partnerships, significant investments in renewable energy, and a commitment to innovation and technology. By addressing global environmental challenges through these strategies, the UAE enhances its sustainability and contributes to global efforts to combat climate change. The UAE's proactive stance in climate diplomacy positions it as a leader in transitioning towards a more sustainable and resilient global future.

XV

References

[1] https://earth.org/the-biggest-environmental-problems-of-our-lifetime/
[2] https://www.wwf.eu
[3] https://www.tariff.com/news-and-insights/the-10-biggest-environmental-issues-of-2024/
[4] https://www.uae-embassy.org/sites/default/files/2024-04/Climate_White%20Paper_04.27.2024.pdf
[5] https://impact.economist.com/perspectives/health/uae-recognises-need-act-climate-change-fast
[6] https://www.undp.org/policy-centre/istanbul/press-releases/samsung-and-undp-award-winners-act28-ai-climate-hackathon-uaes-ai-retreat-2024
[7] https://wam.ae/en/article/b43azr7-uae-lays-out-priorities-for-sustainable
[8] https://mptf.undp.org/news/uae-partners-un-climate-security-mechanism-advance-climate-peace-and-security-agenda
[9] https://www.diplomatie.gouv.fr/en/country-files/united-arab-emirates/events/article/advancing-strategic-bilateral-relations-

highlights-from-the-16th-uae-france
[10] https://www.bbc.com/news/science-environment-67508331
[11] https://www.uae-embassy.org/discover-uae/climate-and-energy/international-engagement
[12] https://www.iris-france.org/181019-cop28-in-the-united-arab-emirates-a-diplomatic-victory-for-the-gulf-states/
[13] https://www.cityweekuk.com/city-week-2024/blog-building-the-uaes-sustainable-finance-ecosystem
[14] https://www.moccae.gov.ae/en/media-center/news/13/3/2024/uae-council-for-climate-action-assesses-progress-in-national-initiatives-aimed-at-achieving-climate-sustainability-and-establishes-action-plan-for-2024.aspx
[15] https://sdg.iisd.org/news/world-bank-to-act-as-host-and-trustee-for-fund-for-responding-to-loss-and-damage/
[16] https://www3.weforum.org/docs/WEF_The_Global_Risks_Report_2024.pdf
[17] https://www.unep.org/news-and-stories/speech/turning-corner-environmental-crises-2024
[18] https://climateactiontracker.org/countries/uae/
[19] https://www.wam.ae/en/article/b43azr7-uae-lays-out-priorities-for-sustainable
[20] https://www.mofa.gov.ae/en/mediahub/news/2024/4/3/3-4-2024-uae-afghanistan

XVI

Cybersecurity and Digital Diplomacy: Protecting National Interests

Cybersecurity and Digital Diplomacy

Cybersecurity and digital diplomacy are critical components of modern statecraft, given the increasing reliance on digital technologies in all aspects of society. In today's interconnected world, where information travels at the speed of light, protecting sensitive data and networks from cyber threats is essential to safeguarding national security and maintaining stability. As more aspects of governance, commerce, and social interaction move online, the need for robust cybersecurity measures becomes ever more pressing. Digital diplomacy, a relatively new but rapidly evolving field, leverages digital tools and platforms to advance a country's foreign policy objectives, engage with international audiences, and shape global perceptions. By understanding the intersections of cybersecurity and digital diplomacy, nations can navigate the complexities of the digital age and harness the power of technology for diplomatic ends.

The Importance of Cybersecurity in Today's Digital Age

In today's interconnected world, the significance of cybersecurity cannot be overstated. As our societies and economies become increasingly digitized, the threat landscape continues to evolve, presenting new challenges and risks that must be addressed proactively. Cybersecurity is not just a technical issue but a critical aspect of national security and a fundamental component of modern diplomacy. Cyberattacks can have devastating consequences, from disrupting essential services to compromising sensitive data and undermining trust in institutions. Governments, businesses, and individuals are all potential targets of cyber threats, and the stakes are higher than ever. In this digital age, protecting critical infrastructure, intellectual property, and personal information requires robust cybersecurity measures to safeguard against malicious actors and ensure the stability and security of our interconnected systems. As more aspects of our lives move online, the need for strong cybersecurity practices becomes even more pressing. The proliferation of internet-connected devices and the rise of artificial intelligence and big data have transformed how we interact, work, and communicate. While these advancements offer tremendous opportunities for innovation and growth, they also create new vulnerabilities that cyber adversaries can exploit. Cybersecurity is not just a technical challenge but also a diplomatic imperative. Cooperation and collaboration are essential in an age where cyber threats transcend borders and impact international relations. By building alliances and sharing information with other countries, the UAE can strengthen its cybersecurity defenses and respond effectively to cyber incidents threatening its national interests. In conclusion, the importance of cybersecurity in today's digital age cannot be understated. As technology advances and connectivity expands, safeguarding our digital assets and infrastructure is paramount. By prioritizing cybersecurity and embracing a proactive approach to cyber defense, the UAE can protect its citizens, businesses, and critical assets in an increasingly complex and interconnected world.

Understanding the Threat Landscape: Cyber Risks and Challenges

In today's interconnected digital world, cybersecurity threats significantly challenge governments, organizations, and individuals. The evolving nature of cyber risks and the increasing sophistication of cyber attackers necessitate a comprehensive understanding of the threat landscape. Cyber risks encompass many threats, including data breaches, ransomware attacks, phishing scams, and malicious hacking activities. These threats can target critical infrastructure, financial systems, government institutions, and private businesses, posing severe implications for national security and economic stability. One of the key challenges in combating cyber threats is the constantly evolving nature of the cyber landscape. Cyber attackers are constantly developing new tactics and techniques to exploit vulnerabilities in systems and networks. This dynamic environment requires continuous monitoring, assessment, and adaptation of cybersecurity measures to stay ahead of potential threats. Moreover, the interconnected nature of the digital world means that geographical borders do not confine cyber risks. Cyber attacks can originate from anywhere worldwide and target entities in any location. This globalized threat landscape underscores the importance of international cooperation and collaboration in addressing cyber risks. As technology advances and digitization becomes increasingly prevalent, the need for robust cybersecurity measures becomes more critical. Protecting national interests in the digital age requires a proactive and multi-faceted approach that combines technical solutions, policy frameworks, and international partnerships to mitigate cyber risks and safeguard critical infrastructure and information assets.

The Role of Digital Diplomacy in Protecting National Interests

Digital diplomacy is crucial in safeguarding a nation's interests in the modern age of technology and interconnectedness. As the digital landscape evolves rapidly, traditional diplomatic practices are increasingly being complemented by digital tools and platforms. In cybersecurity, digital diplomacy is vital in protecting national interests against a wide range of cyber threats and challenges. Digital diplomacy enables governments to engage with other nations, international organizations, and non-state actors in the digital sphere to advance their national security objectives. By leveraging various digital channels such as social media, websites, and communication platforms, diplomats can communicate with a wide audience, shape narratives, and influence perceptions on critical issues related to cybersecurity and national interests. Moreover, digital diplomacy enhances transparency and accountability in cyberspace by promoting responsible behavior and adherence to international norms and agreements. Through digital channels, governments can share information, exchange best practices, and collaborate on cybersecurity initiatives to mitigate risks and build mutual trust. In protecting national interests, digital diplomacy allows governments to share information, coordinate cyber incident response, and joint capacity-building efforts with other countries. By promoting a multilateral approach to cybersecurity through digital diplomacy, nations can collectively address shared cyber threats and vulnerabilities, thereby enhancing their overall security posture. The UAE has recognized the importance of digital diplomacy in protecting its national interests and has proactively engaged in cyber diplomacy initiatives at both regional and global levels. By promoting cybersecurity norms, fostering international cooperation, and investing in cybersecurity capabilities, the UAE has demonstrated its commitment to safeguarding its digital infrastructure and maintaining a secure cyber environment for its citizens and businesses.

Strategies for Enhancing Cybersecurity: The UAE's Approach

The UAE's approach to enhancing cybersecurity is rooted in a comprehensive strategy encompassing various initiatives to safeguard the nation's digital infrastructure and protect its national interests. One key aspect of this approach is the establishment of robust legal frameworks and regulations that govern cybersecurity practices and ensure compliance across all sectors. The UAE has enacted laws such as the Cybercrime Law and the Data Protection Regulation, which provide a legal framework for combating cyber threats and safeguarding data privacy. In addition to legal measures, the UAE strongly emphasizes building a skilled workforce capable of addressing evolving cyber threats. Through initiatives such as the UAE Cybersecurity Strategy and the National Cybersecurity Council, the country invests in training programs, certifications, and capacity building to develop a pool of cybersecurity professionals equipped to mitigate risks and respond to cyber incidents effectively. The UAE's approach to enhancing cybersecurity also fosters collaboration between government entities, the private sector, and international partners. By promoting information sharing, joint exercises, and cybersecurity awareness campaigns, the UAE aims to create a unified front against cyber threats and enhance cyber resilience at both the national and organizational levels. Moreover, the UAE is actively investing in advanced technologies and tools to bolster its cybersecurity defenses. From deploying cutting-edge security solutions to leveraging artificial intelligence and machine learning for threat detection and response, the country continuously innovates to stay ahead of cyber adversaries and protect its critical infrastructure. Overall, the UAE's multifaceted approach to enhancing cybersecurity reflects its commitment to securing its digital assets, promoting a safe cyber environment, and safeguarding its national interests in an increasingly interconnected world. By integrating legal frameworks, capacity-building efforts, collaboration initiatives, and technological innovations, the UAE is well-positioned to address present and emerging cyber challenges effectively.

Capacity Building and Cyber Resilience

Capacity building plays a crucial role in strengthening cybersecurity and enhancing cyber resilience. It involves developing the necessary skills, knowledge, and capabilities within an organization or a country to effectively prevent, detect, respond to, and recover from cyber threats and attacks. In the context of the UAE's approach to cybersecurity, capacity building is a key priority. The UAE recognizes the importance of investing in human capital to address cybersecurity challenges effectively. Training programs, workshops, and certifications are provided to government officials, cybersecurity professionals, and other stakeholders to enhance their expertise in cybersecurity best practices and emerging technologies. By building a skilled workforce, the UAE aims to stay ahead of cyber threats and protect its critical infrastructure and digital assets. In addition to human capital development, the UAE enhances technical capabilities and resources to bolster cyber resilience. This includes investing in advanced technologies and tools for monitoring, threat intelligence, incident response, and recovery. By deploying cutting-edge cybersecurity solutions and infrastructure, the UAE aims to detect and mitigate cyber threats in real time and minimize the impact of potential attacks. Furthermore, the UAE strongly emphasizes collaboration and information sharing among government agencies, private sector entities, academia, and international partners. By fostering a culture of cooperation and coordination, the

UAE can leverage diverse expertise and resources to address complex cybersecurity challenges. Through joint exercises, information exchanges, and public-private partnerships, the UAE enhances its cyber resilience and strengthens its ability to respond to evolving cyber threats effectively. Capacity building and cyber resilience are integral components of the UAE's cybersecurity strategy. Investing in human capital and technical capabilities and fostering collaboration, the UAE is better equipped to protect its critical infrastructure, digital assets, and national interests in an increasingly digitized and interconnected world.

International Cooperation in Cybersecurity: Partnerships and Alliances

International cooperation is essential in cybersecurity to address the ever-evolving nature of cyber threats. The UAE recognizes the importance of collaborating with international partners and forging alliances to enhance its cybersecurity capabilities. The UAE can share information, best practices, and technologies to strengthen its cyber defenses by working with other countries and organizations. Partnerships and alliances in cybersecurity allow for the exchange of threat intelligence and the coordination of response efforts in case of cyberattacks. The UAE engages in joint exercises, workshops, and information-sharing initiatives with its partners to enhance its cyber resilience. Through these collaborations, the UAE can leverage the expertise and resources of other nations to bolster its cybersecurity posture. Furthermore, international cooperation is crucial in setting norms, standards, and regulations in the cyberspace domain. The UAE actively participates in international forums and organizations dedicated to cybersecurity, contributing to developing global cybersecurity frameworks. The UAE can ensure greater interoperability and consistency in its cybersecurity efforts by aligning with international norms and best practices. In addition, partnerships in cybersecurity enable the UAE to address transnational cyber threats that extend beyond its borders. Cybercrime and malicious activities do not recognize national boundaries, making cross-border cooperation vital in combating cyber threats effectively. By collaborating with international partners, the UAE can enhance its ability to detect, prevent, and respond to cyber incidents that have global implications. In conclusion, international cooperation in cybersecurity provides the UAE with a strategic advantage in safeguarding its digital infrastructure and national interests. The UAE can enhance its cybersecurity capabilities, promote cybersecurity norms, and address transnational cyber threats more effectively by building partnerships and alliances with other nations and organizations.

Balancing Security and Privacy in the Digital Diplomacy Framework

Balancing security and privacy in the digital diplomacy framework is a complex and intricate task that requires careful consideration and strategic planning. In an age where digital technologies are increasingly pervasive in all aspects of society, finding the right balance between ensuring national security and protecting individual privacy has become a pressing challenge for policymakers and diplomats worldwide. The United Arab Emirates (UAE) has recognized this challenge and has implemented a range of measures to address it within its digital diplomacy framework. One of the key principles guiding the UAE's approach to balancing security and privacy is the adoption of robust cybersecurity measures that safeguard the country's critical infrastructure and sensitive information. The UAE aims to protect its digital assets from cyber threats and unauthorized access by investing in advanced technologies and cybersecurity capabilities. This proactive stance on cybersecurity enhances national security and helps maintain trust and confidence in the UAE's digital infrastructure. At the same time, the UAE is committed to upholding the privacy rights of its citizens and residents in the digital realm. Through the implementation of data protection laws and regulations, the UAE seeks to ensure that personal information is handled responsibly and ethically by both public and private sector entities. By prioritizing privacy protection, the UAE aims to create a secure and trustworthy digital environment that respects individuals' rights to privacy. In digital diplomacy, the UAE recognizes the importance of open communication and transparency in its interactions with other countries and international organizations. By promoting dialogue and collaboration on cybersecurity issues, the UAE seeks to build trust and cooperation with its partners in the global community. This collaborative approach enhances cybersecurity resilience and fosters a culture of mutual understanding and respect in the digital domain. In conclusion, balancing security and privacy in the digital diplomacy framework is a delicate balancing act requiring a nuanced approach and a commitment to protecting national interests and individual rights. By adopting a comprehensive cybersecurity strategy, respecting privacy rights, and promoting international cooperation, the UAE is well-positioned to navigate the complex challenges of the digital age while upholding its values and interests on the global stage.

Case Studies: Successful Cybersecurity Initiatives in the UAE

The UAE has proactively implemented cybersecurity initiatives to safeguard its national interests and critical infrastructure. One notable case study is the establishment of the UAE Cyber Security Council, which serves as the central authority for cybersecurity policy-making and coordination in the country. The council brings together government entities, private sector organizations, and academia to collaborate on cybersecurity initiatives and share best practices. Another successful cybersecurity initiative in the UAE is the Dubai Electronic Security Center (DESC), which focuses on securing the emirate's digital infrastructure and data. DESC works closely with government entities and private sector organizations to enhance cybersecurity capabilities through training programs, cybersecurity assessments, and incident response coordination. The UAE's national cybersecurity strategy, launched in 2019, outlines the country's vision for cybersecurity and sets clear objectives to enhance cybersecurity resilience. The strategy emphasizes the importance of international cooperation and public-private partnerships in addressing cybersecurity challenges. Furthermore, the UAE has made significant investments in cybersecurity research and development, establishing cybersecurity innovation hubs and centers of excellence. These initiatives help drive innovation in cybersecurity technologies and solutions, positioning the UAE as a regional leader in cybersecurity expertise. One of the key success factors of the UAE's cybersecurity initiatives is its focus on continuous monitoring and threat intelligence sharing. By leveraging advanced technologies and threat intelligence capabilities, the UAE government and private sector organizations can detect and respond to cyber threats in real time, enhancing overall cybersecurity posture. These case studies demonstrate the UAE's commitment to cybersecurity excellence and its proactive approach to addressing cyber threats. Through strategic investments, collaboration, and innovation, the UAE continues to strengthen its cybersecurity capabilities and ensure the security of its digital infrastructure and data assets.

Future Trends and Emerging Technologies in Cybersecurity and Digital Diplomacy

Advanced technologies such as artificial intelligence (AI), blockchain, and quantum computing are expected to shape the future of cybersecurity and digital diplomacy significantly. AI-powered solutions can enhance threat detection and response capabilities, offering real-time analysis of vast amounts of data to identify potential security breaches. Blockchain technology, known for its decentralized and secure nature, can strengthen data protection and authentication processes in diplomatic communications and transactions. Quantum computing, with its immense processing power, may revolutionize encryption methods, making it more challenging for cybercriminals to breach digital defenses. Moreover, the Internet of Things (IoT) poses opportunities and challenges in cybersecurity and digital diplomacy. While IoT devices offer excellent connectivity and efficiency in communication, they also introduce vulnerabilities that malicious actors can exploit. Securing IoT networks and devices will be crucial in safeguarding sensitive information and maintaining diplomatic integrity in the digital realm.

As the digital landscape continues to evolve, collaboration between governments, private sector entities, and international organizations will be essential in addressing emerging cybersecurity threats and ensuring the effective practice of digital diplomacy. Establishing global norms and standards for cyberspace, promoting information sharing and capacity-building initiatives, and fostering a culture of cyber resilience will be key priorities in navigating the future cybersecurity and digital diplomacy trends. Adapting to technological advancements and staying ahead of potential cyber threats will be imperative for governments and diplomatic entities to safeguard national interests and maintain trust and credibility in the digital domain.

In A Nutshell

Based on the search results and the query, here's an analysis of how cybersecurity and digital diplomacy protect UAE national interests:

Cyber Risks and Challenges:

The UAE faces significant cybersecurity challenges as it rapidly digitizes its economy and government services. Key risks include:

- Ransomware attacks, which represent over half of cyber incidents targeting the UAE
- Threats to critical infrastructure, especially in the government, energy, and IT sectors

- Business email compromise and phishing attacks
- Distributed denial of service (DDoS) attacks
- Advanced persistent threats from state-sponsored actors

The UAE Cybersecurity Report 2024 identified over 155,000 vulnerable assets within the country, with 40% of critical vulnerabilities remaining unaddressed for over 5 years. This highlights the urgent need to enhance cyber defenses.

The Role of Digital Diplomacy in Protecting National Interests:

Digital diplomacy plays a crucial role in protecting UAE interests by:

- Promoting the UAE's technological achievements and innovation agenda globally
- Building strategic partnerships on cybersecurity with other nations
- Engaging in multilateral forums to shape global cyber norms and policies
- Using social media and digital platforms to enhance the UAE's soft power and international influence
- Countering disinformation and shaping positive narratives about the UAE online

Strategies for Enhancing Cybersecurity - The UAE's Approach:

The UAE has adopted a multi-pronged approach to strengthen cybersecurity:

- Establishing the UAE Cyber Security Council to coordinate national cybersecurity efforts
- Implementing the National Cybersecurity Strategy
- Enacting comprehensive data protection and cybercrime laws
- Investing heavily in cybersecurity technologies and infrastructure
- Promoting public-private partnerships to enhance cyber capabilities
- Conducting regular cyber drills and exercises, like the "Cyber 193" global exercise

Capacity Building and Cyber Resilience:

The UAE is focused on building long-term cyber resilience through:

- Developing local cybersecurity talent and expertise
- Investing in cybersecurity education and training programs
- Establishing cybersecurity innovation hubs and accelerators
- Promoting cybersecurity awareness among citizens and businesses
- Enhancing incident response capabilities through initiatives like the National Computer Emergency Response Team (CERT)

International Cooperation in Cybersecurity:

The UAE actively engages in international cybersecurity cooperation through:

- Bilateral cybersecurity agreements with strategic partners
- Participation in multilateral cybersecurity initiatives and forums
- Hosting international cybersecurity conferences and events
- Sharing threat intelligence with global partners
- Supporting capacity-building efforts in developing countries

Balancing Security and Privacy in the Digital Diplomacy Framework:

The UAE aims to balance security and privacy concerns by:

- Implementing comprehensive data protection laws aligned with global standards
- Promoting transparency in government data practices
- Engaging with civil society on digital rights issues
- Participating in international dialogues on Internet governance and digital rights
- Investing in privacy-enhancing technologies

In conclusion, the UAE leverages both robust cybersecurity measures and strategic digital diplomacy to protect its national interests in cyberspace. By combining technological solutions, policy frameworks, capacity building, and international cooperation, the UAE aims to secure its digital assets while promoting its image as a global technology leader.

XVII

References

[1] https://www.mitsloanme.com/article/cybersecurity-threats-just-got-worse-in-the-uae-heres-what-you-can-do/
[2] https://cpx.net/media-center/press-releases/state-of-cybersecurity-in-the-uae/
[3] https://ijoc.org/index.php/ijoc/article/viewFile/16150/3583
[4] https://dergipark.org.tr/en/download/article-file/2880716
[5] https://www.cpx.net/media/hocl331j/state-of-the-uae-cybersecurity-report.pdf
[6] https://uae.cysecglobal.com
[7] https://wam.ae/en/article/b1oz4ju-international-cooperation-key-combatting-cyber
[8] https://www.itu.int/hub/2023/11/cooperation-is-key-for-a-safe-and-secure-digital-transformation/
[9] https://www.diplomacy.edu/topics/digital-diplomacy/
[10] https://cms.law/en/int/expert-guides/cms-expert-guide-to-data-protection-and-cyber-security-laws/uae
[11] https://gbsits.com/the-state-of-the-uae-cybersecurity-report-2024/

[12] https://www.tandfonline.com/doi/full/10.1080/23311886.2024.2371665
[13] https://www.cio.com/article/2127704/navigating-the-cyber-security-threat-landscape-in-the-uae-strategies-for-cisos.html
[14] https://www.velatia.com/en/blog/the-united-arab-emirates-organised-a-global-exercise-to-curb-cyber-attacks/
[15] https://www2.deloitte.com/xe/en/pages/risk/articles/advancing-cyber-security-agenda-in-the-uae.html
[16] https://resourcehub.bakermckenzie.com/en/resources/global-data-privacy-and-cybersecurity-handbook/emea/uae/topics/key-data-privacy-and-cybersecurity-laws

XVIII

The Future of UAE Foreign Policy: Opportunities and Challenges

The Evolving Landscape of Global Politics

The global political landscape is continuously evolving, shaped by a complex interplay of factors that impact nations across the globe. In this dynamic environment, the United Arab Emirates (UAE) finds itself at a pivotal juncture, navigating a shifting geopolitical terrain that presents challenges and opportunities for its foreign policy agenda. As we delve into the intricacies of this evolving landscape, it is essential to understand the key drivers and trends shaping the future of global politics. One of the central themes defining this new era of international relations is the emergence of multipolarity, characterized by the rise of multiple power centers and the increasing interconnectivity of nations. As traditional power structures transform, new alliances and rivalries form, creating a more fluid and unpredictable geopolitical environment. This shift towards multipolarity requires the UAE to adopt a nuanced and flexible approach to its foreign policy as it seeks to navigate a complex web of relationships and competing interests on the world stage. At the same time, technological advancements are playing an increasingly prominent role in shaping global politics, with digitization and innovation revolutionizing diplomacy and communication channels. The UAE's embrace of technology as a key driver of economic growth and development positions it at the forefront of this digital frontier, enhancing its capacity to engage with the international community in new and innovative ways. By leveraging technology, the UAE can amplify its voice and influence in global affairs, shaping the discourse on critical issues and fostering closer ties with partners worldwide. Moreover, the growing interconnectedness of economies and societies through globalization has profound implications for the conduct of foreign policy. As borders blur and barriers to trade and communication dissolve, the UAE must adapt to a world where transnational challenges such as climate change, pandemics, and terrorism require collective action and cooperation among nations. Embracing this interdependence, the UAE has the opportunity to play a leading role in driving global solutions to pressing global issues, demonstrating its commitment to multilateralism and international solidarity. In light of these transformative trends, the UAE's foreign policy is undergoing a period of adaptation and evolution as it seeks to position itself as a proactive and strategic player in the rapidly changing landscape of global politics. By embracing innovation, fostering partnerships, and addressing shared challenges, the UAE is poised to shape the course of international relations in the coming years, advancing its interests and contributing to global peace and prosperity.

Shifting Geopolitical Dynamics: Impact on UAE Foreign Policy

The shifting geopolitical dynamics in the global arena have significant implications for the UAE's foreign policy priorities. As traditional power structures evolve and new geopolitical fault lines emerge, the UAE must navigate a complex and dynamic landscape to safeguard its national interests and maintain regional stability. The rise of non-traditional threats such as cyber warfare, terrorism, and climate change further complicates the geopolitical environment, emphasizing the need for a multifaceted and adaptive foreign policy approach. The UAE's strategic location at the crossroads of key geopolitical regions, its robust economy, and its growing influence in international affairs have positioned the country as a key player in shaping regional and global dynamics. As traditional alliances are re-evaluated and new partnerships are forged, the UAE must carefully calibrate its foreign policy to leverage opportunities for economic growth, enhance security cooperation, and promote stability in the region. The UAE's leadership has demonstrated a keen understanding of the evolving geopolitical landscape, consistently prioritizing strategic partnerships and diplomatic initiatives to advance the country's interests on the global stage. By engaging with a diverse array of countries and international organizations, the UAE has effectively navigated geopolitical challenges and seized opportunities for economic development and cultural exchange. As the world continues to grapple with the repercussions of the global pandemic and the economic fallout resulting from it, the UAE's foreign policy will be tested in new and unprecedented ways. Adapting to the evolving geopolitical dynamics, the UAE must remain agile and proactive in responding to emerging challenges while capitalizing on economic opportunities to drive sustainable growth and prosperity for its citizens. In conclusion, the UAE's foreign policy must remain dynamic and responsive to shifting geopolitical dynamics to safeguard its interests and maintain its position as a regional leader in a rapidly changing world.

Economic Opportunities and Challenges in a Post-Pandemic World

The global economy has undergone significant transformations after the COVID-19 pandemic, presenting opportunities and challenges for the United Arab Emirates (UAE). As the world grapples with the economic fallout of the crisis, the UAE finds itself at a critical juncture, poised to navigate the complexities of a post-pandemic world. The pandemic has accelerated digitalization and innovation across industries, highlighting the importance of adaptability and resilience in the face of unprecedented challenges. The UAE's robust infrastructure and strategic investments in technology position it well to capitalize on emerging economic opportunities in a rapidly evolving global landscape. At the same time, the pandemic has underscored the interconnectedness of economies and the need for enhanced cooperation and collaboration at the international level. As the UAE looks to rebuild and revitalize its economy, fostering strong partnerships with global counterparts will be crucial in driving sustainable growth and development. Navigating the economic uncertainties of a post-pandemic world will require a strategic and forward-thinking approach. The UAE's leadership has demonstrated a commitment to economic diversification and innovation, laying the foundation for a resilient and competitive economy poised for long-term success. As the UAE continues to adapt to the shifting dynamics of the global economy, embracing transformation and seizing new opportunities will be key to overcoming the challenges posed by the pandemic and ensuring a prosperous future for the nation and its people.

Embracing Technological Innovation: Implications for UAE Foreign Policy

The UAE's commitment to technological innovation is a cornerstone of its foreign policy agenda. As the world rapidly advances in areas such as AI, blockchain, and renewable energy, the UAE recognizes the need to stay at the forefront of these developments to maintain its competitive edge on the global stage. Embracing technological innovation has profound implications for the UAE's foreign policy, shaping its strategic partnerships, economic diversification efforts, and national security initiatives. One key area where technological innovation influences UAE foreign policy is in the realm of cybersecurity. With the increasing digitalization of societies and economies, the UAE faces growing cybersecurity threats that require nimble and advanced defenses. Investing in cutting-edge cybersecurity technologies and fostering international cooperation on cyber issues, the UAE aims to safeguard its national interests and protect critical infrastructure from malicious actors. Moreover, technological innovation plays a crucial role in the UAE's economic diplomacy efforts. The country's ambitious vision to become a hub for innovation and knowledge-based industries relies heavily on leveraging emerging technologies to drive growth and competitiveness. The UAE is positioning itself as a regional leader in fintech, renewable energy, and smart cities through initiatives such as the Dubai Future Foundation and the Abu Dhabi Innovation Hub. These efforts enhance the UAE's economic prospects and create new avenues for collaboration with global partners. Furthermore, technological innovation has implications for the UAE's soft power projection. As the country pioneers breakthroughs in space exploration and artificial intelligence, it enhances its reputation as a forward-thinking and dynamic nation. This image of innovation and progressiveness strengthens the UAE's appeal as a partner of choice for countries seeking to align with cutting-edge technologies and visionary initiatives. In conclusion, embracing technological innovation is a strategic choice for the UAE and a fundamental element of its foreign policy vision. By harnessing the power of technology to drive economic growth, enhance cybersecurity, and project soft power, the UAE is signaling its readiness to navigate the complex challenges and opportunities of the digital age with confidence and foresight.

Climate Change as a Key Consideration in Future Policy Formulation

Climate change is a defining issue that will significantly shape the future of international relations and foreign policy. As the effects of climate change become more pronounced, countries around the world are increasingly recognizing the need to address this global challenge in a coordinated and proactive manner. The United Arab Emirates, with its ambitious vision and commitment to sustainable development, is well-positioned to play a key role in driving the global conversation on climate change. The implications of climate change for the UAE's foreign policy are far-reaching. As a country heavily reliant on oil revenue, the UAE recognizes the importance of transitioning towards a more sustainable and diversified economy. This shift aligns with global efforts to mitigate climate change and positions the UAE as a leader in renewable energy and clean technologies. By investing in renewable energy projects and setting ambitious targets for reducing carbon emissions, the UAE contributes to the fight against climate change. It enhances its international reputation as a forward-thinking and environmentally conscious nation. Furthermore, climate change has direct implications for regional security and stability. Rising sea levels, extreme weather events, and water scarcity are all factors that can exacerbate existing tensions and conflicts in the region. Therefore, the UAE's foreign policy must consider climate change's impact on regional dynamics and work towards building resilience and cooperation among neighboring countries to address shared environmental challenges. By prioritizing climate change in its policy formulation, the UAE can bolster its security and stability and foster stronger relationships with regional partners. In shaping its future foreign policy, the UAE must continue to prioritize climate change as a key consideration. By integrating climate concerns into its diplomatic engagements, trade agreements, and development projects, the UAE can demonstrate its commitment to sustainability and environmental stewardship on the global stage. Through proactive and innovative approaches to climate change, the UAE can forge new partnerships, drive technological innovation, and contribute to a more sustainable and resilient world for future generations.

Regional Cooperation and Security Concerns: Balancing Act for the UAE

The UAE, situated in a volatile region, faces a delicate balance between fostering regional cooperation and addressing security concerns to safeguard its interests and stability. The Gulf Cooperation Council (GCC) plays a crucial role in the UAE's regional strategy, aiming to enhance collaboration among member states while navigating complex political dynamics in the Middle East. Key security concerns, such as the threat of terrorism and regional conflicts, necessitate a comprehensive approach that combines diplomatic engagement, military partnerships, and strategic alliances to maintain stability and peace. With the evolving regional landscape and new security challenges, the UAE's leadership recognizes the importance of proactive engagement with neighboring states and international partners. Strengthening alliances with countries sharing common interests and security objectives is paramount in advancing regional cooperation and addressing mutual security concerns. The UAE's participation in multilateral forums and initiatives underscores its commitment to promoting dialogue, de-escalation of tensions, and conflict resolution in the region. The UAE's military capabilities and defense partnerships with strategic allies enhance its security posture and contribute to regional stability. The UAE collaborates with like-minded nations to combat security threats and protect shared interests through joint military exercises, intelligence sharing, and counterterrorism efforts. The

UAE aims to create a secure environment conducive to economic growth, investment, and sustainable development by prioritizing security cooperation and building trust with regional partners. Moreover, the UAE's proactive approach to regional security challenges extends to its involvement in peacekeeping missions and humanitarian efforts in conflict-affected areas. By supporting peace initiatives and providing humanitarian aid to vulnerable populations, the UAE demonstrates its commitment to promoting peace and stability in the region. The UAE seeks to mitigate the impact of conflicts through targeted interventions and diplomatic initiatives, address humanitarian crises, and foster long-term peacebuilding efforts in collaboration with international partners. In conclusion, regional cooperation and security concerns represent a delicate balancing act for the UAE as it navigates complex geopolitical realities and emerging security threats in the Middle East. The UAE aims to foster a stable and secure regional environment conducive to sustainable development and peaceful coexistence by prioritizing dialogue, strategic partnerships, and conflict resolution mechanisms. Through proactive engagement, mutual cooperation, and collective action, the UAE continues to play a constructive role in advancing regional security and stability for all stakeholders involved.

Strengthening Global Partnerships: Leveraging Soft Power on the World Stage

The UAE's approach to strengthening global partnerships is deeply rooted in the concept of soft power. Soft power, as defined by political scientist Joseph Nye, refers to the ability to shape the preferences of others through attraction and persuasion rather than by coercion or payment. In today's interconnected world, soft power plays a crucial role in enhancing a country's influence and reputation on the global stage. The UAE has successfully leveraged its soft power assets to build strategic partnerships and foster closer ties with countries worldwide. The UAE's soft power arsenal is diverse and impactful, from its vibrant cultural scene and world-class infrastructure to its commitment to humanitarian initiatives and sustainable development. One key aspect of the UAE's soft power strategy is its emphasis on cultural diplomacy. Through initiatives such as the Louvre Abu Dhabi, the Dubai Expo, and the Sharjah Book Fair, the UAE has showcased its rich cultural heritage and contemporary creativity to audiences worldwide. By promoting dialogue, understanding, and mutual respect through cultural exchanges, the UAE has forged deep-rooted connections with diverse communities across the globe. Furthermore, the UAE's leadership in humanitarian assistance and disaster relief efforts has earned it a reputation as a reliable and compassionate partner on the world stage. Whether providing aid to conflict-affected regions, supporting refugees, or championing sustainable development goals, the UAE's humanitarian initiatives underscore its commitment to positively impacting global challenges. In education and innovation, the UAE has positioned itself as a hub for knowledge exchange and technological advancement. By investing in research and development, fostering innovation ecosystems, and promoting academic collaborations, the UAE has become a magnet for top talent and cutting-edge ideas worldwide. By leveraging its soft power assets effectively, the UAE has enhanced its diplomatic reach, built trust with international partners, and contributed to shaping a more peaceful and prosperous world. As the UAE continues strengthening its global partnerships, its commitment to soft power diplomacy will remain a cornerstone of its foreign policy strategy.

Cultural Diplomacy in the Digital Age: Connecting with Diverse Audiences

Cultural diplomacy is pivotal in shaping a country's image and fostering international relations in the digital age. With the world becoming increasingly interconnected through technology and social media, the UAE recognizes the importance of connecting with diverse audiences through cultural exchange and engagement. The UAE can build bridges with people worldwide and promote mutual understanding and respect by showcasing its rich heritage, arts, and traditions. Through cultural diplomacy, the UAE can share its values, beliefs, and way of life with a global audience, thus strengthening its soft power and influence on the world stage. As the digital landscape continues to evolve, the UAE's cultural diplomacy efforts will be crucial in promoting cross-cultural dialogue, fostering international cooperation, and creating lasting connections with people from different backgrounds. By harnessing the power of cultural diplomacy in the digital age, the UAE can effectively engage with diverse audiences and build meaningful relationships that transcend borders and boundaries.

Humanitarian Leadership: Addressing Global Challenges with Compassion

Humanitarian leadership is a core aspect of the UAE's foreign policy approach. The UAE has consistently committed to addressing global challenges with compassion and empathy. Through various initiatives and partnerships, the UAE has played a significant role in providing humanitarian aid and assistance to those in need worldwide. The UAE's humanitarian efforts are guided by generosity, solidarity, and compassion. The country has been at the forefront of responding to humanitarian crises, whether caused by conflicts, natural disasters, or other emergencies. The UAE's leadership recognizes the importance of helping those in distress, regardless of nationality, religion, or background. One of the key pillars of the UAE's humanitarian leadership is its focus on building strong partnerships with international organizations, governments, and non-profit entities. The UAE can maximize its impact and reach more needy individuals by working with various stakeholders. Collaborative efforts have been instrumental in delivering aid, providing medical assistance, and supporting sustainable development projects in communities affected by crises. In addition to providing immediate relief, the UAE prioritizes long-term development initiatives to address the root causes of humanitarian challenges. Investing in education, healthcare, infrastructure, and economic empowerment, the UAE aims to create sustainable solutions that bring lasting positive change to vulnerable populations. This holistic approach reflects the UAE's commitment to promoting human dignity and fostering hope for a better future. As the UAE continues to navigate the evolving landscape of global challenges, its dedication to humanitarian leadership remains unwavering. By upholding the values of compassion, solidarity, and empathy, the UAE sets a powerful example for the international community. Through its actions and advocacy, the UAE inspires others to join in the collective effort to address global crises and build a more inclusive and compassionate world.

Charting a Path Forward for the UAE's Foreign Policy

As the UAE continues to navigate the complex landscape of global politics, it is evident that proactive and strategic foreign policy approaches are essential for ensuring its continued success and influence on the world stage. By embracing a forward-thinking mindset that incorporates economic, technological, and environmental considerations, the UAE can position itself as a key player in shaping the future of international relations. Through a commitment to humanitarian leadership and compassionate diplomacy, the UAE has demonstrated its willingness to address global challenges and contribute to the well-being of communities worldwide. By prioritizing initiatives that promote peace, stability, and prosperity, the UAE can further enhance its reputation as a responsible and ethical actor in the international community. Looking ahead, the UAE must build on its existing strengths while adapting to emerging trends and challenges. This includes expanding its network of global partnerships, leveraging its soft power capabilities, and investing in innovative solutions to pressing global issues. By remaining flexible, adaptive, and proactive in its foreign policy approach, the UAE can chart a path that aligns with its vision of a prosperous and sustainable future for all. In conclusion, a deep-rooted commitment to excellence, diplomacy, and humanitarian leadership shapes the UAE's foreign policy trajectory. By staying true to its core values while embracing the evolving dynamics of the global landscape, the UAE is poised to continue making significant contributions to global peace, security, and development. As the country navigates the opportunities and challenges, strategic foresight, innovation, and a steadfast dedication to promoting global welfare will be crucial in charting a path forward that advances the UAE's interests and values on the world stage.

In a Nutshell

Shifting Geopolitical Dynamics: Impact on UAE Foreign Policy

The UAE adapts its foreign policy to navigate an increasingly complex geopolitical landscape. The country is moving towards a more pragmatic approach, balancing relationships with traditional allies like the US while also engaging with emerging powers like China. The UAE's recent diplomatic efforts, such as normalizing relations with Israel and improving ties with Iran, demonstrate its commitment to regional stability and adapting to changing dynamics.

Economic Opportunities and Challenges in a Post-Pandemic World

The UAE is positioned for economic recovery and growth in the post-pandemic era. The country focuses on diversifying its economy beyond oil and investing in technology, renewable energy, and tourism. The UAE's Vision 2030 and other strategic initiatives aim to enhance its competitiveness in the global economy. However, challenges remain, including further reducing dependence on oil revenues and creating more job opportunities for Emiratis.

Embracing Technological Innovation and its Implications for UAE Foreign Policy

The UAE leverages technological innovation to enhance its global influence and diplomatic reach. Initiatives like the UAE's AI strategy and investments in space exploration (including the Mars mission) showcase its commitment to becoming a global technology leader. This focus on innovation will likely shape the UAE's future foreign policy, potentially leading to new forms of technological diplomacy and partnerships.

Climate Change as a Key Consideration in Future Policy Formulation

Climate change is becoming a central focus of UAE foreign policy. The country is leading in addressing global environmental challenges, as evidenced by its hosting of COP28 and its commitment to achieving net-zero emissions by 2050. The UAE is also investing heavily in domestic and international renewable energy projects, positioning itself as a leader in sustainable development.

Strengthening Global Partnerships

The UAE continues to prioritize building and strengthening global partnerships. This includes enhancing cooperation within the Gulf Cooperation Council, fostering ties with major global powers, and engaging with emerging economies. The country's approach to partnership-building is multifaceted, encompassing economic, security, and cultural dimensions.

Cultural Diplomacy in the Digital Age

The UAE is adapting its cultural diplomacy efforts to the digital age. The country is leveraging social media and digital platforms to showcase its cultural heritage and promote its values of tolerance and coexistence. Initiatives like virtual exhibitions and online cultural exchanges will likely play an increasingly important role in the UAE's public diplomacy efforts.

Addressing Global Challenges with Compassion

The UAE continues demonstrating its commitment to addressing global challenges through humanitarian aid and development assistance. The country's foreign aid policy, rooted in its cultural values, focuses on reducing poverty and supporting sustainable development in developing countries. This compassionate approach to foreign policy will likely remain a key aspect of the UAE's international engagement.

In conclusion, the future of UAE foreign policy is characterized by adaptability, innovation, and a commitment to global cooperation. While facing challenges such as regional instability and economic diversification, the UAE is leveraging its strengths in technology, sustainability, and cultural diplomacy to enhance its global influence and contribute to addressing pressing global issues.

XIX

References

[1] https://www.weforum.org/agenda/2024/04/megatrends-shape-arab-world-next-25-years/
[2] https://researchme.io/blog/how-uaes-economy-is-shaping-up-post-pandemic
[3] https://www.fairobserver.com/world-news/uaes-revolutionary-world-diplomacy-is-quick-efficient-and-innovative/
[4] https://impact.economist.com/perspectives/health/uae-recognises-need-act-climate-change-fast
[5] https://www.uae-embassy.org/discover-uae/climate-and-energy
[6] https://www.mofa.gov.ae/en/mediahub/news/2023/12/31/31-12-2023-uae-uae
[7] https://meridian.allenpress.com/awg/article/27/2/127/501112/The-Impact-of-Digital-Cultural-Diplomacy-on
[8] https://www.mofa.gov.ae/en/The-Ministry/The-Foreign-Policy/Humanitarian-and-Development-Cooperation
[9] https://carnegieendowment.org/sada/2022/01/the-reshaping-of-uae-foreign-policy-and-geopolitical-strat-

egy?center=global&lang=en
[10] https://www.ragroup.ae/impact-of-covid-19-in-uae-economy-and-recovery/
[11] https://mof.gov.ae/strategic-regional-and-global-partners/
[12] https://www.mofa.gov.ae/en/The-Ministry/The-Foreign-Policy/Cultural-and-Public-Diplomacy

XX

Conclusion - Defining the UAE's Foreign Policy

Recap of UAE's Foreign Policy Evolution: A brief overview of the key milestones and developments in the UAE's foreign policy

The UAE's foreign policy has evolved significantly since its establishment in 1971. Initially focused on securing its sovereignty and regional stability, the country gradually expanded its diplomatic reach to become a key player in global affairs. One of the earliest milestones was the UAE's active participation in forming the Gulf Cooperation Council (GCC) in 1981, signaling its commitment to regional collaboration. Throughout the 1990s and early 2000s, the

UAE emerged as a trade, finance, and tourism hub, leading to a shift towards economic diplomacy in its foreign policy agenda. The country's strategic location and ambitious development plans allowed it to attract investments and forge partnerships with a diverse range of countries. In security and defense, the UAE played a crucial role in supporting regional stability, participating in international peacekeeping missions, and strengthening its military capabilities through strategic partnerships with leading global powers. The country's active involvement in counterterrorism efforts and its support for regional conflict resolution underscored its commitment to promoting peace and security. Cultural diplomacy also became a key aspect of the UAE's foreign policy, as the country sought to showcase its rich heritage and vibrant contemporary culture on the global stage. Initiatives such as the Louvre Abu Dhabi and the Dubai Expo served as platforms for cultural exchange and dialogue, bolstering the UAE's soft power and enhancing its international reputation. Looking to the future, the UAE aims to build on its achievements and continue shaping a dynamic and forward-looking foreign policy agenda. By prioritizing innovation, sustainability, and inclusive growth, the country aspires to strengthen its global partnerships, promote peace and stability, and contribute to addressing the emerging challenges of the 21st century on the international stage.

Vision for the Future: Discussing the UAE's strategic vision for its foreign policy, including key goals and priorities

The UAE's strategic vision for its foreign policy is grounded in a commitment to continued stability, prosperity, and global influence. Central to this vision is pursuing diversified regional and global partnerships to advance mutual interests and address shared challenges. The UAE aims to further promote peace and security in the Middle East and beyond, emphasizing diplomacy and dialogue as key tools for conflict resolution. Economic diversification and innovation will remain focal points of the UAE's foreign policy agenda, focusing on leveraging the country's strengths in key sectors such as technology, renewable energy, and advanced manufacturing. The UAE intends to position itself as a hub for investment, trade, and innovation, attracting global talent and fostering a dynamic economy that drives sustainable growth. Cultural diplomacy will continue to significantly shape the UAE's global image and foster intercultural understanding. The country's rich heritage and vibrant cultural scene will be showcased globally, enhancing its soft power and influence. Additionally, the UAE will continue championing sustainability and environmental stewardship, actively engaging in global efforts to address climate change and promote green initiatives. The UAE will prioritize strategic partnerships and collaborations in security and defense to address emerging threats and challenges, including cybersecurity and regional instability. The country will continue to invest in defense capabilities and capacity-building efforts to ensure its national security and contribute to regional stability. Overall, the UAE's strategic vision for its foreign policy beyond 2024 underscores a commitment to innovation, sustainability, and cooperation on the global stage. By leveraging its economic strength, cultural richness, and diplomatic acumen, the UAE aims to navigate the complex geopolitical landscape and proactively shape a more secure, prosperous, and interconnected world.

Leadership Role: Analyzing the role of leadership in shaping and executing the UAE's foreign policy agenda

The leadership in the United Arab Emirates plays a fundamental role in shaping and executing the country's foreign policy agenda. As a nation emphasizing visionary leadership, the UAE's leaders have been instrumental in steering its foreign relations toward its strategic goals and overarching vision for the future. The leadership's role is multifaceted, encompassing diplomatic relations, economic partnerships, security arrangements, and cultural exchanges. By engaging with key stakeholders both domestically and internationally, UAE leaders have built strong alliances, fostered cooperation, and promoted the country's interests on the global stage. UAE leaders have positioned the country as a key player in regional and global affairs through their proactive engagement and strategic decision-making. They have successfully navigated complex geopolitical landscapes, adapted to changing dynamics, and pursued a foreign policy agenda that is both pragmatic and forward-thinking. Moreover, the UAE's leadership has demonstrated a commitment to promoting peace, stability, and prosperity in the region and beyond. UAE leaders have sought to play a constructive role in addressing regional challenges and advancing shared interests with international partners by advocating for dialogue, diplomacy, and conflict resolution. Overall, the leadership's role in shaping and executing the UAE's foreign policy agenda is integral to the country's standing in the international community and its ability to navigate a rapidly evolving global landscape effectively. By leveraging their vision, expertise, and diplomatic acumen, UAE leaders continue to play a pivotal role in advancing the country's strategic interests and maintaining its reputation as a respected and influential player on the world stage.

Regional Dynamics: Examining the evolving dynamics in the Middle East region and how they may impact the UAE's foreign policy strategies

The Middle East region has long been a focal point of global attention due to its geopolitical significance and complex dynamics. The evolving landscape in the Middle East directly impacts the UAE's foreign policy strategies, shaping its alliances, partnerships, and security priorities. The UAE's strategic location at the crossroads of the Middle East has positioned it as a key player in regional dynamics. The UAE has actively engaged with neighboring countries and regional organizations to promote stability, security, and economic cooperation. The ongoing conflicts and tensions in the Middle East, such as the Syrian civil war, the Yemeni crisis, and the broader regional rivalry between Iran and Saudi Arabia, pose significant challenges to the UAE's foreign policy objectives. The UAE has navigated these complexities by adopting a nuanced and pragmatic approach, balancing its strategic interests with the need for regional stability. At the same time, the UAE has capitalized on emerging opportunities in the Middle East, such as the normalization agreements with Israel and the growing economic ties with countries like Egypt and Jordan. These developments have enabled the UAE to expand its influence and bolster its regional partnerships, contributing to its broader foreign policy goals. The rise of non-state actors, including terrorist groups and militias, has also posed a security threat to the region, prompting the UAE to prioritize counterterrorism cooperation and security partnerships with regional and international allies. The UAE's military intervention in Yemen and its participation in the U.S.-led coalition against ISIS are examples of its proactive role in addressing regional security challenges. Looking ahead, the UAE will continue to closely monitor and adapt to the evolving dynamics in the Middle East, engaging in diplomatic initiatives, conflict resolution efforts, and strategic partnerships to advance its national interests and contribute to regional stability and prosperity.

Global Partnerships: Evaluating the UAE's existing and potential partnerships with key global players and organizations

The United Arab Emirates (UAE) has strategically positioned itself as a key player in the global arena through its proactive approach to establishing partnerships with key global players and organizations. These partnerships are a cornerstone of the UAE's foreign policy, enabling the country to enhance its influence, promote its interests, and contribute to global peace and prosperity. In economic diplomacy, the UAE has forged strong partnerships with leading economies worldwide to drive economic growth and diversification. The country has solidified its position as a global economic hub through initiatives such as the UAE's membership in the World Trade Organization, its active participation in international trade agreements, and its promotion of foreign direct investment. Furthermore, the UAE's partnerships extend beyond economic realms to encompass security cooperation, cultural exchange, and sustainable development. The UAE has established strategic relationships with key global players, including the United States, the European Union, China, and regional partners in the Gulf Cooperation Council (GCC), to address common challenges and seize opportunities for mutual benefit. Looking ahead, the UAE continues to actively engage with global partners to expand its network of alliances and deepen existing relationships. By leveraging its diplomatic expertise, economic strength, and commitment to international cooperation, the UAE is well-positioned to navigate the complexities of the global landscape and play a significant role in shaping the future of international relations.

Economic Diplomacy: Assessing the significance of economic diplomacy in driving the UAE's international relations agenda

Economic diplomacy is crucial in advancing the UAE's international relations agenda. The UAE's economic strength and strategic investments have forged strong partnerships with countries and organizations worldwide. Through economic diplomacy, the UAE leverages its economic power to enhance its global influence and promote its national interests. The UAE's economic diplomacy is characterized by its focus on trade, investment, and economic cooperation. The country has established itself as a key player in the global economy, with a diversified and resilient economy closely integrated into the global market. Its strategic location as a gateway between East and West further enhances its economic significance on the world stage. The UAE's proactive approach to economic diplomacy is evident in its efforts to attract foreign investment, diversify its economy, and strengthen its trade relationships. The country's free trade zones, business-friendly policies, and investment incentives have made it a preferred destination for foreign investors seeking to capitalize on its dynamic business environment. Furthermore, the UAE's economic diplomacy extends beyond its borders through strategic investments in key sectors such as energy, infrastructure, technology, and tourism. These investments drive economic growth domestically and contribute to the country's influence and presence on the global stage. Through economic diplomacy, the UAE has built a network of partnerships with countries and organizations worldwide, fostering mutual economic benefits and enhancing its reputation as a reliable and strategic partner. By leveraging its economic power and resources, the UAE significantly shapes the global economic landscape and promotes its national interests internationally.

Soft Power and Cultural Diplomacy: Exploring the role of soft power and cultural diplomacy in enhancing the UAE's global influence and image

Soft power and cultural diplomacy play a pivotal role in the UAE's efforts to enhance its global influence and shape a positive image on the international stage. The UAE's rich cultural heritage, modern development initiatives, and strategic investments in various sectors have been instrumental in projecting the country as a forward-thinking and culturally vibrant nation. Through initiatives such as the Louvre Abu Dhabi, Dubai Expo 2020, and the Year of Tolerance, the UAE has showcased its commitment to promoting cultural exchange, tolerance, and understanding among nations. The UAE's soft power also extends to its humanitarian efforts and contributions to global development projects. The country's foreign aid programs, philanthropic endeavors, and diplomacy based on mutual respect have earned it admiration and respect from the international community. By leveraging its cultural assets and promoting a message of peace and cooperation, the UAE has built strong relationships with countries around the world and positioned itself as a key player in global affairs. Through promoting Emirati arts, music, cuisine, and traditions, cultural diplomacy has helped the UAE foster connections and create bonds with people from diverse backgrounds. By hosting cultural events, art exhibitions, and heritage festivals, the UAE has been able to share its unique identity with the world and build bridges of understanding and appreciation. This cultural diplomacy showcases Emirati culture's richness and facilitates intercultural dialogue and cooperation, contributing to a more peaceful and interconnected global community. In soft power, the UAE also utilizes media and communication platforms to amplify its voice and share its narrative with a global audience. By engaging in strategic communication campaigns, public diplomacy initiatives, and leveraging digital platforms, the UAE has shaped perceptions, counter negative stereotypes, and promoted a positive image of the country and its values. This comprehensive approach to soft power and cultural diplomacy has proven to be effective in advancing the UAE's foreign policy objectives and strengthening its position as a respected and influential player in the international arena.

Security Challenges: Addressing the security challenges and threats that the UAE faces and how they are being managed in the realm of foreign policy

The UAE faces various security challenges and threats that require careful consideration and strategic response in foreign policy. The country's geostrategic location in a volatile region and the ever-evolving nature of global security threats necessitate a proactive approach to safeguarding its national interests and ensuring regional stability. One of the critical security challenges for the UAE is the threat posed by terrorism and extremism. The country has been targeted by various terrorist groups in the past and continues to face the risk of radicalization and violent extremism. The UAE has adopted a comprehensive counterterrorism strategy at home and abroad, working closely with international partners to disrupt terrorist networks and prevent attacks. In addition to terrorism, the UAE also grapples with cybersecurity threats in an increasingly digital world. As a leader in technology and innovation, the country is highly dependent on secure digital infrastructure to support its economy and critical services. The UAE has invested significantly in building resilience against cyber threats, enhancing its cyber defense capabilities, and collaborating with international partners to address cyber challenges. Furthermore, the UAE faces security challenges related to regional conflicts and tensions in the Middle East. The ongoing conflicts in neighboring countries, the threat of ballistic missile attacks, and the proliferation of weapons of mass destruction all pose significant risks to the UAE's security and stability. The country has pursued a balanced foreign policy approach, engaging in diplomatic efforts and regional initiatives to promote dialogue, de-escalation, and conflict resolution. Moreover, the UAE is mindful of the maritime security challenges in the Gulf region, given its strategic location along major shipping routes. Ensuring safe passage for maritime trade and protecting critical infrastructure such as ports and oil facilities are priorities for the country. The UAE has been involved in maritime security initiatives and coalition efforts to combat piracy, smuggling, and other maritime threats. In response to these security challenges, the UAE has adopted a proactive and multi-faceted approach that combines military capabilities, intelligence cooperation, diplomatic efforts, and strategic partnerships. By engaging with international allies, strengthening its defense capabilities, and investing in advanced security technologies, the UAE aims to enhance its security posture, deter potential threats, and contribute to regional stability and peace.

Climate Change and Sustainability: Discussing the UAE's efforts in addressing global environmental challenges and the integration of sustainability goals into its foreign policy approach

The UAE has recognized the critical importance of addressing global environmental challenges, particularly in the face of climate change. As a country heavily reliant on oil and gas resources, the UAE has proactively integrated sustainability goals into its foreign policy approach. The leadership has emphasized the need to diversify the economy and shift towards renewable energy sources to reduce greenhouse gas emissions and mitigate the impact of climate change. One significant initiative in this regard is the UAE's commitment to the Paris Agreement, which pledged to reduce its carbon footprint and increase the share of clean energy in its overall energy mix. The UAE has set ambitious targets for renewable energy generation, including developing solar power projects and investing in sustainable technologies. In addition to its domestic efforts, the UAE has been actively promoting environmental sustainability globally. The country has hosted numerous international forums and conferences on climate change, highlighting its commitment to addressing this pressing issue globally. By engaging with other nations and sharing best practices, the UAE aims to drive collective action towards a more sustainable future for all. Furthermore, the UAE's foreign policy approach to climate change extends beyond energy considerations. The country has emphasized the importance of water conservation, biodiversity protection, and sustainable urban development in its international engagements. By incorporating these environmental considerations into its diplomatic efforts, the UAE seeks to foster cooperation and innovation in addressing broader sustainability challenges. Looking ahead, the UAE will continue to prioritize climate change and sustainability in its foreign policy agenda. As the global community grapples with the impacts of environmental degradation, the UAE aims to be at the forefront of solutions-oriented approaches that promote a more sustainable future for all. By leveraging its experience and expertise in renewable energy and environmental conservation, the UAE is poised to play a leading role in shaping the international response to climate change in the years to come.

Future Outlook: Providing a forward-looking perspective on the potential opportunities and challenges that the UAE may encounter in the ever-evolving global landscape and how its foreign policy may adapt to these changes

The future of the UAE's foreign policy is intricately linked to the evolving global landscape, particularly regarding climate change and sustainability. As the world grapples with the urgent need to address environmental challenges, the UAE has an opportunity to position itself as a leader in this critical domain. Integrating sustainability goals into its foreign policy approach will enhance the country's reputation and strengthen its strategic partnerships with like-minded nations. One of the key challenges the UAE may face in the future is balancing its economic interests with its commitment to sustainability. As a major player in the energy sector, the country will need to navigate the transition to a more sustainable and green economy while ensuring its continued growth and prosperity. This delicate balance will require careful planning and strategic decision-making by UAE policymakers. Another challenge the UAE may encounter is the increasing complexity of global environmental issues. Climate change is a multifaceted problem that requires coordinated action on a global scale. The UAE must continue engaging with international partners and organizations to drive meaningful progress in combating climate change and promoting sustainability. Despite these challenges, there are also numerous opportunities for the UAE. By investing in renewable energy and clean technologies, the country can reduce its carbon footprint, diversify its economy, and create new job opportunities. Additionally, the UAE's sustainability and climate change efforts can enhance its soft power and influence on the global stage, positioning the country as a responsible and forward-thinking leader. In conclusion, the future outlook for the UAE's foreign policy in climate change and sustainability is both promising and challenging. By embracing these opportunities and addressing the associated challenges head-on, the UAE can continue to play a significant role in shaping a more sustainable and prosperous future for all.

www.ingramcontent.com/pod-product-compliance
Lightning Source LLC
Chambersburg PA
CBHW052132070526
44585CB00017B/1793